Fantasies of music in nostalgic medievalism

MANCHESTER MEDIEVAL LITERATURE AND CULTURE

*Series editors*: Anke Bernau, David Matthews and James Paz

*Series founded by*: J. J. Anderson and Gail Ashton

*Advisory board*: Ruth Evans, Patricia C. Ingham, Andrew James Johnston, Chris Jones, Catherine Karkov, Nicola McDonald, Haruko Momma, Susan Phillips, Sarah Salih, Larry Scanlon, Stephanie Trigg and Matthew Vernon

*Manchester Medieval Literature and Culture* publishes monographs and essay collections comprising new research informed by current critical methodologies on the literary cultures of the global Middle Ages. We are interested in all periods, from the early Middle Ages through to the late, and we include post-medieval engagements with and representations of the medieval period (or 'medievalism'). 'Literature' is taken in a broad sense, to include the many different medieval genres: imaginative, historical, political, scientific and religious.

**Titles available in the series**

40. *Sleep and its spaces in Middle English literature: Emotions, ethics, dreams*
Megan G. Leitch

41. *Encountering* The Book of Margery Kempe
Laura Kalas and Laura Varnam (eds)

42. *The narrative grotesque in medieval Scottish poetry*
Caitlin Flynn

43. *Painful pleasures: Sadomasochism in medieval cultures*
Christopher Vaccaro (ed.)

44. *Bestsellers and masterpieces: The changing medieval canon*
Heather Blurton and Dwight F. Reynolds (eds)

45. *Medieval literary voices: Embodiment, materiality and performance*
Louise D'Arcens and Sif Ríkharðsdóttir (eds)

46. *The heat of* Beowulf
Daniel C. Remein

47. *Hybrid healing: Old English remedies and medical texts*
Lori Ann Garner

48. *Difficult pasts: Post-Reformation memory and the medieval romance*
Mimi Ensley

49. *The problem of literary value*
Robert J. Meyer-Lee

50. *Marian maternity in late-medieval England*
Mary Beth Long

51. *Fantasies of music in nostalgic medievalism*
Helen Dell

# Fantasies of music in nostalgic medievalism

Helen Dell

MANCHESTER UNIVERSITY PRESS

Copyright © Helen Dell 2023

The right of Helen Dell to be identified as the author of this work has been asserted in accordance with the Copyright, Designs and Patents Act 1988.

This book will be made open access within three years of publication thanks to Path to Open, a program developed in partnership between JSTOR, the American Council of Learned Societies (ACLS), University of Michigan Press, and The University of North Carolina Press to bring about equitable access and impact for the entire scholarly community, including authors, researchers, libraries, and university presses around the world. Learn more at https://about.jstor.org/path-to-open/

Published by Manchester University Press
Oxford Road, Manchester M13 9PL

www.manchesteruniversitypress.co.uk

British Library Cataloguing-in-Publication Data
A catalogue record for this book is available from the British Library

ISBN 978 1 5261 7395 9 hardback
ISBN 978 1 5261 9583 8 paperback

First published 2023
Paperback published 2026

The publisher has no responsibility for the persistence or accuracy of URLs for any external or third-party internet websites referred to in this book, and does not guarantee that any content on such websites is, or will remain, accurate or appropriate.

EU authorised representative for GPSR:
Easy Access System Europe – Mustamäe tee 50,
10621 Tallinn, Estonia
gpsr.requests@easproject.com

Typeset
by New Best-set Typesetters Ltd

'The only true paradise is the paradise that we have lost'
*(Marcel Proust,* Time Regained*)*

# Contents

| | |
|---|---|
| Introduction: Music, nostalgia and the medieval | *page* 1 |
| 1 'More real than reality': Nostalgia for the medieval in high fantasy fiction | 38 |
| 2 'Yearning for the sweet beckoning sound': Musical longings and the unsayable in medievalist fantasy fiction | 78 |
| 3 The lost world inside a song: From the book to the record | 109 |
| 4 Exotic sexualities: The countertenor voice in the late twentieth-century medieval music revival | 141 |
| 5 The call of the mother: Music for myth and fantasy in two Arthurian films | 173 |
| Aftermath | 200 |
| Appendix: Listener response analysis methodology | 205 |
| Works cited | 209 |
| Index | 244 |

# Introduction:
# Music, nostalgia and the medieval

> Modernity is haunted by a spectre of paradise, amplified across the Middle Ages, the Renaissance and the early modern period in poetry and medical treatise alike, a dreaming of a pastoral idyll. (Smith, 2019)

This book offers an account of the way three threads – music, medievalism and nostalgia – have been woven together in the fantasies of writers and readers, musicians, musicologists, directors and listeners, film-makers and film-goers. The period between the Second World War and the present has seen an extraordinary rise in the production of medievalist fantasy literature and film. Perhaps J. R. R. Tolkien's greatest achievement in retrospect was in normalising the idea of a secondary world. Although he offers hints that the action of *The Lord of the Rings* (*LOTR*) takes place in the prehistory of our own world, that is not sustained, and to all intents and purposes Middle-earth is a separate creation, operating outside the world of our experience. This has become so standard in modern fantasy that it is not easy to realise how unusual it was before Tolkien. As John Clute described it: '*LOTR* marked the end of apology' (cited in E. James, 2012: 65).

In these genres, music, whether performed or as idea or metaphor, has been essential to the evocation of a medieval fantasy. Over the same period of about seventy years, there has also been an unprecedented interest in the revival, performance and invention of medieval music, an enterprise in which modern fantasies of the Middle Ages have exercised great influence. Together, these developments have placed music at the centre of a nostalgia for an imagined medieval, a longing for a lost past.

Music has been described by Sandra Garrido and Jane W. Davidson as 'one of the strongest ways to evoke memories of previous places and times, whether those memories are of our own past, or of a nebulous and romanticized version outside of our own experience' (2019: 59–60).[1] In the second alternative, the nostalgia for a past one has known only in imagination, sometimes called 'anemoia', may embrace the fantasy medieval to which music can take us (Koenig, 2021: 167).[2] It is a past in the middle, that is – in one sense – at the heart of things.[3] As such it has, in fantasy, become a kind of home – a place within. This book studies the ways in which three fields of creative activity inspired by the medieval – musical performance, literature, cinema and their reception – have worked together to produce and sustain, for some, the fantasy of a long-lost, long-mourned paradisal home.

I have chosen 1950 as a rough starting point for this study. At around that time two events occurred which assisted a shift in the way medieval music was performed, recorded, packaged, heard and imagined. First, the early music revival entered a new, accelerated phase, assisted by the invention of the long-playing ('LP') record in 1948. As a result, more ambitious recording projects became possible. One such project was the 'concept album', that is, a collection of pieces 'unified by a theme, which can be instrumental, compositional, narrative or lyrical' (Shuker, 2005: 7–8), although medieval concept albums arrived considerably later. The Boston Camerata's *Tristan and Iseult* (1987) was one such album, as were Ensemble Gilles Binchois's *Le Vrai Rémède d'amour* (2001) and Alla Francesca's *Le Roman de la rose* (2001). In each case, a pastiche of music and readings were combined to construct a dramatic narrative. Other ensembles found different ways to give unity to a recording. For example, in their 1978 recording, *Llibre vermell de Monserrat*, Hespèrion XX (now Hespèrion XXI) offered a soundscape of bodies, place and movement evoking a pilgrimage. Such strategies give greater scope for an aurally induced fantasy to unfold for the listener over the course of the LP.[4] These kinds of projects are harder to achieve now with the change in listening habits brought about by online listening and purchasing, although some still prefer the CD or vinyl experience.[5]

The second definitive mid-century event was the publication of J. R. R. Tolkien's *The Lord of the Rings* in three volumes (1954–55), and C. S. Lewis's five novels comprising the *Chronicles of Narnia* (1950–56). Tolkien's book in particular, though spurned by critics, broke numerous popularity records. According to Edward James, 'three major surveys of public opinion in Great Britain around the turn of the millennium placed him as the "author of the century" or his book as the most popular work of English fiction' (2012: 62). In the work of these two authors, music is often associated with certain medieval realms which are presented as numinous objects of nostalgic longing, 'more real than reality'.[6] In *The Problem of Pain*, Lewis describes the numinous in this way. In the event of a visitation by 'a mighty spirit':

> You would feel wonder and a certain shrinking – a sense of inadequacy to cope with such a visitant and of prostration before it – an emotion which might be expressed in Shakespeare's words 'Under it my genius is rebuked'. This feeling may be described as awe, and the object which excites it as the *Numinous*. (Lewis, 2009: 6–7; emphasis in original)

It is the sacred glow of the numinous which lends that extra dimension of reality to the medieval fantasy, although, in this fantasy, the awe of the numinous described by Lewis above is tempered by a homeliness.

In high fantasy fiction, numinous moments are often accompanied by music. In the Western world, for as long as we know, there has been an association between music and the magical, the mystical and the sacred.[7] The magic worked by music goes back to Orpheus and beyond. As Sandra Garrido and Jane W. Davidson begin their book, *Music, Nostalgia and Memory: Historical and Psychological Imperatives*: 'Since the beginning of recorded human history music has created a sense of the sacred around key life events such as birth, marriage and death, heightening the experience of these peak moments' (2019: 1).

The word 'enchantment' is derived from the Latin *cantare* (to sing), as is 'incantation', the sung spell. The affective power of music is so great that, however it is interpreted, it always manages to exceed natural explanations and thus to prompt supernatural ones. Joscelyn Godwin observes in the Preface to *Music, Mysticism and Magic: A Sourcebook*: '[M]usic is always the same vehicle for voyages to another world, the same revelation of divine and cosmic laws, the same powerful tool for self-transformation, as it was in ancient and even in prehistoric times' (Godwin, 1987: ix).

4   *Fantasies of music in nostalgic medievalism*

The proliferation of medieval music recording, both scholarly and popular, and of a particular kind of high fantasy fiction in the period since 1950, has allowed a nostalgic vision of the Middle Ages as a magical prelapsarian paradise to reach a wide audience and support a discourse of nostalgic medievalism in which music and its power are central – both audible and imagined music, or music as idea or metaphor.

## Nostalgia for the medieval

The word 'nostalgia' was first coined in the seventeenth century by Johannes Hofer (1669–1752) as an obscure condition of homesickness (*nostos* – homecoming, and *algia* – pain) afflicting Swiss mercenaries (Wilson, 2005: 21). Music, as so often, was the key. In 1720, Theodor Zwinger noted that the trigger for the *Schweizerheimweh* was often the sound of a familiar melody.[8] These Swiss soldiers were reported to throw down their weapons and run for home at the sound of a Swiss melody entitled *Ranz des vaches*, sung or played in Switzerland to call the cows home.[9] Nostalgia has more recently been recognised by Svetlana Boym (2001: xvi) as a 'symptom of our age'. Since Kant, the home of nostalgia has become identified with the past.

Kant wrote, somewhat cynically, in *Anthropology*:

> The Swiss ... are overcome by *homesickness* when they are stationed in other countries. This results from a yearning for the places where they enjoyed the very simple pleasures of life – a nostalgia aroused by recalling images of the carefree and neighborly years of their youth; for when they revisit these places they are greatly disappointed in their expectations and so cured. Though they think this is because everything is changed there, it is really because they cannot relive their youth there. (Kant, *c*.1978: 53–4)

In the terms of this project, nostalgia is still a kind of homesickness, a desire for an imagined state of vanished enchantment which retains a spatial quality within a temporal structure.[10] In the words of Michael Pickering and Emily Keightley in 'The Modalities of Nostalgia', nostalgia is 'driven by utopian impulses – the desire for re-enchantment – as well as melancholic responses to disenchantment' (2006: 936). The nostalgia I am concerned with here may be driven by either. Nostalgia has its moods but the longing for re-enchantment is common to all, based on the 'memory' of a paradisal world, once known and loved, but now lost.

The lost, unfallen home for which nostalgia yearns has become a place/time/state of origin which is sometimes called medieval. Sandra Garrido and Jane W. Davidson have named this form of nostalgia 'historical', that is, one in which 'music can prompt "memories" and a longing for time periods or places that we only know about second-hand' (2019: 54). What John Haines has named the 'enduring vitality of modern nostalgia for the Middle Ages' (2014a: 155) is such a nostalgia and one which shows no sign of abating. I have chosen to use the adjectival, lower case 'medieval' rather than the more stately, capitalised proper noun, 'Middle Ages', because it has a more fluid quality and thus feels more appropriate to the unfolding of nostalgic fantasy narratives.[11]

Nostalgia is theorised in a variety of ways. I speak of it here in terms of the fantasies that desire attaches to the medieval. Linda Austin, in her phenomenological account, has offered an understanding of medieval nostalgia in which secondary memory recollection of the finished past is experienced as primary memory, that is, memory which blends conscious recollection with a bodily response at the margins of consciousness (Austin, 2011: 129). Thus, the medieval past can be 'remembered' as if it occurred in our own lifetime. Although this nostalgia may feel like a memory, I understand it instead as a fantasy in disguise, 'masquerad[ing] as memory' as E. B. Daniels wrote (1985: 84). As will become apparent, my own theorising of nostalgia owes most to the body of psychoanalytic writing on desire that began with Sigmund Freud, most importantly the work of Jacques Lacan.

When the medieval functions as the lost origin of nostalgic longing the question of how we fantasise that origin has a great deal to do with how we understand the medieval past. John Ganim comments insightfully on the 'the pattern woven as much by the scholarly and popular veneration – and execration – of the Middle Ages as by the Middle Ages itself' (2005: 5). He proceeds:

> For the Medieval, almost by the very root of its terminology, has always been imagined by the West as both ourselves and something other than ourselves, as unified and as anarchic, as origin and as disruption, as the hyperfeminine and the hypermasculine. (Ganim, 2005: 5)

Ending his book, Ganim writes: '[W]e still think of the Medieval ... as simultaneously *gemütlich* and *unheimlich*' (Ganim, 2005: 107). Ambiguity is at the heart of medievalist nostalgia. It is part of the paradoxical lure of what I call the *space between* – the place in the middle – in which nostalgia is implicated. Ganim captures this well: '[T]he Medieval ... is that foreign land in which we are always at home' (2005: 107). It is, piquantly, both homely and exotic.[12] The medieval as a paradoxical *space between* opposites is a constant in this book, often announced by oxymoron.[13]

Medieval music partakes of this ambiguity, as Daniel Leech-Wilkinson notes:

> [F]or many (including many scholars) medieval music was another kind of ethnic music, the product of an exotic culture far removed from our own. On the other hand, for others, it was a matter of searching for roots: for them medieval music was *a part* of their culture. (Leech-Wilkinson, 2000: 295)

But it is not necessarily a choice between the native and the exotic. Many listeners require a homeliness in their medieval music, but blended with a spice of the exotic. They desire, that is, that paradoxical space in which opposites are bound together. The *gemütlich* and the *unheimlich*, as Ganim observes, are more intimately related than Leech-Wilkinson's account would suggest.

The ambiguity of the medieval is the ambiguity of home. Home is already *unheimlich*. In the German word *heimlich* (homely) the *unheimlich* (uncanny) is already lurking. Our longing senses this ambiguity and is itself ambiguous. Sigmund Freud, in his essay on the Uncanny, writes: 'The uncanny is that class of the frightening which leads back to what is known of old and long familiar' (1990: 340).[14] It is the juxtaposition that generates the frisson – the monster in the bedroom cupboard, the groping hand under the bed. In support, Freud cites Daniel Sanders's *German Dictionary* (1860, 1, 729) under *heimlich*:

> *Heimlich*, adj., ... I. [B]elonging to the house, not strange, familiar, ... intimate, ... friendly, comfortable. (Sanders, cited in Freud, 1990: 342)

> II. Concealed, kept from sight, so that others do not get to know ... about it ... . To do something *heimlich*, i.e., behind someone's back; to steal away *Heimlich*; ... 'learned in strange *Heimlichkeiten*' (magic arts). (Sanders, cited in Freud, 1990: 344)[15]

Jacques Lacan, with something similar in mind, spoke of 'something strange to me although it is at the heart of me' (1997: 71). The heart, in imagination the hearth of the human person, the deepest, most intimate interior, houses a strangeness. Lacan's word for this strangeness at the heart was *extimité* ('extimacy'), the 'intimate exteriority' (1997: 138). In a sense we are strangers to ourselves.

The ambiguity associated with the medieval is played out also in its gendering, as Ganim points out (2005: 5). If it is gendered feminine then the nostalgic fantasy may associate to desire for the mother and from there to bliss, but also to chaos, shame and disavowal. Since this desire is forbidden, the longing for return may become burdened by fear and guilt. Lacan theorised this complex of fear and longing through an association of the mother with *das Ding*, that which is 'by its very nature alien' (1997: 52). What is most desired is forbidden: 'The Sovereign Good, which is *das Ding*, which is the mother, is also the object of incest, is a forbidden good, and ... there is no other good' (1997: 70). Such a fear may in turn be transposed onto the medieval, understood as history. This theme is explored in Chapters 3 and 5.

On the other hand, gendering the medieval masculine may allow the fantasy to bypass that fear and the medieval to become a site of order and tranquillity, as it functioned for Tolkien and Lewis. Alternatively, it may turn it into a scene of indescribable savagery and sadism, to which the medieval tortures beloved by the media bear witness, as in its famous use in Quentin Tarantino's film *Pulp Fiction* (1994): 'I'ma get medieval on your ass', to which Carolyn Dinshaw's *Getting Medieval* (1999: 184) refers.[16] In this version of the medieval, brutality is the guarantee of realism.

The gender splitting of the medieval may be played out as a battle between Christianity and paganism or between patriarchy and matriarchy, both conflicts appearing in the two Arthurian cinematic events (one a film, the other a TV miniseries) discussed in Chapter 5. It may take shape as a North/South, cold/warm antagonism with gender implications, as it does in Guy Gavriel Kay's *Song for Arbonne* (2002) (a fantastic version of medieval Occitania) where the South is 'a land warm and sun-blessed ... whose sensuous and flamboyant people are dedicated to the worship of the mother goddess', while the North is 'a land of hard, dour northerners – pious in their worship of the god Corannos and rapacious in war' (Kay, 1996: inside back cover).

In recent years, the immense popularity of George R. R. Martin's work suggests that the brutal medieval (or 'mediEvil' as the popular action-adventure video game has it), may have surpassed Tolkien's more idealised version in the popular imagination, but I believe the binary is perpetually in play. David Matthews has argued for a distinction between a '*gothic* or *grotesque* Middle Ages and a *romantic* Middle Ages' (2015: 15; emphasis in original) and, he continues, 'this distinction between a gothicised or *grotesque* and a romanticised medieval is one I take to be fundamental [and] the chief dualism in contemporary understandings of the Middle Ages, whether scholarly or popular' (2015: 15; emphasis in original). I agree, and because of the popularity of Tolkien's and Martin's work in fiction and film, I believe they can stand as central figures in contemporary medievalism as Matthews defines it, with Tolkien representing the romanticised and Martin the 'gothicised' or '*grotesque*' aspects of the term (2015: 15). It is not so clear cut, however. Medievalisms may be romanticised in one aspect and gothicised in another. As Matthews points out, the two 'are not always straightforwardly distinguishable from one another' (2015: 16). What Matthews terms its 'middleness' (2015: 20) can sometimes stand for the ambiguity so often associated with the Middle Ages.

A different kind of ambiguity is addressed in Chapter 4, that exemplified by the countertenor in medieval music, whose presence offered, for some, fantasies of an exotic, polymorphous sexuality which cannot be pinned down as masculine or feminine. Chapter 4 examines a general disquiet about the musical body among scholars, critics and listeners, which can be parsed in terms of a body/soul antagonism also associated with the ancient distinctions that align man with soul and woman with body. Lacan takes up this distinction in Seminar XX: 'So that the soul may come into being, woman is differentiated from it right from the beginning. She is called woman (*on la dit-femme*) and defamed (*diffâme*)' (1999: 85). The body/soul antagonism is part of an asceticism, unproblematically ascribed to the medieval mind, that links as well to a clean/unclean or pure/impure distinction also caught up in the gender distinction. This general disquiet is apparent in some representations of music in Chapter 2.

I argue that we are all, scholars and fans alike (many of us are both), liable to the associational slippages of fantasy and their attendant affects, and that they inflect the theory and the history we make.[17] I am making use here of the psychoanalytic method of free association, arising from the analyst's injunction to 'say whatever comes to mind', but in the looser sense by which words, ideas and phenomena come to be connected in people's thoughts in what they say and write. These various associations and the affinities and antagonisms they raise find an unmistakeable voice in medievalist fantasy fiction (Chapter 2). They also find voice in the way medieval music is made and heard in recordings (Chapter 3) and film (Chapter 5) and argued over in musicology (Chapter 4).

My aim is to follow the trail of these associations as they appear in the words spoken and written by participants in a range of different fields. I am less concerned with the objective truth of what is said than in the fact that someone is saying it and the associations it may illuminate. Such links, often unconscious or implicit, are what structure the medieval fantasy. It is by listening to the slippages between associations and tuning in to the patterns they make that an interpretation of medieval nostalgia and its music can be offered. Absences can also be illuminating. One such comparative absence has been that of nostalgia in the study of medievalism. Within the academy nostalgia has had a somewhat puzzling career.

## Nostalgia and the academy

Within the study of medievalism there has been a tendency for such dubious sentiments as nostalgia to fall under the radar. In medieval studies the term usually surfaces only in denunciations and disclaimers, although even these are comparatively rare. Thomas Prendergast and Stephanie Trigg have shed light on academic anxiety about the 'impurity' of medievalism:

> As [the term 'medievalism'] is applied to post-medieval recuperations of the medieval, the term separates, and we would claim, abjects the study of medievalism in order to retain the 'purity' of medieval studies. (Prendergast and Trigg, 2007: 220)

Similarly, Laurie Finke and Martin B. Shichtman, in 'The Romance of Medievalism', have described how the constellation of signifiers included in the term 'romance', nostalgia among them, have allowed 'those of us who study the Middle Ages to create and perpetuate distinctions between the scholarly and the popular, the artistic and the vulgar, the complex and the simplistic' (Finke and Shichtman, 2014: 295). The term 'medievalism' was created to 'police these boundaries, maintaining the purity of the work done by scholars, historians, and philologists who recover medieval materials against the fanciful speculation that contaminates political legitimation and popularization' (2014: 295). In these distinctions, nostalgia has almost invariably found itself on the wrong, 'fanciful' side of the boundary.

In recent years medievalism has attracted significant and growing academic attention, but in that time little sustained attention has been paid to the nostalgia so often associated with it. Perhaps, as Medievalism Studies now approaches closer in status to Medieval Studies as an academic discipline, the need to exonerate it from the taint of nostalgia becomes more urgent. Medievalism studies, now enjoying more prosperous times, may feel the need to uphold its own hard-won legitimacy by rejecting nostalgia.[18] A few publications have sought to buck the trend. Carolyn Dinshaw, in *How Soon is Now*, is one of the few 'medievalismists' who have given space to the rehabilitation of nostalgia in academia, calling for a 'creative rethinking' (2012: 35). In a 2011 issue of *postmedieval* on medievalist nostalgia ('Nostalgia on my Mind') she asks, provocatively: 'But aren't there ways of thinking about nostalgia that are less suspicious of the effects of desire or longing on our critical capacities?' (Dinshaw, 2011: 226).[19] Finke and Shichtman, as noted, also find value in exploring medievalist nostalgia: 'Once we stop dismissing nostalgia and begin to investigate the mechanisms through which it mediates past and present, the term creates aporias of Derridean proportions' (2014: 296). Bernard Cerquiglini offers another example of medievalist nostalgia, the philologist's endless quest for the elusive original: 'Medieval philology is the mourning for a text, the patient labour of this mourning. It is the quest for an anterior perfection that is always bygone' (1999: 34). That is a quest for Eden.

The gradual entry of nostalgia into medievalism studies is part of an affective turn in the discipline. 'Our approach', write Stephanie Trigg and Thomas Prendergast, 'will often be affective and intuitive – largely based on how our feeling of time is elicited by medieval and medievalist texts' (2018: 23).

On the whole, though, while scholars now speak of passion or desire as fruitfully motivating the medieval scholar, nostalgia is less in evidence. It does not have the savour of those more fiery and active emotions. Yet much that we study in medievalism is precisely 'nostalgia for a past that never was', as David Matthews has termed it (2015: 57). One instance, relevant to this study, is the melancholic regret so evident in *LOTR*. Here is Galadriel: 'The love of the Elves for their land and their works is deeper than the deeps of the Sea, and their regret is undying and cannot ever wholly be assuaged' (Tolkien, 1993: 356). Tolkien's own undying regret is evident in a score of passages lamenting loss, impending or achieved, of a shining Edenic world before a Fall. It is also evident in his letters, in particular this one to his son Christopher in 1945: 'Certainly there was an Eden on this very unhappy earth. We all long for it, and we are constantly glimpsing it: our whole nature at its best and least corrupted, its gentlest and most humane, is still soaked with the sense of "exile"' (Tolkien, 1995: 109). Readers and film-goers find an echo in these sentiments. Perhaps we who study Tolkien's work and the responses of his fans may also find an echo of nostalgia in our own.

In the last decade and more, some medievalism scholars have adopted the term 'neomedievalism' to designate a form of medievalism emerging in this century among practitioners, one which wholeheartedly rejects nostalgia.[20] In 2009 Carol L. Robinson and Pamela Clements wrote: 'Thus, [neomedievalism] is not *anti*-romantic ... but simply *non*-romantic in an anti-nostalgic and decreasingly Eurocentric, and clearly anti-historical sort of way' (2009: 56; emphasis in original). Also: 'A sense of anarchy is a key to this type of neomedievalism; it is a medievalism full of anachronisms ... fully aware and celebratory of the constructed nature of its world(s)' (Robinson and Clements, 2009: 61).

For David Marshall also, neomedievalism is non- or anti-nostalgic: 'The use of the past in neomedievalism thus spurns nostalgia in preference for a "new and improved alternate universe"' (D. Marshall, 2011: 24). And, also from Marshall:

> Other medievalisms (though not postmodern medievalism) incline towards nostalgia – a term coined in the seventeenth century to characterize a sort of homesickness and implying a sense of feeling

alienated from some originary point and a yearning for return. Neomedievalism, indeed, often lacks that, instead tending towards the gross rewriting of the past to suit current predilections. (D. Marshall, 2011: 26)

There are undoubtedly such purely pragmatic medievalisms, but it is puzzling that the nostalgia associated here with *past* medievalisms has, to my knowledge, rarely been fully acknowledged in its supposed heyday, perhaps because in our field it has never really escaped its association with its beginnings as a medical diagnosis; not all are comfortable to freely acknowledge nostalgia in their medievalist pursuits and ideas. The main difficulty with the attitudes expressed in these articles, however, is that nostalgia is considered as unitary, whereas it is multiple, complex and ambiguous. It takes a variety of sometimes incompatible forms. The best-known distinction is that made by Boym, which divides restorative from reflective nostalgias:

> Restorative nostalgia does not think of itself as nostalgia, but rather as truth and tradition. Reflective nostalgia dwells on the ambivalences of human longing and belonging and does not shy away from the contradictions of modernity. Restorative nostalgia protects the absolute truth, while reflective nostalgia calls it into doubt. (Boym, 2001: xviii)

One's sense, reading these articles on neomedievalism, is that the 'nostalgia' in question is always that of the earnest attempt to reconstruct the 'truth' of the medieval world typical of the nostalgia Boym names 'restorative', whereas the nostalgia she describes as 'reflective' seems compatible with the awareness of those described as non-nostalgic in the articles quoted here; those with an appreciation of 'the irreparable gap between medieval and (post)modern' (D. Marshall, 2011: 29).

Irony has also been put alongside nostalgia as a means of questioning the 'absolute truth' of nostalgic visions. Linda Hutcheon wrote, in her conclusion to 'Irony, Nostalgia, and the Postmodern': 'The ironizing of nostalgia in the very act of its invoking may be one way ... that the postmodern has of taking responsibility for such responses by creating a small part of the distance necessary for reflective thought about the present as well as the past' (2000: 6). Boym too has teamed nostalgia up with irony, ending her work with the proviso: 'On the other side of ironic estrangement might be emotion and longing; they are yoked as two sides of a coin' (2001: 354).

Some more recent empirical studies have also turned older associations of nostalgia on their heads, even its supposed negativity, for instance, in this abstract of a 2020 paper:

> Nostalgia is a mixed emotion. Recent empirical research, however, has highlighted positive effects of nostalgia, suggesting it is a predominantly positive emotion. When measured as an individual difference, nostalgia-prone individuals report greater meaning in life and approach temperament. When manipulated in an experimental paradigm, nostalgia increases meaning in life, self-esteem, optimism, and positive affect'. (Newman *et al.*, 2020: 325)[21]

Other recent studies also include optimism in the effects of nostalgia.[22] My point is to suggest that there is no simple or straightforward way to characterise nostalgia's varied emotions. Nostalgia has its ambiguities and ambiguity is not always a comfortable experience. For many, conflicting accounts of a treasured medieval past may prompt anxious or angry responses, as in some arguments about the authentic performance of medieval music discussed in Chapter 4. Books and articles have been written on the subject of ambiguity tolerance and intolerance, recalling Boym's similar distinction between 'restorative nostalgia [which] protects the absolute truth' and 'reflective nostalgia [which] dwells on the ambivalences of human longing and belonging and does not shy away from the contradictions of modernity' (Boym, 2001: xviii). '[R]estorative nostalgia' is also a matter of desire, a desperate attempt to harness one's own unrecognised desire to an unwavering truth – unrecognised because desire must not be perceived. Once it is, claims to 'absolute truth' ring hollow.

Research carried out after the Second World War resulted in the publication of *The Authoritarian Personality* (1949), in which subjects were scored on their tolerance or otherwise to ambiguity and the ambivalence (also named 'emotional ambiguity') which accompanies it (Adorno *et al.*, 2019: 686). The same study found that intolerance to ambiguity appeared 'to be a characteristic of the ethnically prejudiced [and] also appears as part of the explicitly stated ego-ideal of exponents of the Nazi ideology in professional psychology' (Adorno *et al.*, 2019: 688). This research was a matter of great significance at the time it was carried out, following the Second World War and the Holocaust, when the effects of Nazi ideology were everywhere in evidence. It is a matter of significance today when Nazi ideology is again on the rise and an all-white medieval Europe again provides a cherished vision for far-right nostalgia, as Andrew Elliot and others have noted:

> The real trick, for both Hitler and his successors, was to employ the Middle Ages as a seemingly benign mode of nostalgia. In a tense climate of economic depression, widespread misinformation, wounded national pride, and knee-jerk racism, each successive movement promoted a return to the past. The past they invoked was a putatively shared national identity – shared by those whom they considered racially 'pure' – that allowed for a nostalgic use of the past. (Elliot, 2017b: n.p.)

Nostalgia is now employed again, as it was by Hitler and others, to invoke a national identity built on the idea of a shared 'race', comprised of those considered 'pure', and thus requiring an ancestry which guarantees their purity. The 'Middle Ages' of Nazi ideology is one way to provide such an ancestry, however it is established.

If one credits the findings of *The Authoritarian Personality* (whose research methods have been questioned by some),[23] the resemblance between the distinctions made there by Adorno *et al.* and those made by Boym is striking, as are the others mentioned here briefly. The linking of the nostalgia which Boym describes as restorative with the intolerance to ambiguity and the disturbing experience of ambivalence which, for some, accompanies it, emphasises the significance of nostalgia and its effects in our lives. Our memories of the past, whether memories of lived events or those 'anemoic' memories discussed earlier, make up our vision of the world and our place within it. A medieval past which conflicts with this vision can be experienced as an attack on our identity.

These complexities might justly make us wary of medievalist nostalgia but, as an aspect of our identity and our desire, I believe we cannot avoid nostalgia in some form or other. Hating it is not enough, as Alistair Bonnett remarks:

> And why do we need to break from such hostility? Not because nostalgia is a fine and noble thing. Very often it is quite the opposite. It is because nostalgia is a part of what we are. It is not something we can opt in and out of ... To flee it is to run towards it. (2010: 44–5)

Reflection, however, can awaken us to the nostalgic strain in the work we study and in our own research and writing. Reflection can show us how we can recognise and work with nostalgia while avoiding its dangers, especially at this time when it is inciting hatred and violence in many parts of the world. There is a sense of profound loss at the base of nostalgia, whatever its manifestation. Nostalgic fantasies, disseminated from a variety of sources, are challenged by the discipline of research but they are not entirely erased. Nostalgia cannot be completely turned aside by critique. It has its own place. It is part of the emotional component which enlivens and colours our lives and our research. We need to become acquainted with the nostalgic fantasy of the medieval in its various guises, whether it appears in the work we study or in our own work. Now in particular we need to be aware of the medieval nostalgia which is driving one of the most troubling movements of our time: the current upswing of racism across the white world.[24]

### Race, gender and nostalgia in high fantasy fiction

A medievalist nostalgia which thinks of itself as 'truth and tradition', as Boym describes her 'restorative' version, has serious repercussions for our understanding of the Middle Ages and of medievalism. Ambiguity is not well tolerated by some, as the study mentioned indicates. When medievalist nostalgia is fuelled by racist or misogynous hatred and fear it has very serious repercussions in the present and for the future.[25]

White supremacists have rewritten history to retrospectively denude medieval Europe of all but its white inhabitants, as Thomas Prendergast and Stephanie Trigg note in *Affective Medievalism*: 'Medieval myths, narratives, images and heraldic insignia are regularly co-opted by white supremacist groups wanting to promote the medieval past as a period of racial homogeneity or "purity"' (2018: 6). To provide a suitably 'pure' ancestry for their claims, white supremacists attempt to make over, not only the present, but the medieval past as well.[26] An all-white medieval Europe is positioned as the blueprint and justification for a desired present. This is one of the dangers of nostalgia, that we may attribute to the past what we desire in the present, thus providing spurious justifications for our attitudes and actions.[27]

Ancestry is an appropriate term in this context, since it brings to the fore the hereditary aspect of the insistence on a white medieval Europe, as Prendergast and Trigg's words make clear. 'Purity' brings the question of race back squarely to the body. Ancestry is a matter of blood as well as traditions, as it was used, for instance, in the Spanish phrase 'limpieza de sangre', or 'purity of blood'.[28]

But it is not as straightforward as it appears. 'Purity' has an ambiguous relationship to the body. In a different context, 'purity' may stand in for the removal of traces of the body in the performance of medieval song, as discussed in Chapter 4. Such distinctions bring home the range and complexity of the meanings and emotions attached to words which, like purity, are routinely used in association with the medieval world (in particular its music and the listener's relation to it).[29]

Racism needs to be mentioned here for another reason: it has a central place in much medieval fantasy fiction, a fact which has played a role in the advancement of white supremacist attitudes. As Helen Young argues: 'Whiteness as default setting is as much a feature of the Fantasy genre as it is of western culture and society' (2016: 1). In fantasy fiction and film, readers and viewers, especially children and adolescents, are drawn into passionate identifications with or against certain characters or certain peoples. Race may become embroiled in their identifications and racist attitudes transferred to the world outside the book or film.

Some white supremacists have been quick to pick up on fantasy fiction as a mode of recruiting new members, as Young discovered when she first began investigations: 'I stumbled very quickly into the white supremacist love of fantasy, Tolkien especially, specifically in the Stormfront chat forums' (2017: n.p.). Derek Black, a former Ku Klux Klan member, in an interview with Ryan Stone for *The New York Times*, related how he had lured Tolkien fans with a section devoted to *LOTR* on the white supremacist *Stormfront* website: 'And I had founded that section because when [the *LOTR*] movies came out I got super into it, and I figured you could get people who liked with such a white mythos, a few turned on by white nationalism' (2017: n.p.).

*LOTR* has represented, for some white supremacists, an image of a world in which whites fight for and win a deserved victory due to their inherent superiority. Tolkien's work has had a diametrically opposite effect on people of colour. It is to them that his much-read and much-loved works of fantasy have perhaps done their greatest harm, in particular to those reading his work as children or adolescents. These readers speak of their shock in discovering that the only people of colour in *LOTR* and *Narnia* are evil and loathsome, held in contempt by the very characters they most admire and with whom they identify. Christina Warmbrunn relates:

> When I was a child, I was what you would call a J. R. R. Tolkien fangirl. I read The Lord of the Rings over and over. I traipsed around the countryside, imagining it was Middle-earth. With just a flight of imagination, I could be snug in the Shire, exploring the mines of Moria, or even flitting through the woods of Lothlórien.
> When the first Lord of the Rings movie was finally released, I was 14 and so excited to see it. But immediately, I noticed something distressing: no one on screen looked like me … My escapism into fantasy was not as safe as I thought. As an adult, I discovered that my … beloved text was built upon an internally racist foundation that made no room for me, a Black fan. (Warmbrunn, 2020: n.p.)[30]

Where Tolkien recognised racism, in Nazism, he fought it, as in his angry response to his German publisher's enquiry in 1939 as to whether he was *arisch* (Aryan): 'I am not of *Aryan* extraction: that is Indo-iranian. … But if I am to understand that you are enquiring whether I am of *Jewish* origin, I can only reply that I regret that I appear to have *no* ancestors of that gifted people' (Tolkien, 1981: 37; emphasis in original). But he did not always recognise his own racism.

In Tolkien's legendarium the assumption of a racial hierarchy is clear. As Faramir explains to Frodo: 'For so we reckon them in our lore, calling them the High, or Men of the West, which were Númenoreans; and the Middle Peoples, such as are the Rohirrim and the Wild, the Men of Darkness, the wild Easterlings [and] cruel Haradrim' (Tolkien, 1993: 663). This racial hierarchy is apparent throughout *LOTR* and speaks of the habitual assumption of white superiority in Western thought, although it is sometimes undercut. Frodo, as the lowly hobbit turned hero, turns the tables on the hierarchies of being that the world of *LOTR* had established. As Eliza Farrell has argued, 'the hierarchical structure of Middle-earth [can be read as] a dialogic space, where even as Tolkien uses racial generalizations he undercuts these assumptions through the plasticity of his characters and their interactions' (Farrell, 2009: iv).³¹ Frodo's position in the hierarchical structure is ambiguous. In Treebeard's list of the species of Middle Earth, hobbits are not even mentioned. Frodo's status as the humble hero who saved Middle Earth where the great had failed is part of the point of the story. Yet even he is marked out as racially superior, at least to other hobbits. Gandalf describes him as: 'taller than some and fairer than most [hobbits]', the physical characteristics considered most desirable in the racist imagination, the characteristics of northern Europe (Tolkien, 1993: 163). It seems that, in this regard, Tolkien wanted it both ways.

For Tolkien, racism ran deep, 'half-sublimated', as Saladin Ahmed has suggested, in 'Is "Game of Thrones" Too White?': '[Tolkien's] half-sublimated wranglings with race are more complex and fraught than either his shrillest detractors or his most fawning defenders would have us believe' (Saladin Ahmed, 2012: n.p.). Appearance was only part of the picture in Tolkien's *LOTR* version of the 'Great Chain of Being'.³² His assumptions produced in his white characters a more finely honed individuality. In general, non-whites in high fantasy have difficulty emerging fully as individual characters. Sara Ahmed has observed that whiteness is

> a category of experience that disappears as a category through experience, and … this disappearance makes whiteness 'worldly'. To put this simply, what I offer here is a vocabulary for re-describing how whiteness becomes 'worldly'. Whiteness describes the very 'what' that coheres as a world. (Sara Ahmed, 2007: 150)

In this vision all those who are not white are relegated, not just to inferiority, but to a place outside the coherent 'world'. This relegation translates in fantasy fiction as a lack of complexity and of differentiation in writing involving non-whites. They are less intricately written, only rarely emerging beyond their status as part of a group (or horde). In the world of fantasy fiction this means that white characters, above and beyond their narrative centrality, *matter* more; on them is bestowed a heightened, more intimate and more finely crafted reality. Ultimately, the question of whether Tolkien was personally a racist is, as Helen Young has argued, 'secondary to the evidence of [his] creative production when it comes to [his] influence on the fantasy genre' (2016: 16). Even leaving aside Tolkien's influence on the genre, the popularity of his own work and that of the films it engendered have spread its fame far and wide, in some ways for the worse.

In *Narnia*, C. S. Lewis's racism emerges as more conscious and more virulent than Tolkien's.[33] In *The Horse and his Boy*, the Calormenes live below the great desert which separates them from the White lands to the North, much as the Middle East is separated from Europe by the Mediterranean. Calormen is an 'orientalised fantasyland', to use Farah Mendlesohn's terms (2005: 85), but it is an ugly fantasy. Jamison Hartley's map reflects Lewis's Eurocentric *Weltanschauung*, showing us the civilised world of Narnia and Archenland, framed by wildernesses to the north and west and mustard yellow desert to the south, beyond which lies Calormen (Hartley, 2011).

Lewis's Orient has a more elegant side, which appears in Aravis's beautiful, stylised storytelling (2005: 222–4). In her story, if nowhere else in Calormen culture, one might find, in Edward Said's words, 'a place of romance, exotic beings, haunting memories and landscapes' (Said, 1979: 1). In general Lewis's scorn for the inhabitants of Calormen is unabashed: 'In the village [Shasta] only met other men who were just like his father – men with long, dirty robes, and wooden shoes turned up at the toe, and turbans on their heads, and beards, talking to one another very slowly about things that sounded dull' (2005: 205). Even more flagrant is this passage from *The Last Battle*: 'Then the dark men came round them in a thick crowd, smelling of garlic and onions, their white eyes flashing dreadfully in their brown faces' (Lewis, 2005: 682).

Like the orcs in *LOTR*, *all* the Calormenes are dirty, *all* are dull. For the most part, like the orcs, they do not emerge as singular beings, except that, unlike the orcs, they are human, which makes the slur more problematic. Tolkien takes care to present the orcs as inhuman and/or manufactured beings. In the final book of *Narnia*, *The Last Battle*, those who enter the stable, Narnian and Calormene, are claimed either by Aslan or by the hideous demon god of the Calormenes, Tash, who eats his victims. Tash 'had a vulture's head and four arms. Its beak was open and its eyes blazed. A croaking voice came from its beak' (Lewis, 2005: 739). Not for the Calormenes, barring one or two, the super-reality of the heavenly lands. This is the dark side of the 'more real than reality' sites that I am exploring in the work of Tolkien and Lewis. They appear to be whites-only zones. Lewis's contempt for Middle Eastern cultures extends, as John Goldthwaite has argued, to religion: 'As a Protestant fundamentalist, Lewis liked to ridicule other faiths in his pages, attacking Islam in *The Horse and His Boy*, for example' (1996: 224). The ridicule in this book is ferocious.

Lewis's ridicule of Islam and of Middle Eastern culture in general is a blatant example of the need felt by Europeans to deny the role of the Arab world in the formation of the medieval West. As María Rosa Menocal has argued, 'The proposition that the Arab world had played a critical role in the making of the modern West, from the vantage point of the late nineteenth century and the better part of this century, is in clear and flagrant contradiction of [Western] cultural ideology' (2001: 6). Such erasures of non-European influences on medieval Europe have been used to prop up the identities of white Europeans in general. In the work of Tolkien and Lewis, the virtues of Englishness in particular, its quiet, unassuming superiority, are written into the substance of their books – in narrative, appearance, character and, in particular, dialogue.

When it came to gender, similar assumptions were in place for both Tolkien and Lewis, though differently constructed and perhaps less easily maintained in mid-twentieth-century England, where, though white men could possibly isolate themselves from black people, women were harder to avoid.[34] Many men longed, and still long, for the good old medieval days when women supposedly knew their place and could not threaten the assumed superiority of men or trespass on their private, men-only spaces or take their jobs. *LOTR* provided a haven for men in which, by and large, women could flourish (or not) only in very restricted ways, as the tale of the shieldmaiden, Éowyn, attests. Éowyn, once she has fulfilled the prophecy which no man could fulfil, submits to womanhood and exchanges her sword for a distaff (Tolkien, 1993: 943). Michael D. C. Drout has suggested one reason for Tolkien's near-banishment of women on Middle Earth:

> Traditions for Tolkien were inheritances repeated unchanged across many generations, passed from father to son. Thus traditions are a form of what I call 'masculine reproduction', the replication of identities from one man to another without the visible influence of women. Women are almost entirely absent from *The Lord of the Rings*. This attitude towards women in Tolkien's work is generated, I believe, from anxieties intrinsic to masculine reproduction. (Drout, 1996: 26)

Women disturb that masculine reproduction. Perhaps too the form in which women *were* permitted to reproduce, in the flesh, was also a matter of anxiety for Tolkien. The only female in *LOTR* who is seen to feed, bleed and suffer in the flesh is the revolting Shelob, the giant spider.

Girls have more standing in Lewis's Narnia, but it comes at a cost. In Lewis's *Last Battle*, Susan's refusal of the final escapade excludes her (at least temporarily) from entry into the Narnian heaven, because, in Jill's words: 'She's interested in nothing nowadays except nylons and lipstick and invitations. She always was a jolly sight too keen on being grown-up' (2005: 741). Philip Pullman has suggested that 'Susan, like Cinderella, is undergoing a transition from one phase of her life to another. Lewis didn't approve of that. ... He was frightened and appalled at the notion of wanting to grow up' (Pullman, 1998: n.p.).[35] Both Lewis and Tolkien avoided grown-up human women in their stories, substituting elves (Tolkien) or girls (Lewis). The female elves (or half-elves) that we meet, Arwen and Galadriel, seem too ethereal for the actual bodily, sexual, birth-giving aspects of adult womanhood, whereas for Lewis's girls it is all, mercifully, still to come.[36] But Susan is approaching the danger years. For Lewis, I think, Susan's frivolity itself was problematic. He appeared to have been appalled by any signs of frivolity in his fictional children. Girls and boys alike, all were expected to be decent, plain-spoken chaps with no nonsense about them.[37] These are some of the ways in which racism and sexism are ingrained in the nostalgia for the medieval found in high fantasy fiction.

The next section introduces the third element of my study, music, into the blend. Academic attention to the crucial role of music in the fantasies of medievalist nostalgia is a comparatively recent phenomenon, while, on the musicological side, music as an artefact of medievalism has only recently been considered as a subject for study.[38]

## Music and medievalism: Crossing the disciplinary boundaries

Musicology, in the past, has tended towards a positivistic approach to medieval music which has, until this century, largely neglected reception (and invention), while studies in medievalism have focused overwhelmingly on literature, architecture, the visual arts and games, online and off. In the present century musicology has opened its borders. Daniel Leech-Wilkinson, Annette Kreutziger-Herr, John Haines, Kirsten Yri, Stephen C. Meyer, Susan Fast, Elizabeth Randell Upton, Karen Cook and Nick Wilson, among others, have produced valuable work in medievalism studies. With some exceptions, however, the pioneering work of these musicologists has not been sufficiently acknowledged within the general domain of medievalism studies.

The disciplinary border between music and literary or film studies is not an easy one to cross. Musicology has its own special knowledge and language, but then so do all the other disciplines which an understanding of medievalism requires. Yet, until quite recently, music has largely remained separate while the others have found ways to talk to each other. Perhaps this separation owes something to the pervasive hegemony of the visual in the hierarchy of the senses. Music, foregrounding hearing, disrupts a discourse, built up over centuries, which rests on the primacy of sight.[39] However it has come about, this mutual exclusion has resulted in an impoverishment of the discourse of medievalism studies. That barrier has limited both how we think about the medieval past and how we ponder how it is thought, imagined, invented, desired and despised – the province of medievalism. In this study I hope to assist in writing into medievalism studies something of the imagined loss that nostalgia predicates as I read it in the discourses where music is woven into the fabric of the imagining – in medieval fantasy fiction and film, scholarly discourse and professional and fan reviews. Music, because of its seductive power, makes a perfect breeding ground for nostalgia and any discussion of nostalgic medievalism must address its musical aspect.

Fortunately, the gulf between medievalism in music on the one side, and history and the visual and literary arts on the other, is increasingly being bridged. For instance, Anke Bernau and Bettina Bildhauer's *Medieval Film* (2009) has a chapter on music in medievalist film by Alison Tara Walker. Tison Pugh and Angela Jane Weisl (2013) devoted part of a chapter to recent performances of medieval and medieval-inspired music in *Medievalisms*. There is also a chapter on neo-medieval music by Alana Bennett in *The Middle Ages in Popular Culture*, edited by Helen Young (2015), as well as a chapter on music and medievalism which I contributed to *The Cambridge*

*Companion to Medievalism* edited by Louise D'Arcens (2016a). *Studies in Medievalism XXVII: Authenticity, Medievalism, Music* (Fugelso, 2018) has a section devoted to musical medievalism, while Ruth Barrett-Peacock and Ross Hagen's essay collection, *Medievalism and Metal Music Studies: Throwing Down the Gauntlet*, was published in May 2019. In December 2019 a special issue of *postmedieval*, which I co-edited with Andrew Lynch and Elizabeth Randell Upton, was entitled *Music, Emotion, Medievalism*. The *Oxford Handbook on Music and Medievalism*, co-edited by Stephen C. Meyer and Kirsten Yri, was published June 2020.[40] Within Tolkien studies, unsurprisingly, musical medievalism has been more actively addressed, for instance in *Middle-earth Minstrel*, a series of essays edited by Bradford Lee Eden (2010a).

The next section addresses the centrality of desire in the work of Tolkien, Lewis and Lacan. They may seem unlikely interlocutors but they were contemporaries, living through two world wars and their aftermaths, and each wrote about the eternal desire for what is always missing in everyday life, which I explore here. They therefore often found themselves on the same ground, although their understandings of that ground were incompatible.

## Desire in religion and psychoanalysis

Tolkien and Lewis were (and remain through their work) key purveyors of nostalgia for a numinous medieval in which music is central. This book moves between the two lenses of religion and psychoanalysis – with Tolkien and Lewis on one side and Lacan on the other – which their perspectives offer. I aim to bring them into a conversation they never had. All three men had a religious upbringing. All were medievalists, Tolkien and Lewis by trade. Lacan is less explicitly a medievalist but, as Erin Labbie notes, the Middle Ages are crucial to his theory and methodology:

> Jacques Lacan is a medievalist and not merely because he cites courtly love poetics as a means of developing and articulating his theory of desire (although that focus remains a crucial point in support of his medievalism ... Lacan is a medievalist because his methodologies follow those established by the medieval scholastic scholars. (Labbie, 2006: 1–2)

For this study, Lacan's working of desire is central. In his theory desire works through the fabrication of a fantasy, a narrative explanation for loss. Thus, for Lacan, since the object is always inevitably lost, desire includes nostalgia in its basic structure. Nostalgia narrativises the 'loss' of the always already missing object of desire. I have not attempted to distinguish the Lacanian term 'fantasy' (or 'phantasy') entirely from the ordinary usage. They cannot be clearly demarcated, nor is the term a completely unified concept within psychoanalytic theory. It is, however, discussed in Chapter 1.

Tolkien and Lewis have a different part to play in my argument than Lacan. I see their writings, and those of their followers, readers and viewers, as symptomatic of a medievalist nostalgia which Lacan's theories of desire implicitly critique. That is the relation between them posed in this book. It offers a Lacanian interpretation of their work and the influence of the nostalgia they offer the reader in their fiction, Tolkien in particular. This does not make their part any less important or belittle their work. They are central in the production of a medievalist nostalgia in which music figures as a signal of the numinous moment, opening a portal to a greater, more intense reality. They wrote their lost worlds, and the longing that inspired them, with such vividness and passion that their work exemplifies the symptomatology of nostalgia. They – especially Tolkien – strongly influenced the terms in which medievalist nostalgia would be experienced and the part music would play in it, following publication of their fiction.

How it was that Tolkien and Lewis (and again particularly Tolkien) hit the nostalgia button so accurately is a question many have pondered. Theodore Roszak, in his 1969 book, *The Making of a Counter Culture*, wrote Tolkien into the countercultural mix: 'Hippies who may be pushing thirty wear buttons that read "Frodo Lives" and decorate their pads with maps of Middle Earth' (1995: 40). Lev Grossman, looking back on the response to early American editions of *LOTR* in the mid-1960s, wrote:

> [T]he Rings had struck a chord. The burgeoning environmental movement saw in his wasteland of Mordor a strip-mined industrial dystopia. On a deeper level, a country drowning in the moral quicksand of Vietnam and Watergate found comfort in the moral clarity of Tolkien's epic story of a just, clear war. Good and evil are fixed stars in the skies of Middle-earth even as they're starting to look wobbly in ours. (Grossman, 2002)

Grossman was right. A similar phenomenon took hold in Australia in the late 1960s and 1970s, as I witnessed. Many young hippies left the cities and made new homes for themselves in the bush, in an attempt to recreate a harmonious, pre-industrial paradise, a little like the Shire or Narnia. Tolkien was part of a dream of renewal that fired the hearts of many of the first post-Second World War generation, the baby-boomers. Tolkien and Lewis themselves found less comfort than they offered their fans, for whom Tolkien's work was a call to arms. They doubted the value of any political action, looking instead to their Christian faith for escape and consolation.[41] This quest seemed less appealing to many of their hippie followers.[42]

Tolkien and Lewis infected the fantasies of the boomers and the generations that followed. Their immense and continuing popularity is an indication of their accuracy as diagnosticians; their infection found a willing host. They touched for many a wound that would not heal and in doing so revealed it. This was the aim, at least for Lewis, who wrote:

> I am trying to rip open the inconsolable secret in each one of you – the secret which hurts so much that you take your revenge on it by calling it names like Nostalgia and Romanticism and Adolescence. (Lewis, 1980a: 30)

Like Lacan, Tolkien and Lewis were analysts (in Lewis's case both diagnostician and surgeon!) but their analysis of desire was based on their Christian faith in a benevolent God as the ultimate object of desire, the guarantor of truth and the soul's true home, whereas Lacan's was based on an understanding of desire as an effect of the castrations that language imposes on the speaking being.

Lacan finds his place in this book as one who found a way to think the imbrication of language and desire. He turned to language quite early in his career (the cited works below are from the late 1950s and 1960s) and, although his theory evolved over time, he never relinquished his conviction that language played a structuring role for the human subject. For Lacan, we are born into language and structured by it from the word go. In 'Signification of the Phallus' he puts it this way: '[Man's] nature is woven by effects in which is to be found the structure of language, of which he becomes the material, and that therefore there resounds in him ... the relation of speech' (1977a: 284).

The child does not even need to be able to speak in order to learn that 'there is here a path, a defile through which essentially the manifestations of his needs must stoop in order to be satisfied' (Lacan, 1958–59: 9). Here already the constricted path is set for the production of desire through the necessity that all appeals have to be made in a world of beings structured by the principles of language. Even the infant's wordless cry will be structured linguistically by an anxious parent and returned to them in that form: 'are you hungry?', 'are you in pain?'

Lacan dives deeply into the production of desire through language. He speaks of a 'deviation of man's needs from the fact that he speaks, in the sense that in so far as his needs are interpreted as demands, they return to him alienated', not his own. Demand constitutes the Other as 'possessing the "privilege" of satisfying needs, that is to say, the power of depriving them of that alone by which they are satisfied' (Lacan, 1977a: 286). The demand 'open[s] up an immeasurable space, namely that of being a demand for love' (Lacan, 1977b: 311). Any particular satisfaction, by reason of its particularity, 'is reduced to the level of being no more than the crushing of the demand for love' (1977a: 286). Demand is separated from need, and desire appears in that margin of separation:

> Thus desire is neither the appetite for satisfaction, nor the demand for love, but the difference that results from the subtraction of the first from the second, the phenomenon of their splitting. (Lacan, 1977a: 286)

I understand nostalgia as the repeated attempt to identify and make good that loss produced in the margin between the satisfaction of need and the demand for love and at the same time a mourning for the impossibility of the attempt. That is another kind of unbreachable *space between*, between the reasonable and the impossible. The loss cannot be made good because it is not a loss but a fundamental lack produced by the exigencies of speech. Nostalgia is also that which fends off with fantasy the horror of an undifferentiated Real which the past may evoke, as in the vision of Walter Benjamin's 'Angelus Novus':

> His face is turned toward the past. Where we perceive a chain of events, he sees one single catastrophe which keeps piling wreckage upon wreckage and hurls it in front of his feet. (Benjamin, 1970: 259)

In the face of the angel's vision, history itself, viewed as an attempt to narrativise and so make sense of the past and its losses, might be considered as a form of nostalgia.[43] Slavoj Žižek observes:

> [T]he lost quality only emerged at this very moment of its alleged loss. This coincidence of emergence and loss designates the fundamental paradox of the Lacanian object *a*, which emerges as being-lost. Narrativisation occludes this paradox by describing the process in which the object is first given and then gets lost. (Žižek, 1998: 199)[44]

Nostalgia is the narrativisation of the 'loss' of the always already missing object of desire, allowing the hope that what was lost may be found again, as in the second coming of Arthur or the second coming of Christ. Nostalgic fantasies are an attempt to ease the distress caused by the sense of loss by offering an explanation for it: once things worked but then something went wrong; the key ingredient has been lost and cannot be found. Every nostalgic narrative works with this fundamental pattern, beginning with the loss of the Garden of Eden or similar myths of origin and ending with the hope or belief that the garden may one day be re-entered. Religious aspirations are founded on such narratives. The fantasy fiction of Tolkien and Lewis is steeped in that narrative of loss and ultimate recovery. It is an article of their faith. Lacan's theory of the *always* already lost object crushes any such hopes as it crushes the nostalgic narrative itself. It is in that sense that Lacan's work intersects with and analyses their nostalgia.

My arguments rest on the idea that the medieval vision of those to whom I listen is created or fostered by trails of association which they bring, consciously or unconsciously, to the word. When pieced together, these trails can tell us a great deal about the myriad 'medievals' which past and present ages endlessly produce. The medieval, in its turn, has proved fertile ground for an understanding of nostalgia.

## Source material and methodology

This study of medievalism, music and nostalgia covers a variety of sources. Some involve actual musical performance, while in the case of others, for instance, fantasy novels, music plays an important part within the narrative; others again are theoretical and/or ideological sources, such as discussions about music in academia. In the case of performance, my focus is on recordings rather than live concerts. This is partly because, as Elizabeth Randell Upton has written, by enabling repeated listenings, recordings can foster growing familiarity with the music.[45] In this respect a recording is more like a book than a concert. Over time the listener knows the recording well enough to know, at any point, what will come next; each track is pre-echoed in memory at the end of the previous track so that the recording is eventually received in its entirety. In this way, the recording may take on some of the attributes of narrative. This is especially the case with the concept album.

This kind of listening delights in repetition. For these listeners repetition is not associated with increasing boredom. For them, as Kierkegaard insisted: 'That which is repeated has been, otherwise it could not be repeated, but the very fact that it has been makes the repetition into something new' (cited in Eriksen, 2000: 12). For some listeners, as for Kierkegaard, the well-loved music, like the well-loved novel or poem, does not grow stale but comes up fresh every time. For these listeners, paradoxically, along with its beloved familiarity, music still carries with it the sense of wonder usually associated with the new.

In this study, the discourse of nostalgic medievalism in and around music is inscribed in a variety of cultural forms. These are, first, the recordings themselves in terms of their interpretation, presentation, iconography and arrangement of material – both musical arrangement and the temporal arrangement of material on the record; second, the representation of music and its functions in fantasy fiction and film; last, the plethora of material surrounding the performance, recording, marketing and consumption of medieval music; that is, liner notes, promotional material distributed by medieval music groups, musicological arguments, and professional and listener/customer reviews of recorded music. Read together these cultural forms can produce an understanding of the way music figures in nostalgic medievalism.

I have not privileged the music itself over the discourses which surround it; the words are as important as the notes – even more important for my purposes, as they provide the text for a nostalgic fantasy which this book aims to reconstruct. As makers, scholars, performers and listeners we bring our fantasies of the medieval *to* the music, as much or more than we derive them *from* it. It is the nostalgic fantasy of music, often drawn from fantasy fiction, as the key opening the door to a desired medieval paradise, found in all these writings – musical and textual – that I have chosen to investigate. For this reason, this study is organised with the fantasies addressed first and the music later. I understand these nostalgic fantasies as having been with us all along, integral to our status as speaking beings, but nostalgia has only comparatively recently been named as such.

## Chapter summaries

Chapter 1 is devoted to an investigation of nostalgic medievalism via the idea of reality: first, that more real, more intense reality found in certain sites in Tolkien/Lewis fantasy fiction and beyond; second, the realism of violence and savagery espoused by George R. R. Martin and his like; and last, the Real addressed in psychoanalytic theory – undifferentiated matter without the symbolic organisation and the imaginary filters human reason requires. For Tolkien, Lewis and Lacan, the question of what *is* real and what real *means* is the ground on which their fundamental argument lies (or would have if they had acknowledged one another). It is an argument between religion and psychoanalysis in which there is no possible agreement on the nature of human life. The Lacanian real unpicks the coherence of the world to which Tolkien and Lewis, in their Christian faith, clung – a world created and watched over by a loving God through which human beings pass as pilgrims to their eternal home, whether one of reward or punishment. This book follows through the implications of this tacit argument through the writings of these three men.

In Chapter 1 I also explore the pressures to which the fantasy medieval is subjected and the innumerable adaptations it undergoes over the years in response to these pressures. In the Tolkien/Lewis tradition writers sometimes claim to open a way, in their work, to something 'more real than reality' associated with the medieval in its character as an inner space, framed between the classical age and the Renaissance. This medieval is sometimes heard as a negative

– *not* the classical age, *not* the Renaissance – its negativity offering a space framed between two positives that is elusive, mysterious and thus adaptable to fantasies of nostalgic desire – a *space between* – as I have named it. Such a medieval may feel secret and precious, like the *agalma*, the word offered by Lacan for something desirable which is hidden: 'gem or precious object – something that is inside' (Lacan, 2015: 137–8).[46]

The medieval may also be experienced as negative in a different sense, as what must be negated – the repudiated Middle Age as we make of it a repository for the repressed. Ambiguity invariably attends the medieval of fantasy. Chapter 1 also addresses changes in fantasy fiction since *LOTR* and *Narnia*, in the light of the widespread perception that reality is not so stable after all, and considers the various responses by which fantasy fiction and the wider world attempt to come to terms with this perception. One of these responses to instability is a change in the quality of nostalgia.

Each of the remaining chapters addresses a particular discourse in which a range of associative trails link music with the medievalism of nostalgia, however these three terms are understood/fantasised. Chapter 2 broaches the representation of music in medievalist fantasy fiction, in particular the work of Susan Cooper. In her series *The Dark is Rising*, music introduces a 'space between' different temporalities (1973: 244), which may function, like the medieval, as an indicator of something which cannot be directly spoken – the numinous. I have emphasised this *space between* to distinguish its special function. In Chapter 2 the numinous *space between* in medievalist high fantasy may function as a gateway to another world. The *space between*, sometimes signalled by ambiguity or oxymoron, may also signal the presence of something unsayable which slips between oppositions, preventing signification. But in Chapter 2 this space is contested between the apophatic and the didactic impulses of authors: apophatic when music indicates something unsayable between what can be said; metaphoric when the didactic impulse overrides the mystical or poetic and speaking of music becomes instead a way of saying something else. Chapter 3 follows high fantasy discourse from the pages of novels to the music and music literature produced in the medieval music recording industry, especially at the popular end of the spectrum. An indirect conversation flows between these two worlds which allows medieval

Introduction 31

music recordings to be positioned in the numinous place accorded to music in high fantasy novels and to claim to fulfil the promises made there.

Chapter 3, in tracing the flow of discourse between fantasy fiction and the world of medieval music recording, unearths a distinction between listeners who dally with the intensity of the *space between*, taking care to view it from a safe distance, and those who tumble in and lose themselves, becoming the music 'while the music lasts', as T. S. Eliot (1968: 44) has it. This emerges as a crucial distinction, that between desire, ruled by a law of deprivation, and *jouissance*, crossing the line that bounds the pleasure principle, involving a loss of separateness, the loss of an 'I'. In Chapter 3 the *space between* becomes associated with the maternal body surrounding the womb, both longed for and feared.

Chapter 4 engages with the scholarly discourse of musicologists, music historians and aestheticians, and their close collaborators, the directors and performers of medieval music at the scholarly end of the spectrum. The discussion focuses on that enigmatic figure, the countertenor, and his legitimacy or otherwise in the performance of medieval song. I argue that contending fantasies of the body in music helped fuel debates over 'authentic' performance in the 1970s, 1980s and 1990s. The countertenor, too, could be fantasised as occupying a *space between*. Chapter 4 reveals, in the discourse of musicologists and directors, something of what is so strenuously sanitised in purifying accounts of the medieval in music. This purity is expressed as negation – a catalogue of what must be excluded for the sake of authenticity. The countertenor is associated with an excess which must be excised in the performance of medieval music. Whether he is accepted or rejected, the countertenor represents a body excessively but ambiguously sexualised, like his 'ancestor', the castrato. And, because of his perceived kinship with the castrato, the countertenor puts pressure on medieval fantasies of the disembodied, angelic singer, exposing what is repressed in those fantasies – that is, the underbelly of the medieval which is also its improper mirror image. The castrato's *space between* is that of the uncategorisable both and neither.

Chapter 5 is devoted to a discussion of the role of music in Arthurian cinema. Both the film *Excalibur* (1981) and the TV miniseries *Mists of Avalon* (2001) posit a paradisal state of non-separation from nature before a Fall, one (*Mists*) arising from a form of neo-pagan feminism, the other an essentially misogynistic vision associated with the mythopoeic men's movement of the 1980s and early 1990s. I argue that the fantasised paradise is associated with a return to the maternal body, and that this fantasy creates horror as well as ecstasy. Thus, each film finds means, musical and otherwise, to guard against the horror by introducing safeguards into the fantasy. Chapter 5 returns to the *space between* of the medieval maternal body as lost home, its lures and its terrors, in these Arthurian films. What is common to both films is the barrier erected, in different ideological strategies, against a fall into an imprisoning place of archaic irreducibility associated with the maternal body. *Mists of Avalon*, the feminist retelling, invokes a romanticised version of the Goddess Mother as an undifferentiated 'everything', but takes care to scrub her clean of her chaotic associations. The 'englobing' Mother Goddess is castrated and robbed of her horror (Kristeva, 1981: 29).

In each chapter a space emerges, a lost internal place/time, longed for and/or feared, for which the medieval offers itself as a key. It is often marked out by the tensions surrounding it. It is a space intensified by the intense engagement with it of the participants I have studied. This space marks out the place of a fantasy which must be protected, sometimes from its own implications. This book is the product of my engagement with that space, the medieval *space between*, which music may indicate or into which it may precipitate a fall.

## Notes

1 Over the years various studies have borne out the role of music in evoking nostalgia, for instance 'Music-Evoked Nostalgia …' by Frederick S. Barrett *et al.* (2010). In this study, earlier studies are also mentioned as 'implicat[ing] nostalgia as an emotion often triggered by music' (abstract, n.p.).
2 Nostalgia for an unlived past is sometimes known as 'anemoia', a word coined in *The Dictionary of Obscure Sorrows* which means nostalgia for a time you've never known (Koenig, 2021: 167).
3 Similarly, David Matthews notes that 'to be "in the middle", after all, could be thought of as being at the heart of the matter' (Matthews, 2015: loc. 148).

4  Neither recording strategy is a necessary condition, however. Fantasies can be pieced together solely by the susceptible ear and mind.
5  'Why do some people still buy CDs when there's Spotify and iTunes?' is a question asked by Quora (n.d.). Some listeners still want to own a physical CD, one they can hold in their hand, admire the artwork and read the commentary. Some wish to honour the artist's arrangement and presentation of their music. There are other sites asking the same question, for instance Reddit ('u/dacara 1615', 2018).
6  'Numinous' is derived from the Latin 'numen': 'Divinity, god; a local or presiding power or spirit.' (*Oxford English Dictionary*, 2020). See Rudolf Otto's *The Idea of the Holy* (1990), which influenced Lewis.
7  In *The Tough Guide to Fantasyland*, Diana Wynne Jones playfully suggests: 'Music is very important, always GOOD and probably MAGIC, especially if played on a HARP. It seems that DARK LORDS are tone-deaf. They have never been known to employ Music ... on the side of Good, Music has enormous power. It can amplify SPELLS, summon supernatural help, and inspire superhuman courage' (D. Jones, 1996: 131–2).
8  Zwinger revised Hofer's dissertation on nostalgia in 1710. Cited by Austin (Austin,2003: 41).
9  Bernard Romanens sings 'Ranz des Vaches': www.youtube.com/watch?v=e0xAw2oXhJY. Listening to Romanens, it is not hard to imagine the response of those Swiss soldiers to the song. Jean-Jacques Rousseau, however, thought otherwise: 'We shall seek in vain to find in this air any energic accents capable of producing such astonishing effects. These effects, which are void in regard to strangers, come alone from custom, reflections, and a thousand circumstances, which, retrac'd by those who hear them, and recalling the idea of their country, their former pleasures, their youth, and all their joys of life, excite in them a bitter sorrow for the loss of them. The music does not in this case act precisely as music, but as a memorative sign' (Rousseau, 1779, trans. Waring).
10  As Robert Mills expresses it, the medieval can function, not only as an era, but as 'a fluid and floating category of otherness, one that operates spatially ... as well as temporally' (Mills, 2018: 1).
11  As Richard Utz states, this is precisely the affective response Jacques Le Goff rejected when he became a historian, despite it being what drew him to the medieval age in the first place (Utz: 2017: 5).
12  See also Renée Trilling: 'Because of its dialectical structure, nostalgia can point both to a place of absolute alterity and a place that we recognise as our lost home' (Trilling, 2011: 220).

13 The '[f]igure that binds together two words that are ordinarily contradictory' (Eidenmuller, 2001).
14 As Prendergast and Trigg have noted, the Middle Age is one of those places, at once homely and unfamiliar (Prendergast and Trigg, 2019: 11).
15 Freud adds: 'What interests us most in this long extract is to find that among its different shades of meaning the word "*Heimlich*" exhibits one which is identical with its opposite, "*unheimlich*"' (Freud, 1990: 345).
16 See the Urban Dictionary: To physically torture or injure someone by means of archaic methods, usually involving tools frequently used for blacksmithing or traditional feudal era torture. Example of such include thumbscrews, flesh peeling and branding. First coined by Marcellus Wallace in Quentin Tarantino's *Pulp Fiction* (1994). 'What now? Let me tell you what now. I'ma call a coupla hard, pipe-hittin' niggers, who'll go to work on the homes here with a pair of pliers and a blow torch. You hear me talkin', hillbilly boy? I ain't through with you by a damn sight. I'ma get medieval on your ass.' See also: 'The medieval era is the dumping ground of the contemporary imagination, rife with torture, refuse in the street, rape, slavery, superstition, casual slaughter, and every other human vice we supposedly stopped indulging in once we became "enlightened"' (Kaufman, 2016: 56–7).
17 Tison Pugh and Angela Jane Weisl, in *Medievalisms* (2013: 2), cite the writings of Leslie Workman to suggest that 'even academic studies of the Middle Ages become implicated with such nostalgia'. I think the 'even' is redundant.
18 See for instance David Matthews's suggestion that perhaps medievalism now 'threatens to take over the parent discipline [medieval studies?]' (2015: 167).
19 In the same issue, *The Medievalism of Nostalgia*, edited by myself, Louise D'Arcens and Andrew Lynch, a variety of instances and types of medievalist nostalgia are examined. See also my 2018 essay, 'What to Do with Nostalgia in Medieval and Medievalism Studies?' (274–91).
20 'Neomedieval' when applied to music has a different signification. For Alana Bennett, 'unlike pure neomedievalism, however, neo-medieval music is inspired by a keen sense of nostalgia' (Bennett, 2015: loc. 1516).
21 See also the abstract for a paper by Constantine Sedikides *et al.*: 'Nostalgia: Past, Present, and Future': 'Traditionally, nostalgia has been conceptualized as a medical disease and a psychiatric disorder. Instead, we argue that nostalgia is a predominantly positive, self-relevant, and social emotion serving key psychological functions. Nostalgic narratives reflect more positive than negative affect, feature the self as the protagonist, and

are embedded in social context. Nostalgia is triggered by dysphoric states, such as negative mood and loneliness. Finally, nostalgia generates positive affect, increases self-esteem, fosters social connectedness, and alleviates existential threat (Sedikides *et al.*, 2008: 1).

22 For instance, the paper 'A Prologue to Nostalgia: Savouring Creates Nostalgic Memories that Foster Optimism' (Marios Biskas *et al.*, 2019).
23 See, for instance, Budner (1962).
24 As Jason Wilson of the Australian *Guardian* wrote: 'White nationalist hate groups in the US increased 55% throughout the Trump era, according to a new report by the Southern Poverty Law Center (SPLC), and a "surging" racist movement continues to be driven by "a deep fear of demographic change"' (2020: n.p.).
25 'Postelection Surrealism and Nostalgic Racism in the Hands of Donald Trump' is a 2017 article which accurately predicted the carnage, seen in the USA and elsewhere, unleashed by Trump's brutal rhetoric. In the abstract the authors write: 'Our response reflects upon two currents that characterize this postelection moment: first, the surreal mix of gendered and racialized nostalgia embedded in Trump's iconography and message, and second, the intensification of white racism as Trump's rhetoric of patriotic nationalism becomes government' (Goldstein and Hall, 2017: 397). Also on racism in the USA, see an article on the part played by nostalgia in white Southerners' attachment to the Confederacy (Vinson: 2021).
26 Purity (with its spiritual connotations) has a special association with the colour white. In music, for instance, 'white' voices, that is voices without vibrato, are considered purer, although the term is rarely used nowadays. The same colour coding is apparent in *LOTR*. Gandalf the *grey*, for instance, when he returns to Middle Earth after his encounter with the Balrog, has been purified. He is now Gandalf the *white*, his brightness bedazzling the eyes of his former companions (Tolkien, 1993: 483).
27 For a thoroughgoing account of the use of the Middle Ages in racist and nationalist agendas, see Amy S. Kaufman and Paul B. Sturtevant's *The Devil's Historians: How Modern Extremists Abuse the Medieval Past* (2020). See also Helen Young's *Race and Popular Fantasy Literature: Habits of Whiteness* (2016) for a study of the place of fantasy fiction in fuelling such agendas.
28 'In 1604 Felipe III granted the descendants of Pablo de Santa Maria [Jews whose families had converted to Christianity], the privilege of limpieza de sangre, "purity of blood", or equality with "old Christians"' (Roth, 1995: 148). Paradoxically, this privilege of 'purity of blood' could apparently be 'granted' to the descendants of converted Jews. See also

the various appropriations of the term in Uli Linke's *Blood and Nation*, as in the Preface: 'Blood, with its diverse fields of meaning and diverse manifestations, consists of a dominant metaphor or gestalt, mapping fundamental cultural assumptions about gender, sex, and race' (Linke, 1999: vii).

29  A different but related form of nostalgia is that expressed by American whites whose neighbourhoods have changed due to a rise in the number of black residents. Here real memories are subtly reframed to preserve desired identity narratives. A 2012 American study by Michael Maly *et al.* examines the nostalgic narratives of white residents whose neighbourhoods undergo 'racial transition' (Maly *et al.*, 2012: 758). Based on interviews, they found that 'nostalgia narratives are useful in framing white racial identity along the themes of innocence and virtuousness as well as powerlessness and victimhood' (2012: 757). These two nostalgic narratives, the medieval and the contemporary, converge along a path of wounded righteousness and entitlement, the right to a white Europe or a white neighbourhood. Also related is the 'mourning for what one has destroyed' discussed in Renato Rosaldo's 'Imperialist Nostalgia' (1989: 107). Here it is the 'mood of nostalgia [which] makes racial domination appear innocent and pure' (1989: 107). Nostalgias are not always innocent. Like all forms of human memory, they are liable to silently shift in the direction which frees the one who remembers from responsibility.

30  I have wondered too whether children and young people may have failed to recognise black or brown characters in *LOTR* until they saw them on screen, having never heard the unfamiliar words 'swart' or 'swarthy', which Tolkien frequently used to describe them.

31  See also Dimitra Fimi: 'Tolkien's Middle-earth is definitely hierarchical, with divisions and subdivisions within different groups of beings. But, at the same time it is not a consistent world' (Fimi, 2010: 159).

32  Aristotle's work *History of Animals* was based on his detailed observations of different species which he arranged into hierarchical order, from the simplest to the most complex. This ordering, in terms of the value placed upon each species, has become known, since the Middle Ages, as the Great Chain of Being.

33  David Holbrook begins the preface to his book *The Skeleton in the Wardrobe* by citing a psychotherapist 'who would not allow his children to read the [Narnia] books because they were "so filled with hate"' (Holbrook, 1991: 9).

34  Consider Lewis's attempt to introduce his wife Joy into the Inklings.

35  David Holbrook wrote in the same vein: 'Lewis cannot bear the growth to maturity' (1991: 201).

# Introduction 37

36 '[Leslie A. Donovan] argues persuasively … [that] one characteristic shared by Tolkien's primary female characters is their association with light' (Reid, 2013: 101).

37 Unless Aslan is in charge of the romp, as in *Prince Caspian*, when Bacchus and his maenads join in the fun (Lewis, 2005: 388).

38 John Haines remarked: 'Considering the interest in reception since the 1970s, it is something of a surprise that studies in the reception of medieval music have taken so long to appear' (2004a: 3).

39 *postmedieval* 3 (4) (Winter 2012), is an issue devoted to unsettling this hegemony. It aims, in the words of its editors, 'to challenge the reign of the gaze as determiner of subjectivity, power, and pleasure in/with the other' (Dugan and Farina, 2012: 373–4).

40 I have drawn here on previous work (Dell, 2019b).

41 Lee D. Rossi was right to name Tolkien's and Lewis's writing a 'literature of political despair': 'For both writers, then, the motive for fantasy is essentially an attempt to liberate themselves from the ugliness and moral impasse of the modern world' (Rossi, 1984: 4).

42 As David Matthews has written: '*The Lord of the Rings* and hippies met where they shared antimodern distrust of technology and love of nature. They shared little else' (Matthews, 2015: 32).

43 Susan Stewart wrote that 'the past [nostalgia] seeks has never existed except as narrative and hence, [is] always absent' (Stewart, 1993: 23).

44 Susan Stewart's comment that '[t]his point of desire which the nostalgic seeks is in fact the absence that is the very generating mechanism of desire' is another way of writing the paradoxical temporality of desire which she termed a 'future-past' (Stewart, 1993: 23).

45 'In contrast [to a performance], recordings allow performers and listeners to respond to the stylistic choices and sonic qualities of other musical performances. The ability to re-listen to the same performance prompts listeners to pay greater attention to musical elements of timbre and phrasing that would vanish instantly in live performance. With live performance, the sonic presence of music vanishes as it is produced, leaving a memory of the work. With recordings, the performance remains present' (Upton, 2012: n.p.).

46 Lacan is drawing on Alcibiades' speech in Plato's *Symposium*.

# 1

## 'More real than reality': Nostalgia for the medieval in high fantasy fiction

> You have made us for yourself, O Lord, and our heart is restless until it rests in you. (Augustine, 1998: 3)
>
> If I find in myself a desire which no experience in this world can satisfy, the most probable explanation is that I was made for another world ... I must keep alive in myself the desire for my true country, which I shall not find till after death. (Lewis, 1977: 77)
>
> Oh distance is like the future. An enormous glimmering oneness lies before our soul ... but alas! When we hasten there, when there becomes here, everything is as it was, and we stand in our poverty, in our finiteness, our soul thirsting for the refreshment that has slipped away. (Goethe, 2005: 32)

High fantasy fiction frequently presents us with a world which is medieval in one sense or another.[1] As Charles Butler comments, 'following Tolkien and Lewis, the "default" fantasy setting is a medieval one' (2006: 20). Between them, these two authors cemented an association between fantasy and the medieval which persists today. The association was there already, in the work of, among others, Alfred, Lord Tennyson, William Morris, George MacDonald, Lord Dunsany and E. R. Eddison, but the fiction of Tolkien and Lewis marked a pivotal point. *The Lord of the Rings* (*LOTR*) (published 1954–55) and *The Chronicles of Narnia* (*Narnia*) (1950–56) spawned a host of imitators and created a mass audience for a brand of medievalist fantasy fiction that continues to flourish today. The films of *LOTR* and *Narnia* have maintained the public appetite for the brand. Since Tolkien and Lewis, it has become almost impossible to write fantasy fiction that does not indicate in some way an awareness of their work.[2]

Each of these men has given his own particular twist to the medievalism of fantasy fiction, and each of these particular twists, due to their influence, have become ingrained in the default setting. The fantasy authors cited in this book are all, in different ways, heirs (or, occasionally, forebears) of the Tolkien/Lewis tradition.[3] In this tradition, medieval allusions may be only fleeting or indeterminate or they may be explicit and saturate the story at every level. But however these references are handled, they indicate a perception, shared by writers and readers, that fantasy and the medieval have a privileged link, or are even interchangeable, as Rebecca Barnhouse (2000: 79) has suggested.[4] Readers seem to believe that to enter the medieval world is to step off the mundane world into a fantasy, and fantasy writers present them again and again with this opportunity. As Nickolas Haydock observes, 'The very alterity of the Middle Ages works to make it an especially potent preserve of fantasy, the realm par excellence of the imaginary' (2008: 7).[5]

The Tolkien/Lewis medieval fantasy has a curious feature: it is sometimes presented as 'more real than reality itself'. That is a quotation from artist Jack B. Yeats, brother of the poet W. B. Yeats: 'Even in mere phantasy there often are things inseparable from truth, or things more real than reality itself. It is the very world a true artist lives in' (Yeats, cited in Pyle, 1991: 109). Picasso also used the term. Lidia Ruth Ferrara speaks of 'the possibilities of the "sur-réal", a term coined by Picasso to describe "something more real than reality"' (2020: Abstract). Francis Bacon spoke in a similar way of his work as 'not illustration of reality but ... a concentration of reality' (Bragg, 1985: n.p.). These artists saw or felt or desired a more intense, more concentrated reality. That vision or felt lack drove their work.

This real is distinct from the historically verifiable, although it may invoke historical validity.[6] The phrase can suggest, depending on one's point of view, either that human artifice is required to transmute reality into something more real, more intense or concentrated, or that the artist brings forth an essence, something already there, latent, beyond or within the mundane, that is more real and underwrites whatever reality the mundane retains. For Tolkien and Lewis, it was the second.[7] This is the kind of fantasy Rosemary Jackson called 'transcendentalist', that is, fantasy 'claimed as "transcending" reality, "escaping" the human condition and constructing superior alternate, "secondary" worlds' (Jackson, 1981: 2). That more real reality, felt to be lacking in ordinary life, is what nostalgia yearns for. That is the connection between them.

Another word for the more real might be 'presence', which Tolkien would have recognised from the 'real presence' of Christ in the Eucharist. Ralph Harper's idea of presence is that which 'is inextricably mixed with the perishable world [... b]ut does not perish with it' (Harper, 1966: 112). Harper suggests that 'we come alive through presence' (1966: 113). That idea of imperishable life shining in and through the perishable world offers another way of expressing the experience of the more real.

Wherever the *more* real of fantasy is placed it is framed in some way – within a painting, a poem, a novel, a film or a song. It is this framing which often represents and thus produces a deeper, intensified reality in the same way as a magical portal opens into a fresh, new world. At the end of *The Last Battle*, Lewis likens the deeper reality of the new, heavenly Narnia to a beautiful landscape seen through a window reflected in a looking glass. The frame provided by the window intensified by the further frame of the looking glass deepens its reality (Lewis, 2005: 759–60). And if the fantasy is required to be *more* real than reality it follows that mundane reality is not felt to be real enough.

John Clute speaks of the response in fantasy fiction to what he names 'wrongness. Some small desiccating hint that the world has lost its wholeness' (2016 [2007]: loc. 543). 'Wrongness', the desiccation and loss of wholeness, sounds close to what I call the felt loss of reality. When something is missing, the realm of fantasy may become, by default, where the real missing from the mundane is located. If the real deserts reality we turn to fantasy to find it.

That is what Tolkien and Lewis did. Both wrote of a reality the unreal of fantasy could offer to a receptive reader, Lewis (1966a) in 'On Stories', Tolkien (1966) in 'On Fairy-Stories'. Lewis writes: '[A story] may not be "like real life" in the superficial sense: but it sets before us an image of what reality may well be like at some more central region' (1966a: 15), that 'central region' being 'the only real "other world" we know, that of the spirit' (1966a: 12).[8] Embedded here is the idea that the spirit is more real than the body and most real when detached from the body, a Platonic notion which has had a profound effect on medieval fantasy fiction and also on the performance of medieval music, especially vocal music. 'Purity', as applied to medieval singing, is the watchword for this tendency – a signal that traces of the body, like vibrato or the heard breath of the singer, have been diminished or, if possible, eliminated. 'Ethereal', a word often applied to medieval music, especially singing, has a similar effect.

For Tolkien, as for Lewis, there was an 'underlying reality' of which fantasy could offer a glimpse:

> Probably every writer making a secondary world, a fantasy, every sub-creator, wishes in some measure to be a real maker, or hopes that he is drawing on reality ... If he indeed achieves a quality that can fairly be described by the dictionary definition: 'inner consistency of reality', it is difficult to see how can this be, if the work does not in some way partake of reality. The peculiar quality of the 'joy' in successful Fantasy can thus be explained as a sudden glimpse of the underlying reality or truth. (Tolkien, 1966: 87–8)[9]

Both these realities invoke the sacred. The medieval worlds Tolkien and Lewis created in story carry the scent of the 'central region', the numinous realm of heaven for which the heart longs.[10]

Here a proviso is in order. Lewis wrote massively, in fiction and non-fiction, about these matters of desire and reality and their religious import. Tolkien was more reticent. His non-fictional works are fewer and his fictional works less didactic. Tolkien was rarely an apologist for Christianity. He left the apologetics to Lewis and took care to avoid explicit references to religion in *LOTR*. Their differences as thinkers and as writers were profound. Tolkien admitted to Roger Lancelyn Green that he 'disliked [*The Lion, the Witch and the Wardrobe*] intensely', according to Humphrey Carpenter (2006: 223). Carpenter suggests that Tolkien found the inconsistency of the secondary world of *Narnia* intolerable (Carpenter, 2006: 223). Nonetheless, there is enough similarity between the two across these different registers to outline a way of thinking and of desiring. Tolkien and Lewis placed their bets bravely on their desire for God's reality. The two had enough in common to make it possible to speak, hesitantly, of a Tolkien/Lewis tradition.[11] The real that fantasy offered, and the desire for it, have, for generations of readers, audiences and film-goers, been filtered through these authors' desires and the fantasy worlds their desires created.

Lewis encouraged seekers after the divine to read Rudolf Otto's *The Idea of the Holy* (1990; originally published 1923). It was this book which familiarised for modern readers the seventeenth-century term 'numinous', from the Latin 'numen'.[12] Otto, writes David C. Downing, 'identifies six common features of numinous experiences':

> Fear, awe, holy dread
> Fascination, attraction, yearning
> A sense of unspeakable magnitude and majesty
> Energy, urgency, intense dynamism
> Wonder, astonishment, stupefaction
> Mystery, Otherness, incomprehensibility. (Downing, 2005: 65)[13]

Otto's language evokes the sublime. There are links between nostalgia and the sublime, although not direct correlations, as J. M. Fritzman has observed:

> The relation between the sublime and nostalgia is not one of identity. … [T]here occurs a certain transversing of nostalgia and the sublime. … That is, there exists a line of intersection that shares characteristics of both. This transversing allows the two concepts mutually to illuminate each other. (Fritzman, 1994: 171)

There is also a connection between romanticism and the sublime, one in which music is implicated, as Charlotte Purkis (2010) suggests in 'Listening for the Sublime: Aural-Visual Improvisations in Nineteenth-century Musical Art': 'Arguably, music can be seen as the "keynote" to the sublime'. Romanticism lingered on in music, she maintains, into the late nineteenth-century age of positivism. She cites Richard Wagner (1870), among others, as bearing witness to this: 'Surveying the historical advance which the art of Music made through Beethoven, we may define it as the winning of a faculty withheld from her before: in virtue of that acquisition she mounted far beyond the region of the aesthetically Beautiful, into the sphere of the absolutely Sublime' (Wagner, cited in Purkis, 2010: n.p.).

Tolkien and Lewis (especially Tolkien), inherited Wagner's sense of music as a channel for the numinous or sublime, often associated with nostalgia for a lost past. The 'common features of numinous experiences', outlined by Downing, can be found over and over again in medieval fantasy fiction of the Tolkien/Lewis tradition, often heralded by or expressed through music.[14] Wordless music, or music in which the words cannot be understood, is a particularly apt channel for an experience of 'Mystery, Otherness, incomprehensibility'. This association can also be heard in some performances and recordings of medieval music. The Middle Ages has many moods for post-medieval nostalgia, as John Haines writes (2014a: 4). The one promulgated by Tolkien and Lewis and their successors was this mood of wonder, mystery and yearning and, due in large part to their influence, it became indelibly associated with the medieval world, particularly through music.

For Tolkien and Lewis, any touch of the mundane was fatal to that glimpse of the numinous reality. Lewis discovered that for himself when Arthur Conan Doyle claimed to have photographed a fairy. Lewis did not believe Conan Doyle's claim, 'but the mere making of the claim – the approach of the fairy to within even that hailing distance of actuality – revealed to me at once that if the claim had succeeded it would have chilled rather than satisfied the desire which fairy literature had hitherto aroused' (Lewis, 1992: 204).

For Lewis, the real of fantasy needed no validation from historical or scientific evidence. It was of a different, higher order. He maintained, rather, that 'far from dulling or emptying the actual world, [fairy land] gives it a new dimension of depth. [The child] does not despise real woods because he has read of enchanted woods: the reading makes all real woods a little enchanted' (Lewis, 1966c: 30).[15] That added dimension of reality is the gift of fantasy to the mundane world. In Lewis's sense, depth was a way of communicating that enhanced reality and thus a critical word in his lexicon. There is another form of realism, however, far removed from the Tolkien/Lewis brand – the supposed realism of medieval violence.

## The realism of medieval violence

The realism of violence is that offered as justification by fans of George R. R. Martin (of *Song of Ice and Fire* and the television drama series *Game of Thrones*) for scenes of sexual and other forms of violence. For instance, in the comments section of an article on Gizmodo.com (a design, technology, science and science fiction website) 'Erik the Red' argues:

> I think people tend to equate GRRM's writings with his beliefs. Just because he depicts rape doesn't mean he's indifferent toward it. There is also incest, patricide, child killing and slavery among others belonging in the 'fucked up' category. Doesn't mean he condones them, but to build realism in this world, some of these things are necessary; otherwise you'd have another Narnia or Lord of the Rings series. (Anders, 2012: n.p.)

Martin himself has used similar justifications on the grounds of authenticity:

> Rape and sexual violence have been a part of every war ever fought, from the ancient Sumerians to our present day. To omit them from a narrative centred on war and power would have been fundamentally false and dishonest, and would have undermined one of the themes of the books: that the true horrors of human history derive not from orcs and Dark Lords, but from ourselves. (Itzkoff, 2014: n.p.)

Both quotations contain the same dismissive attitude to Tolkien's moral landscape, underlining Martin's superior claims to historical and individual authenticity. But such justifications tend to bypass the awkward question of authorial choices (after all, fantasy fiction writers are not bound by an injunction to tell the truth!), and the still more awkward question of enjoyment, to which 'realism' can never be a sufficient answer. Shiloh Carroll writes: 'Fantasy literature is, by its nature, speculative. It rarely takes place in the historical Middle Ages as they existed on Earth, but instead in a fictional world that borrows the flavor of our Middle Ages' (Carroll, 2018: 13).

In a fictional world, she continues: 'recreating the Middle Ages in a way that could be called "realistic", "authentic", or "accurate", is impossible ... there is always some sort of agenda' (Carroll, 2018: 14). In this case, I suggest, part of the agenda is enjoyment. Martin's works – *A Song of Ice and Fire* (*ASOIAF*), a series of currently seven novels, and *Game of Thrones* (*GOT*), the HBO adaptation of the novels – cater to a contemporary obsession with medieval violence, justified by the platitude of the brutal Middle Ages. 'Realism' provides a respectable cover for graphic scenes of medieval rape and slaughter.[16] Violence, whether in books or onscreen, is always in demand, and medieval violence especially so. The medieval functions in some contexts as a guarantee of violence as well as an excuse for it. As Matthew Gabriele writes:

We tend to think of the European Middle Ages as a particularly violent time and place. It's now such a commonplace that it's almost a cultural norm. Fantasy video games such as *The Witcher*, TV shows like *Game of Thrones*, movies like *Braveheart*, and books such as the *Broken Empire* series promote the myth of rampant violence, using a background of knights and castles to link their fictional worlds in our minds to the Middle Ages. (Gabriele, 2018: n.p.)

Tolkien's love of fantasy and its relationship with reality is entirely different. He and Lewis, as I have suggested, reserved the word 'real', used in a particular sense, for a numinous intensity that touches on the sacred. For Tolkien earthly evil was all too real. He, Lewis and other writers of his time had had 'direct first-hand experience of some of the worst horrors of the twentieth century', as Tom Shippey writes, leaving them 'bone-deep convinced that they had come into contact with something irrevocably evil' (2011: 368). Both fought in the First World War and experienced the horrors of the trenches, seeing their comrades dying around them. Lewis was wounded at the Somme, Tolkien hospitalised with trench fever. They and other contemporary authors were driven to search for an understanding of the evils they experienced, in and through their writing, needing 'to find some way of communicating and commenting on them' (Shippey, 2011: 39).

Both Tolkien and Lewis included supremely evil characters in their novels – Sauron and the White Witch among them. In *ASOIAF*, however, evil is so pervasive that the element of probability is ruled out. Jessica Walker comments that Lady Fortuna, rather than being the guiding hand of Providence, rules events in the novels, as: 'unlike providence, Fortune does not seek to punish ill or reward good; her only motivation is movement, her only constant change itself' (J. Walker, 2015: 77). The difficulty with that view is that Lady Fortuna is at least impartial, whereas the predominance of evil in *ASOIAF* and HBO's *GOT* leaves impartiality far behind.

Kavita Mudan Finn (2019) sees *ASOIAF* and *GOT* more as refractions than reflections of the reality of medieval and early modern Europe:

> Reflections offer a mirror image, a glimpse into the medieval as it was; refractions, conversely, require that we look awry – to use Shakespeare's phrasing from *Richard II* – and see not what actually happened but our own skewed perspective that shows us what we

want to see. If our goal is to view the medieval as a Dark Age, safely tucked away behind centuries of progress, refraction is how we get there. (Finn, 2019: n.p.)

Yet another brand of 'realism' is that found in Lacanian psychoanalysis. I have found Lacanian psychoanalytic theory helpful as a way of understanding the lure of Tolkien/Lewis fantasy, in particular as it touches on the question of what *is* real and what the real *is*.

## The real of Tolkien and Lewis versus Lacan's Real

Tolkien and Lewis never mentioned Jacques Lacan, nor he them, although Lewis took an interest in Freud and argued, even after his conversion to Christianity, that Freud should be treated with respect on his own ground, 'the actual medical theories and technique of the psychoanalysts' (Lewis, 1977: 89). He also declared that psychoanalysis was 'not in the least contradictory to Christianity', again provided it stuck to its own turf (which, I suspect, would have been fairly limited territory) (Lewis, 1977: 89). Lacan, for his part, never underestimated the power of religion, although for him religion and psychoanalysis were alternatives. He held no great hopes for the future of psychoanalysis, stating, in *The Triumph of Religion*: 'Yes. [Religion] will triumph over not only psychoanalysis but over lots of other things too' (Lacan, 2013: 64).

Armand M. Nicholi, Jr (2003) has written the debate Freud and Lewis never had, on 'God, Love, Sex, and the Meaning of Life'.[17] I should like to stage here a similar debate between Tolkien, Lewis and Lacan on the subjects of desire and reality. Medieval or medievalist music would be central in this debate since, in the Tolkien/Lewis tradition (literary and cinematic), music is frequently introduced as announcing or transmitting the presence of a greater, more intense reality. The debate staged here is one between religion and psychoanalysis and the question of what is real is at its heart. Lewis would not have made the concessions for Lacan that he made for Freud. Nonetheless they would have agreed on the 'desire which no experience in this world can satisfy' (Lewis, 1977: 76) and its relevance to the question of reality. But for Tolkien and Lewis, the desirable reality which could be glimpsed in fantasy fiction truly awaited the saved soul in the world to come, the 'true country' – our longed-for homeland. That ultimate reality validated the promise offered by the glimpses.

Lacan turned this arrangement on its head with the notion that reality is itself a fantasy, held in place by desire. He maintained that

> the whole of human reality, is nothing other than a *montage* of the symbolic and the imaginary ... [T]he desire, at the centre of this apparatus, of this frame that we call reality, is ... what covers ... the *real*, which is never more than glimpsed. Glimpsed when the mask, which is that of phantasy, vacillates. (1966–67: 6)

For Lacan, it is the Real, not reality, which is glimpsed when the fantasy wavers. The problematic 'object' of desire, which Lacan called *objet (petit) a*, is the means (in its absence) by which the mechanism of fantasy is sustained: '[T]he barred S[ubject] of desire, props up the field of reality ... and this field is sustained only by the extraction of object *a*, which nevertheless gives it its frame' (Lacan, 1977a: 223). From this perspective, mundane reality, like the reality offered by high fantasy, is a framed world, propped up by a fantasy of desire for an object always extracted from it.[18]

*Objet a* is impossible to represent or signify, although we inevitably attempt to bring it into the fields of signification and representation. That is where fantasy comes in. Lacan used the matheme $\$\lozenge a$ to designate fantasy (for example, in 1977a: 315); fantasy intervenes between the split subject and the impossible *objet (petit) a*, disguising its nothingness:[19] 'Phantasy is the support of desire' and what sustains the subject as desiring (Lacan, 1981: 185). Subjectivity cannot be supported without it. It is in the fantasy that our representations and significations are bound up. Medievalist fantasy fiction of the Tolkien/Lewis brand, though differently interpreted, supports a fantasy for the reader in this psychoanalytic sense, in that it provides a means to sustain nostalgic desire and the desiring subject through its representations of a lost medieval home. By these means, fantasy preserves the reader from a glimpse of what Lacan called the Real.

Lacan distinguished reality, as produced by fantasy, from the Real. Reality is a coherent construct – a whole – although it takes hard work on the part of the human subject to maintain its coherence, its appearance of rationality. That is the role of fantasy. Lacan argued: 'What is called the "Reasonable" is a phantasy. It is quite manifest at the beginning of science ... A phantasy is not a dream, it is an aspiration' (1977e: 4). Reality is a construct made from desire for the reasonable, the meaningful, and this is what religion offers. Science also, in a different way. For Lacan, the analyst is, instead, one who experiences (and bears) 'the intrusion of the real' (2013: 67). This Real is undivided, unwhole, beyond meaning; it is not the domain of discrete objects. There are no *spaces between*. From the point of view of the world divided by language, the Real is chaotic. For Lacan it is 'the world of words [which] creates the world of things – the things originally confused in the *hic et nunc* of the all in the process of coming-into-being' (Lacan, 1977b: 65). The Real is 'unassimilable' 'trauma[tic]' (Lacan, 1981: 55).

The frame of reality functions as border protection against the trauma of the Real. The medievalist fantasy that we are exploring claims a (divinely appointed) reality beyond the mundane which is found wanting, but it avoids a brush with the Real.[20] It goes further and rejects it. Its reality, founded on the extraction of *objet a*, is pre-ordered, pre-symbolised. It fills the *space between* which otherwise reveals no-thing. In fact, it can be seen as an improved fantasy of reality, an expurgated version. Tolkien said of his mythology for England that it should be '"high", purged of the gross' (1995: 143). *LOTR* is certainly purged of any grossness.[21] It is also purged of the nagging incoherencies that beset humanity. But it claimed to be more – a glimpse into a deeper, abiding reality.

Lewis and Tolkien would say that the sense of another reality, more real, more vibrant than the mundane, aroused a profound desire that nothing accessible could satisfy. It was that desire which they sought to foster in the readers of fantasy fiction.[22] In Lacan's terms it would be truer to say that desire itself necessitated the idea of another reality, better than our own. Desire is the constant for all three men, but for Lacan it is differently positioned. *Objet (petit) a* as object-*cause* of desire throws a spanner into the usual notions of priority and causation. For Lacan, what looks like the object of desire, 'out in front', is actually its cause, driving desire from behind (1962–63: 2). This theme of the object–cause became a basis for much of Lacan's later work. For instance, in Seminar XX: 'the substance of what is supposedly object-like ... is in fact that which constitutes a remainder in desire, namely, its cause, and sustains desire through its lack of satisfaction ... and even its impossibility'

(Lacan, 1999: 6). The effect precedes the cause. *Objet a* can be seen as a kind of blip in the circular machinery. The question of what constitutes reality is one which keeps returning in this study, but no final agreement is possible between these contenders. 'Real' is one of the qualities that has become attached to the medieval in the Tolkien/Lewis tradition. There are many others, both within and outside that tradition. The 'middle' in Middle Ages as a *space between*, allows a wide range of associations, each leading to still more, some of which are unconscious. The next section offers an account of some of these associations between ideas, fantasies, emotions and judgements which the term 'medieval' gives rise to.

## The medieval: Associations and implications

The signifier 'medieval' is not the only instance of a fantasy identified as more real than reality, although it is particularly apt for the purpose. 'Childhood' is another realm where the real missing from reality may be situated, offering a link in imagination between childhood and the Middle Ages. In Wordsworth's words, the infant arrives on earth 'trailing clouds of glory ... from God, who is our home' (1977: 523). At length, however, 'the Man perceives it die away / And fade into the light of common day' (526). Looking back, we glimpse childhood, and so whatever we look back on becomes a kind of childhood, as the French medievalist Michel Zink has pointed out (1998: 13). And, in the Romantic imagination which Tolkien and Lewis inherited, the radiance of childhood, 'apparelled in celestial light' (Wordsworth, 1977: 523), must give way to the 'common' light of adulthood. Like Wordsworth, they knew 'That there hath past away a glory from the earth' (524). Wordsworth's 'Ode: Intimations of Immortality from Recollections of Early Childhood' is a hymn to nostalgia in which, for those two latter-day Romantics, Tolkien especially, human history mirrored the same irreparable loss (Wordsworth, 1977: 524).

The association between the medieval and childhood is widespread. Both, in looking back to an origin, are adaptable to fantasies of nostalgia. Childhood, since it was taken up by the Romantics, has become associated with the primitive or the primeval, the childhood of the species. Friedrich Schiller (1796) spoke of a longing for a time of innocence, 'humanity's infancy prior to the beginning of culture' (cited in Wagner, c.2004: 27). T. J. Jackson Lears, in *No Place of Grace*, gives a valuable account of the way childhood was constructed by the Romantics and Victorians as a repository for a number of traits lost in adult life: innocence, spontaneity, sincerity, vitality and 'unrepressed emotional and imaginative experience' (Lears, 1981: 143–7).[23] The slippage from childhood to the primitive occurred, Lears suggests, through 'the common tendency to analogise individual and social development' (1981: 147). This idea was formalised and given scientific authority in 1866 by the biologist Ernst Haeckel, who was responsible for the proposition that 'Ontogeny recapitulates philogeny'.[24] The association between childhood and the medieval depends on an established association of both childhood and the medieval with the primeval. This double association was well established when Johan Huizinga wrote, in 1919, of a medieval 'child-life' of wild vitality and spontaneity (Huizinga, 1999: 3).[25] That intensity of experience also associates to the numinous.

It is apparent that Tolkien/Lewis medievalism has continued to haunt fantasy writers and readers up to the present. It is their Middle Ages that constitutes the first introduction, sometimes the only introduction, for many readers, and shapes, to some extent, individual and collective medievalist fantasies since publication of their fiction. Nonetheless, whatever attributes might qualify the medieval as real or childlike or primitive, and whatever visions and desires Tolkien and Lewis may have left imprinted on the minds and hearts of their readers, the medieval of fantasy fiction is first and foremost an effect of the signifier of periodisation which places it, retrospectively, in the middle and offers it as a place for a fantasy – in one sense an *empty* space, in so far as it is defined by what it is not. Its significance is topographical; it becomes a *space between*, as I have argued.[26] The 'medieval' is hospitable to fantasy first and foremost by virtue of this negative or empty status, as defined only in relation to the ancient and modern worlds; the 'Middle' produces the Age as having no title of its own.[27] By functioning as an empty signifier it creates a blank canvas which lends itself to the production of fantasies. The influence of Tolkien and Lewis is felt most in the linking of medieval fantasy with the evocation of a numinous reality and the experience of longing associated with it. Also important is their own infectious nostalgia, so evident in their writing, Tolkien's in particular.

It is the status of the medieval as framed which gives it the location of a *space between*, bestowing on it the radiance of a secret, intimate and magical place. This is the fantasy provided by Tolkien, Lewis and their followers while, in Lacan's terms, the frame is what fences the fantasy of reality. In its negative character, the medieval is 'what is not modern' (M. Alexander, 2007: xxvii), modernity's necessary other against which it defines itself, although it is also what is not ancient and thus may represent for modernity a falling away – a 'decline and fall' – from the pinnacle of classical civilisation into the 'dark ages' associated with more cruel and bloodthirsty fantasies. As Bruce Holsinger has pointed out:

> In the Western tradition's clichéd narratives of intellectual and cultural progress, the modern begins in the Renaissance, which in turn reanimates the intellectual and literary heritages of the ancient world as horizons for our own. The Middle Ages, by contrast, persist imaginatively as the dark age preceding the Renaissance discovery of the individual. (Holsinger, 2005: 12)

Placed as a declivity by this recursive logic, the medieval becomes a more apt repository for the childhood of humanity than the classical. Post-Renaissance deference prevents any association of classical Greece and Rome with the childish or the primitive, whether the childish or the primitive is to be praised or despised. In fantasy, phylogenetic infancy skips a generation – the medieval throws back to the primitive, the primordial or the prehistoric.[28] The medieval of fantasy became and has remained the archetypal primitive, allowing it, like childhood, to function as an origin.

To put it another way, while it is difficult to fantasise the classical or Renaissance 'ages' as other than 'civilisations', that title does not cling so tightly to the Middle Ages. In so far as it functions negatively, it lends itself to the label *un*civilised, in comparison to other ages. Any attribute of the medieval tends to be associated with negativity in the sense that something is lacking to it.[29] Sven-Olov Wallenstein defines nostalgia as 'a form of a more general historico-philosophical trope, where the origin is that which must disappear for there to be time and history, and for historicity to become thinkable as such' (Wallenstein, n.d.: 1).[30] The trope of nostalgia places an obligation on the medieval as fantasy. As it must be what is not modern, so it must also be what is not history, in order to function as the missing origin upon which history is constituted. It must remain a prehistoric age, however much historians have to say about it.[31] This is the *before* that nostalgia references – a paradise before the Fall into history. As such it also references the pre-symbolic, before the word and before time.

In its negative sense, the medieval is placed in the role of being what we, in so far as we identify ourselves as modern, must repudiate. We repudiate it in order to define ourselves as modern, but then we find we are also dissatisfied with the adulthood of modernity in its belief in an endless and inevitable progress towards perfection. It is the same with childhood, as Lears points out. He speaks of the widespread assumption, in late nineteenth-century Europe and America, that

> nineteenth-century liberalism was the maturest outlook known to man. From this dominant view, childish traits characterized any society which did not conform to the model of Western industrial capitalism. The 'civilized world', having put childish things in its medieval past, had reached social adulthood. [But] suspicion grew that social adulthood might be indistinguishable from overcivilization [and] admiration for childhood, both individual and 'racial' began to receive scientific sanction. (Lears, 1981: 147)[32]

Into one pile labelled 'medieval' we can heap all that we repudiate – Carl Rubino's 'despised and rejected' Middle Ages (Rubino, 1985: 54) – while into the other, also named 'medieval', we can heap all that we lack and long for in our experience of modernity. The medieval is a sinkhole for what moves us, positively or negatively; a site of profound ambiguity.[33] And the distinction between the positive and negative is not straightforward, since we may also long for precisely what we repudiate. Our moment is not that of nineteenth-century liberalism,[34] but the periodising signifier is still with us, beyond and within academic borders, and still functions as a bolt-hole for fantasy. 'We cannot not periodize', as Fredric Jameson observed (2002: 29). Nor have positivism and the belief in continual progress died out. Ideas of social evolution, while theoretically debunked, still function in national and global discourses. Lears's comments hold true in the twenty-first century: as in the moment of late nineteenth-century liberalism, social evolution breeds its own backlash of doubt and ambivalence. The postmodern condition too, as Linda Hutcheon points out, has a 'mix of the complicitous and the critical at its ambivalent core' (2000: 2). It is this uneasy complex that I consider under the general heading of nostalgia.[35]

At this point you might question the identity of this 'we' of the present to which I allude: are 'we' moderns, postmoderns, post-postmoderns or something else, and which 'we' am I talking about?[36] I think we are all of them and more.[37]

In 1995 Walter Truett Anderson saw postmodernism as one of four 'typological world views':

> These four worldviews are the Postmodern-ironist, which sees truth as socially constructed; the scientific-rational, in which truth is found through methodical, disciplined inquiry; the social-traditional, in which truth is found in the heritage of American and Western civilization; and the neo-romantic, in which truth is found through attaining harmony with nature and/or spiritual exploration of the inner self. (Anderson, 1995: 111)

Nostalgia would perhaps, in our time, be most at home in the neo-romantic, but it could fit into any of Anderson's worldviews or in more recent versions. The postmodern condition itself breeds a nostalgia for the certitudes of the scientific-rational or the social-traditional. The pattern of desire and repudiation repeats itself in every context. If we now inhabit an age called posthuman by some, or some other title which supposedly encapsulates our era, one thing is certain. Nostalgia will accompany us because it is in our very marrow.

This means that each of us inhabits a variety of presents, even those we consciously reject, and each of those presents spawns a variety of pasts.[38] Each present, moreover, adopts its own attitude to these different pasts. Inhabitation of these different presents entails different patterns of nostalgic desire and repudiation. As we read, watch and listen in our daily lives we are obliged to be constantly on the move between one present and another and, as we move, our pasts move with us. We cannot be coherently identified as belonging to any one of these pasts or presents no matter how hard we try. It is an aspect of our homelessness in an age without certitudes. The imagined medieval is subjected to all these pressures and changes in response to each of them.

That is one 'we' that claims all of us living in the 'West' in the last few decades, in Anderson's four worlds and what may follow. The other 'we' to which we belong, as I understand human nature, is the 'we' of the split subject of Lacanian psychoanalysis, described in 'The Signification of the Phallus': the subject of language, '[whose] nature is woven by effects in which is to be found the structure of language, of which he becomes the material, and that therefore there resounds in him ... the relation of speech (Lacan, 1977a: 284). What Lacan called 'a crisis in relation to the object' (1997: 99) is an effect of the structure of language which, by introducing absence into the Real, makes desire eternal. Since, as I understand it, nostalgia is one manifestation of desire, this 'we' is not confined to any era: it is the fate of all of us in whom the relation of speech resounds. One aspect of the split in the subject is that which pertains to the conscious/unconscious divide. The idea of an unconscious is a useful, perhaps a necessary, construction for the incoherence of the subject. And having said earlier that we may long for precisely what we repudiate, it is difficult to avoid the idea of a medieval unconscious.

## Medieval unconscious

This 'medieval unconscious' is not that which Michael Camille observed in 'parodic marginal compositions' in medieval manuscripts which 'challenge the authority of the [central] text and deny its presentation of the "whole truth"' (Camille, 1985: 142), nor is it of Paul Strohm's medieval texts which are 'not only unwilling but unable to tell us all they know' (2000: xii), although it shares with both the characteristic of repression. Camille and Strohm speak of the unconscious *of* medieval texts and images. *This* medieval unconscious is one in which it is the unconscious that is medieval, marginal in relation to the central text of modernity or postmodernity.

Lears does not avoid the idea of a medieval unconscious. He writes:

> For Mark Twain and for many of his contemporaries, an imaginary medieval realm focused those yearnings [for a realm of fantasy and an instinctual vitality] and medieval mentalities – like primitive mentalities in general – took on many characteristics of the unconscious

mind. Like the individual child, the medieval childhood of the race seemed to represent unconscious mental life at its least repressed. ... Yearnings for unconscious vitality underlay a mounting challenge to the modern superego. (Lears, 1981: 166)

Freud (1915) wrote that *'the essence of repression lies simply in turning something away, and keeping it at a distance, from the conscious'* (1991: 147; emphasis in original). In Freudian theory, what is repressed is the prohibited. Freud stated that, in clinical experience,

> we ... learn that the satisfaction of an instinct which is under repression would be quite possible, and further, that in every instance such a satisfaction would be pleasurable in itself; but it would be irreconcilable with other claims and intentions. It would, therefore, cause pleasure in one place and unpleasure in another. It has consequently become a condition for repression that the motive force of unpleasure shall have acquired more strength than the pleasure obtained from satisfaction. (Freud, 1991: 147)

So, for Freud the unconscious housed those desires we cannot satisfy without deriving from that satisfaction a greater degree of unpleasure than pleasure. Following this trajectory, whatever is consciously repudiated as the primitive medieval – savagery, greed, superstition, incest, unrestrained and indiscriminate sexuality, violence, excess of all kinds (everything that evokes horror in the media) – may be unconsciously desired. Freud argued that negation is 'the hallmark of repression, a certificate of origin' (1961: 236), because the repressed idea can only be made conscious via negation. We signal our unconscious desires in the act of denying them.[39]

Thus the medieval is negative in two senses. It functions first as what is *not* something else and any positive characteristics it may acquire are based on this primary negativity. For nostalgia, of course, the fundamental quality is the negative: 'no longer present'. Second, 'the medieval' is subject to negation. This negative status makes it hospitable to whatever is desired and/or repudiated, so there are many Middle Ages, perhaps as many as there are minds to create and receive them and historical moments in which they may emerge.[40]

For the fantasies of nostalgia, signifiers such as childhood and the medieval act as wildcards; chameleon-like, they take on whatever characteristics desire might attribute to them. I am concerned here with the Tolkien/Lewis medieval, which has its own flavour or, more precisely, range of flavours. It is a genus, or perhaps family, within which each author provides his or her particular blend. For consumers of it, the enormous popularity of Tolkien's and Lewis's work and that of their heirs could only assist the effect of the signifier and the inbuilt assumptions it inherits, in eliding the medieval with fantasy. Certain medieval otherworlds presented in Tolkien/Lewis fantasy fiction, or select regions of them, are offered to the reader as more real than reality, sites of plenitude and presence for which the heart longs.[41] Below I provide an introduction to a few of these sites of super-reality in the Tolkien/Lewis universe and my understanding of their significance.

## The super-real in fantasy fiction

These sites of enhanced reality are offered as imagined accommodation for readers in the fantasy fiction described by A. S. Byatt as creating a 'shiver of awe', like 'Keats's "magic casements, opening on the foam / Of perilous seas, in faery lands forlorn"' (Byatt, 2003: n.p.). Avalon, in Marion Zimmer Bradley's *Mists of Avalon*, is such a world: 'more real than any other place you have ever seen' (1993: 151). C. S. Lewis's new, purified Narnia of the final chronicle, *The Last Battle*, is another. There it is 'the real thing', the real of Plato's essential reality, neither shadow nor copy (Lewis, 2005: 759). Our world, in comparison, is 'the Shadowlands' (Lewis, 2005: 766).[42] The explicitly Christian version of Aslan's country appears as Heaven in Lewis's novel *The Great Divorce*: 'Heaven is reality itself. All that is fully real is Heavenly. For all that can be shaken will be shaken and only the unshakeable remains' (Lewis, 1946: 43). Other such lands in fantasy fiction are Tolkien's Lothlórien and Elvenholme, the Summer Country of Lloyd Alexander's Prydain series, Guy Gavriel Kay's 'hidden isle' made for the lios alfar (*Darkest Road*) or the lost province of Tigana in his 1999 novel of the same name, Susan Cooper's (and George MacDonald's) 'land at the back of the North Wind'.

For Lewis, there was a fully real and a way to it which he strove tirelessly to convey through story as well as his many works on Christian apologetics. He said of this unshakeable real that it 'meant more' (Lewis, 2005: 760). In *The Last Battle* the narrator tries to explain the difference between the old and the new, real Narnia:

> You may have been in a room in which there was a window that looked out on a lovely bay of the sea or a green valley that wound away among mountains. And in the wall of that room opposite to the window there may have been a looking glass. And as you turned away from the window you suddenly caught sight of that sea or that valley, all over again, in the looking glass. And the sea in the mirror, or the valley in the mirror, were in one sense just the same as the real ones: yet at the same time they were somehow different – deeper, more wonderful, more like places in a story: in a story you have never heard but very much want to know. The difference between the old Narnia and the new Narnia was like that. The new one was a deeper country: every rock and flower and blade of grass looked as if it *meant* more. (Lewis, 2005: 759–60; my emphasis)[43]

To understand the difference, one would need to ask what meaning meant for Lewis, as Charlie W. Starr (2007) does. For Lewis, meaning was that extra dimension that comes with myth and is what distinguishes reality from truth: 'What flows into you from the myth is not truth but reality (truth is always about something, but reality is that about which truth is)' (Lewis, 1970: 66). In Lewis's sense, meaning is 'the antecedent condition both of truth and falsehood, whose antithesis is not error but nonsense' (1980b: 265). Whatever is accessible to mundane perception (the world outside the window) and mundane knowledge (the knowledge of true and false) is not this real conveyed by myth. A frame, placing the view at one remove, is necessary to transform or condense reality into the essence of itself and bring about the numinous moment, like the toy garden on a biscuit tin lid which entranced Lewis as a child. He wrote: 'As long as I live my imagination of Paradise will retain something of my brother's toy garden' (Lewis, 1955a: 7).

Meaning, for Lewis, is beyond the confinement of true and false, but myth 'becomes the father of innumerable truths on the abstract level' (Lewis, 1970: 66). For him, the Christian story is both true and real, historical fact but retaining all the properties of myth (1970: 67). Tolkien agreed, or rather, Lewis relates, it was Tolkien who convinced him of it and in doing so assisted his conversion to Christianity:[44]

The Gospels contain a fairy-story, or a story of a larger kind which embraces all the essence of fairy-stories ... But this story has entered History and the primary world; the desire and aspiration of sub-creation [i.e. the world of fantasy] has been raised to the fulfilment of Creation. (Tolkien, 1966: 88)

It is not history or science that validates the Gospels but God, whose fairy-story Creation is.

Tolkien's Lothlórien (Lórien) provided the classic model of deep reality for his heirs to draw on. In Lórien it is Galadriel whose presence accounts for the luminosity, she whose presence lights and enlivens the world. When Frodo first sees Lórien,

> it seemed to him that he had stepped through a high window that looked on a vanished world. A light was upon it for which his language had no name. All that he saw was shapely, but the shapes seemed at once clear cut, as if they had been first conceived and drawn at the uncovering of his eyes and ancient as if they had endured for ever. ... On the land of Lórien there was no stain. (Tolkien, 1993: 341)

When Sam speaks his admiration of Lórien, the elf Haldir comments approvingly: 'You feel the power of the Lady of the Galadhrim [that is, Galadriel]' (1993: 342). Through the high window one steps into Lórien. The frame becomes a portal – a means of access into the otherworld (the fantasy), like Alice's looking-glass, or the door of the wardrobe through which the children step into Narnia in *The Lion, the Witch and the Wardrobe*, or the picture of a ship in *The Voyage of the Dawn Treader*.[45] The heroes of fantasy fiction can sometimes step through the portal into that deeper world, saturated with reality. When the travellers depart the light goes out, reality dims. Beyond Lórien the world is 'dreary and cold' (Tolkien, 1993: 370). The scene is dismal; they are back in the grey, mundane world, stricken with loss. For the nostalgic this grey world is the one in which we are obliged to live, haunted by the 'memory' of that saturated reality which, in Wordsworth's words, has 'fade[d] into the light of common day' (1977: 526).

The next section engages with the thread in post-Tolkien/Lewis fantasy which tackles the question of a fading reality in which characters were now obliged to live. In Lewis's writing nothing might shake the heavenly real; it was the imperishable original of which our world is the faint copy. There has been a widespread perception, however, within fantasy fiction and more generally, that reality is not what it used to be. It has undergone mutations over the last seventy years or so since Lewis was writing.

## Living in post-reality

Fantasy fiction has changed, as much by the weight of its own tradition as by anything else. Authors would never have got away with simple repetitions of Frodo's breathless discovery of Lórien. The note of wonder wears thin if it is overdone. But, beyond the need for variety, fantasy since Tolkien also reflects (and fuels) the widespread perception that essential reality is on the wane.

Fantasy fiction writer Diana Wynne Jones has frequently exploited the link between fantasy and the real, although her real is not linked to a creator God.[46] In *The Merlin Conspiracy* (2003), the heroine, Roddy, is speaking of a figure who, it turns out, embodies the Isles of Blest (the British Isles in a parallel universe):

> I was not sure at first that she was really there. I could see right through her, to trees and stars in the sky. She was just a sort of whiteness faintly across these things, like a cloud. Then she looked at me with huge eyes and I saw that she *was* real. She seemed to be about my age, but I was fairly sure that she was older than the garden and *more real than I was*. (Jones, 2003: 281; my emphasis)

Here the being of ordinary mortals is merely contingent; they come and go, flickering in and out of existence, but they lack essential reality. That is the preserve of certain beings like the spirit of the Isles of Blest. The confusion surrounding her existence is an indication that there are different orders of reality. Hers is not to be confused with the mundane; on the mundane plane she would not be real. In fantasy fiction only the 'sensitives' like Roddy can see such beings – those with whom the reader can proudly identify. Instead, the spirit of Blest partakes of the real that high fantasy offers and claims as a greater real – the real Tolkien and Lewis called mythic. This being is the animating, 'realifying' principle of the land. She is the land itself in its essence – its 'Real Presence'. 'I never knew you were alive before,' Roddy confides to her. 'Of course I am,' she replies. 'So is every land' (Jones, 2003: 458). She represents precisely that lively, inner flame that is felt to be lacking or is simply not perceived in mundane reality.

Jones's *The Homeward Bounders* (1981) has a more complicated take on reality.[47] Here Jamie, the young hero, gives a detailed account of a realifying process. A Prometheus figure, Uquar, freed by Jamie, returns to his native home. At first the land, which 'ought to have been one of the most beautiful places you ever saw ... seemed faded. It wasn't faded the way things fade in autumn. It was more the way an old photograph goes, sort of faint and bleached. The grass wasn't green enough and the rocks were pale' (1981: 247). As they walk through the land, however, 'colour seemed to be draining back into the place. The sky turned bluer. The streams dashed along sharper, and seemed to nourish the grass to a better green' (247). When they arrive at the house 'everywhere was pretty beautiful and the birds were singing their heads off ... the valley seemed to be getting brighter and brighter' (247). Uquar's temple-like dwelling-place marks the centre, the point of the most intense reality. Like the spirit of the Isles of Blest, it is Uquar who makes the land real, enlivens and illuminates it simply by his indwelling; you could say he is the life of the land.

*Homeward Bounders* also offers an explanation for *de*-realification:

> A place is less real if it is seen from outside, or only seen in memory; and also ... if a person settles in that place and calls that place Home, then it becomes very real indeed ... if reality were removed from the worlds, it could be concentrated in one place. And reality could be removed if someone to whom all the worlds were home never went to any world, but only remembered them. (D. Jones, 1981: 249)

In *Homeward Bounders* reality is unstable. The luminosity of the eternal real that Lewis and Tolkien worked so hard to maintain *as a given* cannot be relied upon.[48] It can be stolen away and concentrated in another locality, as it is here, by beings only identified as *They* and *Them*, always italicised and capitalised, who can then play games with unreal worlds. Underpinning instances of realification and de-realification is the notion of reality as mutable and multiple, detachable and mobile. There is less sense of a deeper, *guaranteed* reality in the background that nothing can shake, nor of a providential hand guiding events towards it, other than the habit of narrative by which things turn out more or less right in the end regardless.[49]

The hand of Providence is still functioning in the ghostly form it assumes in fantasy narrative, but it is challenged. At the end of *Homeward Bounders*, the existence of a home to go to hangs on the renunciation of home by one person, Jamie:

> You see how it works, do you? As long as I ... keep moving and don't think of anywhere as Home, I shall act as an anchor to keep all the worlds real. And that will keep *Them* out. Funny kind of anchor that has to keep moving ... The more I move, the longer it'll take ... I'm going to keep *Them* out as long as I can ... But you wouldn't believe how lonely you get. (D. Jones, 1981: 266–7)

In *Homeward Bounders*, written in the less stable atmosphere of 1981, when faith in an immutable, eternal reality had waned, reality is only anchored for as long as the anchor, one boy, keeps moving. There could be no stronger metaphor for the effort required to maintain reality. His sacrifice is not new – it is a staple in the genre – but the uneasy and conditional state of the real represents a change. Jamie takes on the punishment of Prometheus in a different form and, presumably, someone else will have to come along to take over from him. *They* are only waiting for a chance to return.

It was not so much the inessential, mundane reality that mattered in the work of Tolkien and Lewis, but a deeper, essential reality. In *LOTR* the enemy reappears in every age and it is the duty of all good creatures to fight him, but beyond the shadow the heavens endure. As Sam and Frodo struggle through Mordor Sam looks up:

> There, peeping among the cloud-wrack ... Sam saw a white star twinkle for a while. The beauty of it smote his heart, as he looked up out of the forsaken land, and hope returned to him. For like a shaft, clear and cold, the thought pierced him that in the end the Shadow was only a small and passing thing: there was light and high beauty for ever beyond its reach. (Tolkien, 1993: 901)

The vicissitudes of mortal life could be borne provided there was a reality beyond their grasp.

That reality has become less certain. A parody can identify and sum up a generic trope as no single, 'straight' instance can. In Terry Pratchett's *Moving Pictures*,

> at least nine-tenths of all the original reality ever created lies outside the multiverse, and since the multiverse by definition includes absolutely

everything that is anything, this puts a bit of a strain on things. Outside the boundaries of the universe lie the raw realities, the could-have-beens, the might-bes, the never-weres, the wild ideas, all being created and uncreated chaotically like elements in fermenting supernovas. Just occasionally where the walls of the worlds have worn a bit thin, they can leak in. And reality leaks out. (Pratchett, 2002: 21)[50]

Here reality has run amok. It is leaking out, like the reality that leaks out of the universe in certain series of *Doctor Who* (for instance Series 5, 'Cracks in the Universe'), taking history with it and backdating the excision so that, eventually, nothing will ever have existed. More importantly, in all this leakage the distinction between real and unreal (or less real), between original and copy, is leaking as well, worn down by constant assaults. Similarly, in Pratchett's *Moving Pictures*, the city Ankh-Morpork is remade as a movie set, more real than the original, more 'genuine' (Pratchett, 2002: 206): 'The new city was the old city distilled [which] when it was finished would make Ankh-Morpork look like a very indifferent copy of itself' (207). This distillation looks like an inverted version of Lewis's unshakeable real, only achievable by simulation – a Plato's cave in reverse, where the shadows on the firelit wall are more real than the bodies from which they are projected.

These gyrations are not confined to fantasy fiction. Reality has been on the slide everywhere. Many have noted the slow seepage, including Jean Baudrillard. In his scheme there are four 'successive phases' of the image in its passage from representation to simulation:

- it is the reflection of a basic reality
- it masks and perverts a basic reality
- it masks the absence of a basic reality
- it bears no relation to any reality whatever: it is its own pure simulacrum. (Baudrillard, 1983: 11)

For Gilles Deleuze, similarly, the simulacrum takes matters out of the realms of representation altogether:

So 'to reverse Platonism' means: to make the simulacra rise and to affirm their rights among icons or copies. The problem no longer has to do with the distinction Essence–Appearance or Model–Copy. This distinction operates completely within the world of representation ... The simulacrum is not a degraded copy. It harbours a positive power which denies *the original and copy, the model and the reproduction*. (Deleuze, 2004: 299; emphasis in original)

Once reality starts to leak, it is difficult to avoid the conclusion that it has *always* been so, that reality (as in *Doctor Who*, Series 5) has never been real (will have never been real) and 'that God himself has only *ever* been his own simulacrum' (Baudrillard, 1983: 8; my emphasis). Reality is not (and *now* has never been) guaranteed. It was in the hope of preventing such a rockslide that Tolkien and Lewis worked so hard. They never imagined it was easy to maintain reality.

That was where faith came in. Tolkien wrote to his son Michael that 'faith is an act of will inspired by love' (1995: 337). Tolkien knew that that underlying reality was always in danger of sliding and must be, in the end, a matter of faith. Faith was the constant work needed to hold it in place: 'But the act of will of faith is not a single moment of final decision: it is a permanent indefinitely repeated act/state which must go on – so we pray for "final perseverance". The temptation to "unbelief" is always there within us' (Tolkien, 1995: 338). Belief must be fought and prayed for, as it is for the father in Mark 9:24 who 'cried out, and said with tears, Lord, I believe; help thou mine unbelief' (*King James Bible*, 1970: NT 30).

In *Mere Christianity* Lewis devoted two sections to faith. In the first he maintained that faith is a virtue because, although the convert to Christianity may have decided that 'the weight of the evidence is for it, [there] will come a moment when there is bad news, or he is in trouble, or is living among a lot of other people who do not believe it, and all at once his emotions will rise up and carry out a sort of blitz on his belief' (Lewis, 1977: 78). Faith in this sense 'is the art of holding on to things your reason has once accepted in spite of your changing moods' (78). Lewis recommended 'daily prayers and religious readings and churchgoings' to combat the loss of faith (78). Tolkien prescribed 'Communion [as] the only cure for sagging ... faith' (Tolkien, 1995: 338). Both insisted on the need for frequency and regularity in these exercises – faith must be constantly fed if it is to survive. The ultimate reality had to be held in place by a sustained effort every bit as demanding as Jamie's lengthy peregrinations as the moving anchor in *Homeward Bounders*. What changed in fantasy fiction was the kind of work being done.

The turning away from faith viewed as a temptation, or as an inadequacy on the part of the sinful soul, still assumes a listener. If one can still pray 'Lord, I believe; help thou my unbelief', the fight to maintain reality still has a divine assistant. Once the listener has left the scene and *now* has never been there, the battle changes shape. No one is left to uphold reality – if it is to be upheld – but someone like Jamie, who, unlike Christ, offers himself as a completely human sacrifice. No supreme being is watching or listening or will lend a hand. Help may come from a variety of sources, human or otherwise; Doctor Who races about through time, devising schemes, Uquar rallies the troops to fight *Them*. There may even be gods (uncapitalised) but, generally speaking, the official, supreme deity is neither in the foreground nor the background and is no longer expected: 'Postmodern man has stopped waiting for Godot', as Steinar Kvale wrote (1996: 25).

The writing of reality has become more complicated, more riven; witness the distance between the hushed, quasi-religious tone of Tolkien's passage on Lórien of the 1950s and Pratchett's slick, postmodern knowingness of the 1980s. But, as they knew, Tolkien and Lewis were already fighting a rearguard action. The slide from the fantasy Rosemary Jackson called 'transcendental' into a 'disenchanted' form has a longer history (R. Jackson, 1981: 18). Jackson focuses in the main on 'those fantasies produced within a capitalist economy', beginning around 1800 (1981: 4). Citing Jean-Paul Sartre, she observes:

> There was no facile transition from faith to disbelief: transformations of fantasy were slow and fluid and the survival of the 'marvellous' in twentieth-century works indicates that mode's continuing seductiveness. (R. Jackson, 1981: 18)

Indeed, the seductions of the marvellous have been given new power since Jackson's *Fantasy: The Literature of Subversion* was published in 1981. Owing to its massive success in the cinema, the Tolkien/Lewis brand now encompasses every corner of popular culture and shows no sign of diminishing.[51] Disenchantment has not killed (and cannot kill) the marvellous; the more it is debunked the more desirable it becomes.

Tolkien and Lewis did not usually call their writing of reality 'nostalgia', because to do so would be to acknowledge that faith in reality was sliding or had already slid. Their response to disillusion, a rearguard action, was to write all the harder to shore up their reality by presenting it as beyond attack. Since *Narnia* and *LOTR*, what Tolkien and Lewis called faith is now more likely to be called nostalgia: mourning for a past that has never been. The past tense has intervened, even as its object has disappeared. The current ubiquity of the term 'nostalgia' is an uneasy or a knowing acknowledgement of the silent evacuation of reality from time and eternity.

Fantasies of an unshakeable reality are not relinquished, but they lose their naivety; they must find a way to accommodate scepticism and a half-shamed deprecation. For Tolkien the 'secondary world' of the fantasy writer must ring true 'while you are ... inside. The moment disbelief arises, the spell is broken' (Tolkien, 1966: 60). Pratchett and the makers of *Doctor Who*, by mixing nostalgia with irony, manage to exploit both the nostalgic's longing for a real reality and the ironist's sense of superiority for knowing better.[52] The Urban Dictionary (n.d.) carries thirty-seven nostalgia derivatives which amply attest the chic superiority of the 'nostalsceptics' or the 'nostironics' who can indulge in an orgy of nostalgia without for one moment taking it seriously.[53] They appear to dance happily with postmodern undecidability and never miss the ground of a reliable metanarrative under their feet, although one might suspect some bravado in their claims.[54] Being human involves this loss and thus involves us in some form of nostalgia, however it may be experienced, understood and addressed. It may be nostalgia for precisely that bedrock of reality that life erodes for the speaking being.

## Nostalgia for reality

Many have written of the nostalgia of those forced to leave the beloved home of their childhood. In a world in which displacement is common this nostalgia is all around us. This is the grief that first gave nostalgia its name, as we have seen and many have written about, beginning with Hofer, taken up by Rousseau and the Romantics and surviving into the twentieth century in the works of, among others, Tolkien and Lewis. The nostalgia I am concerned with here arises from the sense that reality has leaked out – the 'realifying', indwelling spark has been removed; it is not where it ought to be (even if one cannot say why it ought to be there), and the world is left impoverished and disenchanted. Baudrillard comments: 'When the real is not what it used to be, nostalgia assumes its full meaning'

(Baudrillard, 1983: 12), but if 'God ... has only ever been his own simulacrum' (8), the real has never been 'what it used to be'.[55] The loss of 'reality', 'authenticity', an 'aura' (Benjamin, 1970), an 'origin', which nostalgia mourns has come under increasing scrutiny in the twentieth century and in our own,[56] but it has always accompanied us in one guise or another, as David Lowenthal has noted (1985: 8). The real is always elsewhere and elsewhen, precisely the reverse of the worlds of *Homeward Bounders* where '[a] place is less real if it is seen from outside, or only seen in memory; and ... if a person settles in that place and calls that place Home, then it becomes very real indeed' (D. Jones, 1981: 249). In our world home is not this very real Home. For nostalgia, home is more real in memory or in fantasy than in the present.

It is true that nostalgia takes on different forms in different historical moments because longing is always couched in terms of present circumstances and perceived present lack. As Andrew Lynch writes, 'the desire in nostalgia is always a desire formed by the pressures of the present' (Lynch, 2011: 203). Rosemary Jackson has argued that fantasy fiction 'characteristically attempts to compensate for a lack resulting from cultural constraints: it is a literature of desire, which seeks that which is experienced as absence and loss' (Jackson, 1981: 3). The second part of her statement has validity, but the first is more doubtful. Within the Lacanian framework which I follow here, the particularity of contemporary constraints affects only the narrative of desire, not its basic structure, which, in my understanding, is founded on a constitutive lack in human experience – the lack of the always already missing *objet a*.

Mircea Eliade rightly maintained that nostalgia is 'a specific condition of Man in the cosmos' (Eliade, 1996: 383) and that humanity has always sought the means to address it. Eliade shared that longing, as Ansgar Paus has argued: 'Eliade's longing for a life of fulfilment penetrated by the sacred dominates each of his works. In them his nostalgia for a lost paradise is manifest' (Paus, 1989: 146). I think the idea of sacredness, in particular of being penetrated by the sacred, may be another way to speak of the 'more real than reality' which haunts humanity with its absence, even, for some, its occasional presence.

Lacan, although as a rule he made little mention of nostalgia as such, spoke, in his *Ethics* seminar, of a nostalgia expressed in the idea that the Ancients were closer than we are to the instinct [which] perhaps means no more, like every dream of a Golden Age or El Dorado, than that we are engaged in posing questions at the level of the instinct because we do not yet know what to do as far as the object is concerned. To set out to find the instinct again is the result of a certain loss ... of the object. (Lacan, 1997: 99)

This is 'instinct' (as opposed to drive), that is, the notion of a natural, uncontaminated impulse such as the animals appear to enjoy. Lacan is speaking here in the context of what he identifies as Freud's nostalgia for the 'simple, natural love of two human beings of the pastoral tradition' (Lacan, 1997: 98). Here is something unchanging, the classic nostalgic fantasy which assumes another time and place in which something worked, an Eden where life was natural and harmonious as opposed to the present. Svetlana Boym describes such a world as enchanted: 'Modern nostalgia is a mourning for ... the loss of an enchanted world with clear borders and values ... the Edenic unity of time and space before entry into history' (2001: 8).

James Cameron's 2009 film *Avatar* provides a perfect instance of an unfallen world where the instincts still function properly in speaking beings who are both animal and human. The split between nature and culture has not arisen. History is not abandoned, Lacan insists, noting a change from the ancient to the medieval world in the eruption of courtly love, a 'historically and socially specific' form of fantasy (Lacan, 1997: 99), but beneath the social and historical differences 'lies a certain lost chord, a crisis in relation to the object' (99) which is common to both.

For Lacan, loss and longing are inevitable for speaking beings, since what we can only deem to have once been real, what we are convinced *ought* to be real, is hollowed out for us through the inauguration of absence which constitutes language. 'In Function and Field', 'the symbol manifests itself first of all as the murder of the thing and this death constitutes in the subject the eternalization of his desire' (1977b: 104).

In the fantasy of the nostalgic, reality is mutilated by this murder, made incomplete, insubstantial, tarnished, faded, tawdry – like a Fun Park seen through the eyes of an adult, by daylight. Robbed of that always already missing piece it loses luminosity; it is a corpse. The present has no presence, no life, no immediacy, no authenticity;

it is not the real thing. The nostalgic seeks not so much the object as the 'world' – a home-world – which its restoration would supposedly make real.

Many have been moved to find ways of speaking about nostalgia. Eliade named the eternal longing for something real a *'nostalgia for Paradise* ... the desire to be always, effortlessly, at the heart of the world, of reality, of the sacred, and, briefly, to transcend, by natural means, the human condition' (Eliade, 1996: 383; my emphasis). George Steiner's 'nostalgia for the absolute', in his book of the same name, offers an account of a nostalgia afflicting 'western man', so bitter that it destroys all traces of Eden wherever they were found:

> Possessed, as it were, by some archetypal rage at his own exclusion from the Garden of Paradise, by some torturing remembrance of that disgrace, we have scoured the earth for vestiges of Eden and laid them waste wherever we have found them (1974: 32).

Less vengeful and despairing nostalgias keep searching for whatever promises to restore the real, to provide a *real* place 'at the heart of the world', for 'the true heaven, the true light, and the true earth' of which Plato speaks in the *Phaedo* (2002: 148),[57] where 'the gods *really* dwell' in the temples dedicated to them (148; my emphasis). It is this longing that Lewis evokes in his retelling of the Psyche myth, *Till We Have Faces*: 'the [Greek] masters who have taught that death opens a door out of a little, dark room (that's all the life we have known before it) into a great, real place where the true sun shines' (Lewis, 1980c: 73).[58] In this vision one can see religion as a product of a human nostalgia for a world more real than reality. Henry M. Seiden has also invoked the ancient Greeks in his assertion that psychoanalysis

> would be deepened by an explicit broadening of our psychoanalytic thinking to include the importance of a longing for home. Indeed, I have come to think of Odysseus – and not Oedipus – as the figure from antiquity most representative of the universal psychological experience of our species (2009: 204).

The longing for a real place can be heard in Frodo's introduction to Lothlórien, where he 'saw no colour but those he knew, gold and white and blue and green, but they were fresh and poignant, as if he had at that moment first perceived them and made for them names new and wonderful' (Tolkien, 1993: 341).⁵⁹ The real of medievalist fantasy fiction, though it is not usually explicitly Christian, carries that breath of the sacred or the spiritual.⁶⁰ Plato's god who *really* dwells in the temple dedicated to him is that enlivening, illuminating force. It is spiritual in George Bataille's sense, that which 'arises from ecstasy' (Bataille, *c*.2001: 21).⁶¹ Often in fantasy fiction the special radiance associated with the homely place is condensed into one precious object with special magical powers and a special significance – the lost object.

## The lost object of longing

The lost object which has the power to heal the world is at the heart of quest fantasy. And as if to illustrate Lacan's point that it can never be found, the 'object', like Hitchcock's MacGuffin, is ultimately 'nothing at all' (Digou, 2003: 270), or perhaps anything at all, because whatever it is, that's not it. Lacan said often in his seminars: 'I ask you ... to refuse what I offer you ... because that's not it' (Lacan, 1999: 126). In Seminar XX he added, '[y]ou know what "it" is; it's object *a*. Object *a* is no being' (1999: 126).

In quest fiction it is never enough to find the object because, when found, 'that's not it'. It could not be it if *objet a* is no being. The glamour, the 'it', must then be displaced onto another object. There is always another object to be sought, a further quest, another book. A certain restraint in the matter of desirable objects of power is the mark of a good fantasy writer, because as the number grows the numinous loses its shine and the reader's sense of wonder diminishes. Tolkien demonstrated the lure of the distant object in fiction when he described the attraction of *LOTR* as

> an attraction like that of viewing far off an unvisited island, or seeing the towers of a distant city gleaming in a sunlit mist. *To go there is to destroy the magic*, unless new unattainable vistas are again revealed. (Tolkien, 1995: 333; my emphasis)

Tolkien reveals his Romantic ancestry here; he might be paraphrasing Goethe's Werther: 'Oh, distance is like the future! An enormous glimmering oneness lies before our soul ... but alas! When we hasten there, *when there becomes here*, everything is as it was, and we stand in our poverty, in our finiteness, our soul thirsting for the refreshment that has slipped away' (Goethe, 2005: 32; my emphasis). The mundane dogs the heels of the traveller no matter how far they travel.

The object of longing in fantasy fiction must always remain just out of reach. It recedes as we advance in a *mise-en-abyme*, leaving desire as an inexhaustible residue: 'To go there is to destroy the magic'. When C. S. Lewis's children are in England they yearn for Narnia, but when, in the world of Narnia, they catch a breath of Aslan's country their yearning is redirected there, for instance towards the end of *The Voyage of the Dawn Treader* (Lewis, 2005: 538–9).

In Lewis's own longing, as he describes it in the Preface to the third edition of *The Pilgrim's Regress*, there is a further twist: '[T]hough the sense of want is acute and even painful, yet the mere wanting is felt to be somehow a delight. ... [T]his desire, even when there is no hope of possible satisfaction, continues to be prized, and even to be preferred to anything else in the world, by those who have once felt it' (1992: loc. 69). There is 'a peculiar mystery about the *object* of this desire' (loc. 77). Nothing will satisfy it. Lewis finds, after an extensive search that, '[e]very one of these supposed *objects* for the Desire is inadequate to it' (loc. 85). Lewis's desire, if one could discount his hope in a heavenly future, would look distinctly Lacanian.

Viewed from the understanding of nostalgia as a structure of desire, the crucial point is that the object is missing from wherever – or whenever – it is supposed to be because if it were to materialise it would not be *the* object. *That* object can only ever be lost. It is in its nature to be lost.[62] Since the object can never be anything other than an absence, desire can never be other than circular.

That circularity offers a different perspective on the temporality of nostalgia. Even to ask whether we yearn backwards to a vanished 'past' or forwards to an uncertain 'future' is problematic. Fantasy fiction plays it both ways. In the yearnings of nostalgia, past and future, origin and eschaton, are ambiguously related. Nostalgia arises from our attempts to place loss in a linear temporality, a *narrative*, when desire is circular. Nostalgic desire turns its face towards a 'future-past', as Susan Stewart terms it (1993: 23), since to *return* to a 'past' – for the good times to come *again* – one must go via a 'future', as in the prophesied return of Arthur, the once and future king; that is, the 'pastness' of the object is an effect of a sense of loss for which history cannot account, while its 'futureness' is an effect of the structure of desire which requires a 'future' in order to function.[63] To speak of nostalgia as a function of memory is to sidestep its problematic temporality. To quote Susan Stewart, the past of nostalgia is

> a past that has only ideological reality. This point of desire which the nostalgic seeks is in fact the absence that is the very generating mechanism of desire ... [N]ostalgia is the desire for desire. (Stewart, 1993: 23)

The next chapter brings in the third term of my enquiry, music, as approached through literature. There I consider the place of music and musical ecstasy as represented and evoked in fantasy fiction.

## Notes

1 High fantasy is generally set, at least in part, in a fictional, 'secondary' world. As Farah Mendlesohn points out, however, all such classifications are difficult to sustain. She argues: 'High fantasy is traditionally a fully built world ... Low fantasy is "this world" fantasy [but] I have come to find this categorization rather unhelpful' (Mendlesohn, 2005: xxx–xxxi).
2 'In the field of fantasy, eras are measured as B.T. or A.T. – Before Tolkien or after Tolkien' (Gunn, 1998: n.p.).
3 Fred Inglis more slightingly termed it 'the Tolkien formation' (Inglis, 1981: 238). Most of the authors cited in this study are included by Inglis in that category.
4 See also L. O. Aranye Fradenburg on 'the Middle Ages [as] a marker *of* fantasy and excess' (Fradenburg, 1997: 210; emphasis in original).
5 As Haydock also notes, scholarly knowledge is no antidote for a well-entrenched medieval fantasy (2008: 7). See also: 'In the popular imagination, the Middle Ages has become virtually synonymous with fantasy and with a distinctly modern form of nostalgia for a past organic society' (Finke and Shichtman, 2014: 108).
6 As Mary McAleer Balkun notes in *The American Counterfeit*, 'the ostensibly real thing may not be "authentic" and the fake may have an authenticity of its own' (Balkun, cited in Pugh and Weisl, 2013: 111).
7 The Tolkien scholar Verlyn Flieger (1997) uses a similar phrase. She is quoting a character from Tolkien's *Notion Club Papers*, Ramer, 'who

"fell wide asleep" into a dream more real to him than waking reality' (Flieger, 1997: 198). See Lewis, quoting Sappho, 'more gold than gold', with reference to the form of goodness (Lewis, 1986: xii).

8  God's centrality is based on a reversal of the traditional cosmic design which placed earth at the centre. Drawing on Dante, Lewis argues that 'the universe is thus, when our minds are sufficiently freed from the senses, turned inside out' (Lewis, 1967: 116).

9  Tolkien's joy is different from Lewis's. For Tolkien, 'Joy' is the sensation experienced at the 'eucatastrophe' of a story, its 'happy ending' (although Tolkien disputes the idea of any absolute ending in fairy-story). It is the 'good catastrophe', 'a sudden joyous "turn" [and] miraculous grace: never to be counted on to recur' (1966: 85–6). For Lewis, joy was an intense desire for desire itself (Lewis, 1955a: 16–18).

10  See Colin Manlove: '[T]he "real" world is often not our universe [...] but is equated with the final Reality from which all worlds stem' (Manlove, 1975: 2).

11  Their religious differences (Tolkien – Catholic; Lewis – Protestant), may have also played a part. As Andrew Lynch suggested to me, 'Lewis seems more focussed on atonement and obedience, Tolkien on channels of grace' (personal communication, 2020).

12  'Divinity, god, a local or presiding spirit' (*Oxford English Dictionary*, 2020: s.v. 'numen').

13  See Otto's (1990) *Idea of the Holy*, especially pp. 8–40.

14  Otto's 'numinous' or 'Holy' in turn links back to the 'sublime' of Edmund Burke's (1998) *A Philosophical Enquiry into the Origin of our Ideas of the Sublime and Beautiful* (originally published 1757) and Immanuel Kant's (2011) *Theory of the Sublime* (originally published 1764). Arguably, music can be seen as the 'keynote' of the sublime.

15  Lewis makes the same claim for Tolkien's 'myth', that 'it takes all the things we know and restores to them the rich significance which has been hidden by "the veil of familiarity"' (Lewis, 2004: 14).

16  As Kavita Mudan Finn asks, if realism is the goal why is it that programmes like *Game of Thrones* never investigate 'the more positive aspects of that "realism" as well as its darkness'? (2020: 43).

17  See also the 2009 play, *Freud's Last Session*, by playwright Mark St Germain, which takes their imagined debate to the stage, selections of which can be seen on YouTube (St Germain, 2010).

18  See also Oscar Zentner: '[T]he main function of the fantasm is not withdrawal and compensation from reality but rather the constitution of reality' (Zentner, 2000: 82).

19  In Michael Plastow's words, 'the fantasm appears in the place of an object that is lacking' (Plastow, 2000: 35).

20 Cf. Rosemary Jackson: 'The moral and religious allegories, parables and fables informing the stories of Kingsley and Tolkien move away from the unsettling implications which are found at the centre of the purely "fantastic". Their original impulse may be similar, but they move from it, expelling their desire and frequently displacing it into religious longing and nostalgia' (Jackson, 1981: 9). I would suggest, however, that religious longing and nostalgia are also forms of desire.
21 Tolkien's Middle Earth, like the Middle Ages described by Pugh and Weisl, 'must be stripped of its offensive medievalness before it can be repackaged as wholesomely medieval' (Pugh and Weisl, 2013: 50).
22 Gary K. Wolfe has rightly called the 'matter' of fantasy 'the geography of desire' (2002: 16).
23 See Peter Coveney's (1967) *Image of Childhood* for a discussion of the Romantic construction of childhood, also Linda Austin's (2003) more recent 'Children of Childhood'. See also John Ganim's *Medievalism and Orientalism* on the Romantic refiguration of 'medievalist discourses' in which the primitive is redeemed, 'no longer an indication of a fall from grace or a decline from a higher and more noble form, but a point of origin, even a source of vitality' (Ganim, 2005: 6).
24 See Stephen Jay Gould's *Ontogeny and Phylogeny* for discussion and history of the terms (1977: 1). Ganim also links childhood, 'a childhood to which we can never return', with the medieval (Ganim, 2005: 22).
25 This vision of the medieval era as a period of childhood is common in Victorian English Chaucer criticism, for instance Adolphus William Ward's condescending remarks in his volume on Chaucer in the series English Men of Letters: 'About our national life in this period, both in its virtues and in its vices, there is something – it matters little whether we call it – childlike or childish ... it lacks the seriousness belonging to men and to generations, who have learnt to control themselves, instead of relying on the control of others' (Ward, 1879: 41–2).
26 See Pugh and Weisl, who note the '"in between" quality of the period that makes it so challenging to fix' (2013: 5).
27 See Carl A. Rubino's Middle Ages, 'that long, dark era which has even been denied a name of its own' (1985: 55), and Jeffrey Jerome Cohen's musings on the implications of being the Age in the middle (2003: 21). See also Brian Stock: 'The Renaissance invented the Middle Ages in order to define itself; the Enlightenment perpetuated them in order to admire itself; and the Romantics revived them in order to escape from themselves. In their widest ramifications "the Middle Ages" thus constitute one of the most prevalent cultural myths of the modern world' (Stock, 1990: 69).

28 See again Pugh and Weisl, who note that '"medieval" in its current form may be constructed on analogy with "primeval", an unwitting suggestion of many of the assumptions of primitivism so often assigned to the period' (2013: 5).
29 See Paul Strohm's 'totalized medieval world', leading 'a continuing shadow existence ... under a sign of negation' (Strohm, 2000: 159).
30 The disappearing origin bears a resemblance to *objet a*, whose extraction constitutes reality.
31 Wallenstein credits Rousseau as the father of the trope. See Arthur Lindley's (1998) 'The Ahistoricism of Medieval Film' for another take on the ahistoric Middle Ages. E. M. Cioran's Golden Age or Eden, where nothing happens, shares the attributes of the medieval of nostalgic fantasy, 'an eternal present, that tense common to all visions of paradise, a time forged in opposition to the very idea of time' (Cioran, 1998: 99).
32 In a different version of Victorian nostalgia, Alice Chandler wrote, in 1970: 'Both aspects of medievalism – the political and the metaphysical – saw materialism and mechanization as inimical to the human. The return to the Middle Ages was conceived of as a homecoming' (Chandler, 1970: 7–8).
33 That ambivalence is what has allowed the medieval to be invoked for every ideological purpose. Susan Aronstein offers an overview of the range of ideological medievalisms from the fifteenth century onwards (Aronstein, 2005: 11–27). John Ganim, in his Introduction to *Medievalism and Orientalism* (Ganim, 2005: 1–16), points out the ambiguity of medievalist ideologies in the 'identity crisis' of the West (2005: 3). See also Fradenburg on the American 'overvaluation of modernity ... and disavowal of our hatred of modernity' (Fradenburg, 2009: 87).
34 Although, as Linda Hutcheon pointed out (2000: 7), 'it has become a commonplace to compare the end of the nineteenth century to the end of our own', that is, the twentieth.
35 Lears, writing in 1981, 'hope[d] to cast light on the soul-sickness which emerged in the late nineteenth century and spread throughout the twentieth – the sense that modern life has grown dry and passionless, and that one must somehow try to regenerate a lost intensity of feeling' (Lears, 1981: 142). That late-Victorian soul-sickness has not been cured.
36 See this term in Robinson and Clements (2009: 61).
37 According to Gregg Henriques and Daniel Görtz (2020): 'Metamodernism is the cultural code that comes after postmodernism'.
38 This is a paraphrase of the introduction to the first volume of *postmedieval*: '[W]e propose that the post/human present and future are predicated upon a plurality of different, discontinuous and heterogeneous

temporalities: there are many different Nows existing alongside each other and within each of them, multiple pasts' (Joy and Dionne, 2010: 6).

39  Steve Guthrie has suggested that, in the current (American) climate, '[p]opular usage still associates "medieval" with violent physicality and the absence of centralized, organized authority, but people no longer resist these things in themselves as they may once have done' (Guthrie, 2012: 100). An *un*repressed, *un*repudiated violence identified with the medieval is perhaps becoming disturbingly popular.

40  As Umberto Eco pointed out, anything 'between Nazi nostalgia and occultism' (Eco, 1986: 61–2), can pass muster as medieval. We are most familiar with the usage of repudiation, especially familiar since 9/11, whose aftermath spawned numerous instances of medieval as a term of abuse, for instance, 'The horrific attacks of September 11 have made it painfully clear that a technologically sophisticated band of medieval barbarians have declared war on America' (Timothy Lynch, cited in Holsinger, 2001: 8).

41  Susan Stewart refers to these realms where '"authentic" experience … is placed' as 'fictive domains', 'the beyond in which the antique, the pastoral, the exotic [and, I would add, the medieval], are articulated' (Stewart, 1993: 133). The term 'authenticity' accommodated something of that longing, particularly in late twentieth-century arguments concerning medieval music performance. In these arguments the term became weighted with the anxiety and hostility ignited by competing medieval fantasies, as discussed in Chapter 4. See also my 2019 essay, 'A Single, True, Certain Authenticity' (Dell, 2019b).

42  See Plato's theory of forms in *The Republic* and his simile of the cave (Plato, 1993: 278–86).

43  The enhanced real of fantasy fiction often includes this sensation of added depth. In Alan Garner's *Owl Service*, for instance, the familiar world suddenly changes and Gwyn feels 'that the trees and the rocks had never held such depth, and the line of the mountain made his heart shake' (Garner, 2006a: 34).

44  See Lewis's letter to Greeves on his conversation with Tolkien and Hugo Dyson (1988: 268).

45  See Chapter 1 of Farah Mendlesohn's (2008) *Rhetorics of Fantasy* for a discussion of 'portal fantasies'.

46  Diana Wynne Jones was a student of both Tolkien and Lewis at Oxford (Marcus, 2006: 85–6). She acknowledged a debt to her own Middle Ages: 'What I, personally, think of as the Middle Ages has to have been an abiding influence on me – I know that, and it's not simply because I happen to be married to a medievalist' (Jones, 2012: 214).

47 The loss of reality, however, is not a pure, one-way development in fantasy fiction. Reality is more abiding in *The Merlin Conspiracy* (2003) than in *Homeward Bounders* (1981). Colin Manlove, writing in about 2003, dubbed the 1980s as the decade of postmodern 'playing with reality' (Manlove, c.2003: 141), to be replaced in the 1990s by other, less 'literary' modes of narrative (169). It cannot be said, however, that the mainstream Western world has made good on the losses incurred during the 1980s.

48 See also Diana Wynne Jones's *The Pinhoe Egg* (2006), in which, '[e]ven though he could see far off through the trees, there was no depth to the place. It only seemed to touch the front of his mind, like cardboard scenery' (2006, 92).

49 There is always a cost, however.

50 Pratchett's Discworld, he tells us, 'started out as a parody of all the fantasy that was around in the big boom of the early '80s' (Pratchett, 2007). In this he supports Manlove's view that playing with reality was a motif of 1980s fantasy.

51 As John Haines (2014a: 153) notes: '*The Hobbit* ... broke all previous records. In the history of cinema, no movie until that December [2012] had ever made as much money in its opening weekend: $200 million worldwide.'

52 Linda Hutcheon rightly observed that 'irony may not be so much a defence against the power of nostalgia as the way in which nostalgia is made palatable: invoked but at the same time undercut' (Hutcheon and Valdés, 1998–2000: 7).

53 See headings under nostalgia in the Urban Dictionary. 'Nostalsceptic' and 'nostironic' are not there – I take responsibility for them.

54 See also D'Arcens (2011), Lynch (2011) and Dell (2011a) for discussions of nostalgias which maintain *nostos* and *algia* in uneasy cohabitation.

55 As Paul Hegarty notes, Baudrillard fails to recognise his own nostalgia (Hegarty, c.2004: 52). See also Paul Strohm, who spots a similar inconsistency in Baudrillard's *Symbolic Exchange* (Strohm, 2000: 159).

56 See, for instance Jacques Derrida's idea of an 'origin ... thought to be simple, intact, normal, pure, standard, self-identical' (Derrida, 1988: 236).

57 Shades of Lewis's 'central region' (Lewis, 1966a: 15).

58 See also Plato's myth of Er (in *The Republic*).

59 See Plato's *Phaedo* (2002: 147).

60 Fantasy fiction fulfils the need, once catered to by a range of beliefs, rituals and practices, in an age where the spiritual quest is often a more relaxed, do-it-yourself affair. See, for instance, the Religious Tolerance website: 'The New Age is in fact a free-flowing spiritual movement; a

network of believers and practitioners who share somewhat similar beliefs and practices' (Robinson, 2015). Lewis would have been uncomfortable with this 'free-flowing' tolerance. It is not what we think that matters, he wrote: 'What God thinks of us is ... infinitely more important' (Lewis, 1980a: 38).
61  For Tolkien and Lewis, however, ecstasy must guide the soul to a predetermined destination, hence Lewis's anxieties about mysticism. There was no knowing where the soul might fetch up! Ecstasy itself must be constrained within the limits prescribed by law. See *Letters to Malcolm* on mystics: 'the experience [of setting out] vouches for nothing about the utility or lawfulness or final event of their voyages' (Lewis: 1964: 64).
62  'It is in its nature that the object as such is lost' (Lacan, 1997: 52).
63  See Stewart on the 'false promise of restoration' (1993: 150).

# 2

# 'Yearning for the sweet beckoning sound': Musical longings and the unsayable in medievalist fantasy fiction

> For most of us, there is only the unattended
> Moment, the moment in and out of time,
> The distraction fit, lost in a shaft of sunlight,
> The wild thyme unseen, or the winter lightning
> Or the waterfall, or music heard so deeply
> That it is not heard at all, but you are the music
> While the music lasts.
> (Eliot, 1968: 44)

> Heard melodies are sweet, but those unheard
> Are sweeter; therefore, ye soft pipes, play on;
> Not to the sensual ear, but, more endear'd,
> Pipe to the spirit ditties of no tone.
> (Keats, 1970: 208)

This chapter addresses the place of music in medievalist fantasy fiction, in particular the writing of Susan Cooper. As before, I approach this conjunction from two angles, that of the Tolkien/Lewis legacy and that of Lacanian psychoanalytic theory, where they meet and where they diverge – in particular on the questions of what is real and what 'real' means. Tolkien and Lewis invented worlds that were real in the sense of radiant and meaningful, worlds that worked, whereas for Lacan 'The real is the difference between what works and what doesn't work. What works is the world. The real is what doesn't work' (Lacan, 2013: 61). Another point of divergence is between the joy infused with meaning, guaranteed by God, which Tolkien and Lewis espoused, and the *jouissance* beyond meaning of Lacanian psychoanalytic theory.

In Tolkien/Lewis fantasy, music is frequently invoked in relation to these radiant worlds – the numinous realms in fantasy fiction.

Sometimes it is there as a faint, tantalising intimation of their presence, just out of reach, intermittent, impossible to locate, as in Susan Cooper's *The Dark is Rising*, the second book of her *Dark is Rising* sequence.[1] Sometimes it is the mechanism by which characters are transported to the otherworld, as in Alan Garner's *Elidor*. Sometimes it frames the place itself, as when, in *Lord of the Rings* (*LOTR*), Frodo's faithful servant, Sam, at his first sight of Lothlórien says: 'I feel as if I was inside a song' (Tolkien, 1993: 342).

The notion of music as providing access to an otherworld has medieval antecedents. Karen Ralls-MacLeod, who has researched this connection in *Music and the Celtic Otherworld*, observes: '[The early medieval Celts] believed that this world and the supernatural world dynamically interact with each other, often with music as the bridge between the two' (Ralls-MacLeod, 2000: 172). She concludes her book by connecting this interaction with humanity's continuing search for Eden: 'Perhaps, then, the Otherworld and its beautiful music is beckoning us to "Come Home" again, to restore the universal Lost Chord' (184–5). In this way, music plays a central role in the lost home fantasies of nostalgia.

That nostalgic association between music and a lost home has descended into the imaginary of medievalist fantasy fiction. By now any one of these three words: 'medieval', 'music', 'otherworld', prompts an association with the other two for fantasy, including fantasies of access. But the song Sam refers to can also be thought of as a way of alluding to something unsayable about Lórien. Music has the power to immerse the listener in something beyond the power of speech to convey.

The background to Sam's remark is important. Frodo and Sam have stayed in the Elvish land of Rivendell, where songs bespell the listener:

> Frodo began to listen. At first the beauty of the melodies and of the interwoven words in elven-tongues, even though he understood them little, held him in a spell, as soon as he began to attend to them. Almost it seemed that the words took shape, and visions of far lands and bright things that he had never yet imagined opened out before him. (Tolkien, 1993: 227)

Here the singing voice has the power, literally, to open up for the listener a vista of 'far lands and bright things'; a spell is cast by music. Part of the promise of *LOTR* is that a luminous world is spun for the listener out of the substance of the singing voice, even – or perhaps *especially* – when (like Frodo) one cannot fully understand the language of the words or the music. In Lórien and in Rivendell there is for Frodo a residue, unavailable to understanding. This unknowable residue, so often called into play, starts to look essential to the spell cast on character and reader alike, although for readers another step is required. They must start from scratch with only the words to guide a musical fantasy. But again, this may be an advantage if the words do their work. To the extent that fantasy is a private, idiosyncratic affair, it may do better with less. For one whose fantasies begin in the dark and silence of the book, the music of the *LOTR* movies (P. Jackson, 2001–3) may seem out of joint or overblown, as the images of film sometimes do. The residue, the unheard and unseen, shaped only by words on a page, is a good place for a fantasy to germinate, especially when mystery is part of the fantasy. Such fantasies may not erupt as fully fledged perceptual experiences. The fantasies aroused by text may instead come across as a vague amalgam of the five senses and the sixth which amalgamation produces.

The quotation in my title comes at the end of Susan Cooper's *The Dark is Rising*. Cooper is one of the most musical authors in the Tolkien/Lewis tradition. Her youthful protagonist, Will Stanton, is the last-born of the immortal Old Ones, chosen to assist the Light in its long struggle against the Dark. In this passage Will sees the 'tall carved doors that led out of Time' (Cooper, 1973: 244) slowly open. Portals are one version of the frames which intensify reality discussed in Chapter 1, in this case a frame through which one enters an otherworld. The Old Ones have a curious relation to time. Merriman (who is Merlin), tells Will:

> We of the Circle are planted only loosely within Time. The doors are a way through it, in any direction we may choose. For all times co-exist, and the future can sometimes affect the past, even though the past is a road that leads to the future ... but men cannot understand this. (Cooper, 1973: 54)

As the Doors open, Will hears

> that haunting bell-like phrase that came always with the opening of the Doors ... Will clenched his fists as he listened, yearning towards

the sweet beckoning sound that was the space between waking and dreaming, yesterday and tomorrow, memory and imagining. It floated lovingly in his mind, then gradually grew distant [as the Doors] swung slowly together, until silently they shut. Then as the last echo of the enchanted music died, they disappeared. (Cooper, 1973: 244)

What Will yearns for is not any particular time but a 'space between' (255), leading from one time into another, a timeless crevice between times.² Here is an instance of the fantasy of the *space between* as more real than reality, which I associate with the 'middle' of medievalism. It is what Georges Bataille calls 'the projection of [an] instant into the infinite' (Bataille, c.2001: 24), which for Will, as so often in the book, is associated with music.

The portals also open to the sound of music in Theresa Whistler's *The River Boy*, when Rose, the old pony, watched by Nathaniel,

> sprang full at the curtain of water [and] the waters closed behind her ... The pipes no longer played 'Come and rest' but 'come and dance' ... For a moment Nathaniel caught, through [the door], a glimpse of some unimaginable country, folded in a dazzling deep blue darkness. The Old Rose, with a whinny of joy, had passed through, and the narrow door was softly closing. The music faded away [and] it seemed to Nathaniel that a great unbearable silence had fallen on all things. (Whistler, 1976: 33)

Nathaniel, like Will, is left with an unbearable longing for the doors to open again and admit him. The same three crucial ingredients are present for each: the portals, the music and the yearning. For Will, each actual 'time' in which he finds himself carries its own hardships and dangers, once he is *there*. It is the field of action and narrative, the field of chronological time. There are deeds to be done, battles to be fought, choices to be made. The shift between times is different, it 'floats'. This crack between times, for Will, is the ecstatic realm. That floating quality is essential to it, in that it lies in a moment outside the perimeters of chronological time (and geographical space), the ultimate instance of the temporal disjunction to which fantasy fiction so often alludes.³

Time travel allows many adventures but carries its own dangers. The heroes and heroines of fantasy fiction are rarely scripted to live out their days in the blissful realms, although they may visit them. These are not places where ordinary mortals dwell, or only at their peril. The disjunction between them and the mundane world is often expressed as a temporal distortion, perilous in itself.[4] Temporal distortion is one of the commonest tropes of high fantasy, an almost inevitable side effect of hopping between worlds, like an interworld jetlag. You might spend twenty years in the otherworld and yet return at the very instant of your departure, as the children do in *The Lion, the Witch and the Wardrobe* (Lewis, 2005: 196); alternatively, you might return that same day and find that ten years had elapsed in the mundane world, as Alveric discovers in Lord Dunsany's *The King of Elfland's Daughter*, when he escapes from Elfland with the princess (Lewis, 1999: 27).[5] I propose that all instances of temporal distortion gesture towards this moment of ecstasy, inaccessible to chronological time. No mortal could *dwell* in such a place because it has no duration. Lewis alludes to such moments in 'On Stories' (*In Other Worlds*): 'In life and art both we are always trying to catch in our net of successive moments something that is not successive' (Lewis, 1966b: 38). Such instants between the flow of ordinary time and that which Walter Benjamin called a 'time filled by the presence of the now' (Benjamin, 1970: 293), signal a drastic break with the familiar and this break is a chief concern of fantasy fiction in this tradition. And so often, in such instants, as Ralls-Macleod writes, music accompanies or figures 'the bridge between the two' (Ralls-MacLeod, 2000: 172). This is the ecstatic *between* space for which the term medieval can stand, making the medieval the perfect setting for high fantasy.

If the heroes of fantasy fiction do eventually set sail for the blessed isle, others, always including the reader, are left behind on the final page, still yearning. Aslan's country is the exception to this rule, except that the characters, by the time they reach it, are all dead! The reader is left alone, the last survivor (Lewis, 2005: 755). Lewis's afterlife allows no nostalgic yearnings. It is the final homecoming where everything of value has been retained. There is nothing to yearn for. Unlike Nietzche's longing for a state of pre-nostalgia (Boym, 2001: 26), Lewis longed for a state of post-nostalgia where all desires would be satisfied.

Some heroes choose to join the ranks of the mortals who must remain, so as not to be parted from them. Taran, in Lloyd Alexander's *The High King*, forgoes the delights of the Summer Country, preferring to 'dwell in sorrow instead of happiness' in order to mend the wounds of his country (Alexander, 2006: 236). Most notably, Arwen, in *LOTR*, chooses to stay and bear mortality with Aragorn, 'the sweet and the bitter' (Tolkien, 1993: 952). In both cases, mortal life, with its inevitable sorrow and loss, has its own allure, and especially for the reader. High fantasy devotees love to read of such sunderings; the very sound is seductive. Tolkien uses the word to great nostalgic effect in *LOTR*, for instance in Galadriel's song: 'While here beyond the sundering seas now fall the elven tears' (Tolkien, 1993: 363).[6]

Yearning, Will discovers, is endemic for the Old Ones: 'An Old One ... was doomed always to feel the same formless, nameless longing for something out of reach, as an endless part of life' (Cooper, 1973: 123). The Old Ones are alien, never able to belong. But Will is speaking for the initiated – and in this case that is everyone who reads the book. Through our knowledge as readers, we enter that privileged zone. We are interpellated as Old Ones, doomed to exile. Not for us the sweets of forgetfulness dealt out to ordinary mortals, as they are to the mortal children in Cooper's (2000a) *Silver on the Tree*, the last in the *Dark is Rising* cycle: 'And none of you will remember ... because you are mortal and must live in present time, and it is not possible to think in the old ways there' (2000a: 273). But as readers we are not obliged to forget. It is we who 'think in the old ways'. Will represents us, speaking *our* yearning, the yearning of alienated mortals with a yen for the immortal, a 'memory' even of the immortal.[7] The *space between* in fantasy fiction, like the age in the middle, suffers from the ambiguity to which any middle (as neither one thing or another) lends itself. Language subjects us to an anxiety about any word and the concept to which it is insecurely attached. Indeed, so disturbing is ambiguity for some that a *space between* may be ecstatic or terrifying or both at once. As I have argued, the 'middle' of Middle Ages allows the medieval to act as a *space between* the clarity of the classical age and the Renaissance. In the next section I explore further this ambiguous *space between*.

## The formless space between

The ambiguity of the 'Middle Ages' as a fantasy *space between* makes it liable to transformations. It may, for instance, be stripped of its historical content and reduced to a screen on which nostalgic fantasies of a timeless, Edenic presence and plenitude can be displayed, but dimly rendered rather than clearly delineated.[8] Will might encounter the ecstasy of the *space between* but readers, though included among the initiated, do not. They stand at one remove from an encounter with the utterly formless and nameless.

Diana Wynne Jones describes a dangerously formless 'Place Between', which Christopher, from her *Chrestomanci* series, has to traverse in order to travel to other worlds:

> Christopher thought it was probably a left-over piece of the world, from before somebody came along and made the world properly. Formless slopes of rock towered and slanted in all directions ... and none of it had much shape. Nor did it have much colour ... There was always a formless wet mist hanging round this place, adding to the vagueness of everything. You could never see the sky. In fact, Christopher sometimes thought there might not *be* a sky. (D. Jones, 2000a: 9)[9]

This between place looks very like Chaos, for instance in Ovid's *Metamorphoses*:

> Before there was any earth and sea, before the canopy of heaven stretched overhead, Nature presented the same aspect the world over, that to which men have given the name of Chaos. This was a shapeless, uncoordinated mass, nothing but a weight of lifeless matter, whose ill-assorted elements were indiscriminately heaped together in one place. (Ovid, 1955: 29)

This Place Between also conjures up associations with Lacan's traumatic Real, 'absolutely without fissure' (Lacan, 1991: 97), and with what Kristeva names the abject (as opposed to the object) 'which draws me towards the place where meaning collapses' (Kristeva, 1982: 2). For Kristeva the abject is 'what disturbs identity, system, order. What does not respect borders, positions, rules. The *in-between*, the ambiguous, the composite' (Kristeva, 1982: 4; my emphasis). The abject is a space undivided by the organising principle of difference. Kristeva's abject is not Lacan's Real. What they have in common, however, is a sense of the horror of the uncategorised and uncategorisable which fantasies of reality seek to cover. Kristeva's abject is horrifying because it is viewed from the point of view *of* order (Kristeva, 1982: 3). The paradisal fantasy of the 'more real than reality', an enriched version of faded everyday life explored in Chapter 1, protects us from this horror.

When Christopher returns to the Place Between as an older child, he is terrified:

> His eyes tried to make sense of the shapeless way the rocks slanted and couldn't. The formlessness stirred a formless kind of fear in him, which the wind and the mist and the rain beating in the mist made worse. (D. Jones, 2000a: 92)

As I have previously argued, in the high fantasy tradition the non-signifying, shapeless, engulfing *space between* does not threaten the reader. It is pre-digested and robbed of its trauma (and its ecstasy) by words on the page when we encounter it. This is not Gothic horror. L. O. Aranye Fradenburg, drawing on Lacan's work, describes the double lure of the medieval in terms which could describe such fantasy fiction:

> [M]edievalism still 'screens', in both senses, *jouissance*. It still, that is, points out the way to the ecstatic location of the subject's finitude, the place where the subject would encounter the non-identity that is within him; but it also defends against the deadly consequences of such an encounter. (Fradenburg, 1997: 210)

It is important to distinguish, as Fradenburg does, between the fantasy of a space or place between and that ecstatic 'location' where everything, including the subject, is undone.[10] Lacan's *jouissance* is that which 'goes beyond the limits imposed, under the term of pleasure [Freud's pleasure principle] on the usual tensions of life' (Lacan, 2007: 48). The moment of ecstasy and/or horror (Lacan's *jouissance* carries both) beyond the limits of pleasure, cannot be fantasised. The floating 'time' has nothing with which to build a fantasy. Will's object of longing may be formless and nameless but, for the reader, something is screened, however dimly. Fantasy needs the coordinates of time, place and narrative. There must be a narrative, no matter how minimal, for a fantasy to be spun. It is possible, however, to fantasise *about* such a moment. It is possible to create an alluring fantasy in which one is projected into the infinite instant to the imagined admiration of one's friends.

Lacan suggests, in his seminar *Formations of the Unconscious*, that the desirer 'enjoys desiring and this is an essential element of his *jouissance*' (Lacan, 1957–58: 284).[11] Yet, on the other hand, he proposes in the Anxiety seminar that desire can function as a limit to *jouissance*: 'The will to *jouissance* ... is a will which fails, which encounters its own limit ... in the very exercise ... of ... desire' (Lacan, 1962–63: 5). This is the distinction to which Fradenburg (1997) alludes: desire may function as a support to one *jouissance* but as a barrier to another. The screen on which desire's fantasies are displayed can protect against that other, vertiginous *jouissance* which undoes the imaginary coherence of the self. Ecstasy can kill. Those of us with an instinct for self-preservation shelter behind that barrier, enjoying in comparative safety the fantasies of nostalgic desire.

It is this second form of *jouissance* that fantasy fiction generally provides (at least in novels of the Tolkien/Lewis tradition), drawing back from the horror of that encounter with the Real. But, in Fradenburg's words, 'it points out the way'. The medieval *space between* in fantasy fiction offers itself as that strangeness at the heart – Lacan's 'extimacy'. Music dangles the same double lure, as listeners know. You can lose yourself in it or you can instead fantasise that you do. Mladen Dolar, speaking of the voice as *objet a*, makes a similar point: '[M]usic evokes the object voice and obfuscates it; it fetishises it, but it also opens the gap that cannot be filled' (Dolar, 2006: 31). Listeners may draw back from the horror of the voice as *objet a* but music also points the way. Fantasy fiction, by splicing music to the medieval, intensifies the ambiguous allure of both. Their fusion lights a spark of recognition, confirming for readers that they have glimpsed the strange but familiar territory, that *space between* where, nostalgia insists, all losses are restored.

The music Will hears in the passage quoted earlier *is* the *space between*: 'the sweet beckoning sound *that was* the space between'. What is the nature of this relation? It is not presented as one of representation or metaphor but of absolute identity. But how is it meaningful to say that one object is another object, as in the Mass when the priest says, raising the wafer of bread, 'this *is* my body'? It is a writing that raises questions about the status of the object.

## Writing the musical space between

Authors have a variety of devices for indicating, while not describing, the characteristics of between-ness (for which the Middle Ages can stand), for instance the juxtaposition in the quotation the last section: 'the space *between* waking and dreaming, yesterday and tomorrow, memory and imagining', or, in George MacDonald's *Lilith*, 'the hush that lives *between* music and silence' (MacDonald, 2000a: 208). Cooper also alludes to a 'silent music' (Cooper, 1973: 50).[12] This drawing together of opposites, tending towards oxymoron, subverts the usual logic of speech, pointing towards an impossible *space between* where opposites fuse. In everyday language waking is *not* dreaming, yesterday is *not* tomorrow, memory is *not* imagination and music most certainly is *not* silence, or how could we communicate?

The only way yesterday can mean anything is by *not* being tomorrow or today or next week. As Ferdinand Saussure asserts, 'each linguistic term derives its value from its opposition to all other terms' (Saussure, 1974: 88). In language what a thing is depends on what it is not. The signifier 'sound' cannot signify without its absent counterpart: 'silence'. But juxtaposition serves as a means to indicate something unsayable by jamming the oppositions together, as a jazz pianist plays two notes a semitone apart as a way of indicating the quartertone which is missing on a normally tuned piano. By destabilising language this juxtaposition goes further. In defying the logic of non-contradiction, it defies the categories upon which Western metaphysics is constituted, Father Parmenides' law of non-contradiction:

> This [Parmenides says] should not ever prevail in your thought: that the things that *are not*, *are*; Rather do you keep your mind well shut off from just this way in searching. (Plato, 1996: 41; emphasis in original)[13]

Oxymoron, by revealing the degree to which being depends on the shaky foundations of signification, throws being itself into doubt. Oxymoron returns us to the absence of *objet (petit) a* and the ontological fragility of the desiring subject. The 'more real than reality' promised by fantasy fiction is not this slippery reality endowed by the signifier; it is rather on the side of what subverts it.

Such textual devices as oxymoron rest on a fundamental premise: that the longed-for object cannot be described any more than it can be possessed. It resists the formulation of attributes.[14] Tolkien, in 'On Fairy-Stories', says, of the 'perilous realm' of Faërie, that it 'cannot be caught in a web of words; for it is one of its qualities to be indescribable, though not imperceptible' (Tolkien, 1966: 39). The object of enchantment cannot be fully represented or fully comprehended. Something escapes 'the web of words' and the comprehension of the perceiver. Once you have attributed qualities to it, that is not it.

This applies equally when the enchanting object is music. Will cannot identify the instruments playing his music. They will not coalesce into solid, material entities. Invisible (acousmatic) instruments are the stuff of fairy story and myth. The enchanting elven music Frodo hears in *LOTR* is marked with the same trait of unknowability:

> One clear voice now rose above the others. It was singing in the fair elven-tongue, of which Frodo knew only a little, and the others knew nothing. Yet the sound blending with the melody seemed to shape itself in their thought into words which they only partly understood. (Tolkien, 1993: 78)

In this case *between-ness* lies between the melody and the singing voice, but like Will's bell-*like* instruments, it resists the domination of knowledge.[15] There will be no ultimate revelation, however carefully the net of words is spread. There is no lack of words, but they come with a disclaimer; the reader is warned that they will always fail.

This urge to keep the mystery intact is at war, however, with an equal urge towards explication, impelled by, among other things, the exigencies of plot. Mysteries call for explication, but then clarification produces new mysteries in its wake to drive on the narrative, particularly in the case of a quest. Even more so this becomes the case as fantasy fiction series lengthen towards infinity. But the conflict goes deeper for Christian fantasy. Lewis's attempt to marry Romanticism and Reason in his defence of Christianity illustrates the dilemma. Lewis's Romantic side, he tells us, was led to God by *Sehnsucht* (longing).[16] That came first. He said of himself that 'the imaginative man in me is older, more continuously operative, and in that sense more basic than either the religious writer or the critic' (Lewis, 2007: 516). When as a young man Lewis first read George MacDonald's *Phantastes*, 'romantic enough in all conscience', he said that what it did 'was to convert, even to baptise [his] imagination' (Lewis, 2014: xi).[17] Once a Christian and an apologist for Christianity, however, Lewis had to come to terms – and persuade others to come to terms – with God as the true object of desire, the God who is also Creator and Judge. Romanticism had to make room for the urgent need to save souls from damnation, his own included. Hence the need for submission and obedience at all costs; the unknowable object of *Sehnsucht* was now the God who will one day call the soul to judgement and not all will be saved.[18] This God must be placated.

I think this necessity accounts for a kind of schism in Lewis's fiction in which music is caught up. Like Apuleius's Psyche, determined to know the identity of her lover at whatever cost,[19] Lewis sacrifices an intimacy founded on indistinctness for the sake of clarity. In his writing there is, on the one hand, a kind of brisk sorting of the sheep from the goats in which nothing is permitted to cloud the accurate judgement of right and wrong. This sorting occurs precisely at moments of judgement, like the White Witch's comeuppance in *The Lion, the Witch and the Wardrobe* (Lewis, 2005: 191), the abrupt disappearance of the damned in *The Last Battle* (Lewis, 2005: 751), or the horribly explicit fate of the people at N.I.C.E. in *That Hideous Strength* (Lewis, 1955b: 343–7).[20] On the other hand there are moments when a confusion of categories may be safely permitted, as here, in *The Voyage of the Dawn Treader*, on the verges of Aslan's country:

> It brought both a smell and a sound, a musical sound ... Lucy could only say, 'It would break your heart.' 'Why,' said I, 'was it so sad?' 'Sad!! No,' said Lucy. (Lewis, 2005: 539)

Fantasy fiction following Tolkien and Lewis may ignore Christianity or find it wanting. In Cooper's *Dark is Rising*, the Rector, trying ineffectually to exorcise the forces of the Dark when they turn up at his church, is reduced to the condition of a 'frightened animal' without the 'powers of speech and movement' (Cooper, 1973: 143–4). Christianity is not going to save the day here. Something is retained in Cooper's world of a crucial choice between different paths and it is still a moral choice (usually involving sacrifice) with weighty consequences.[21] The ghostly hand of the Christian fantasy tradition is still writing. Tolkien and Lewis would recognise their offspring, though they might have difficulties with her moral landscape (Lewis perhaps more so).[22] The difference is that Cooper's work is not burdened in the same way, or to the same extent, by the imperative to judge correctly at every turn.

The second quality of the musical object in fantasy fiction concerns a different kind of elusiveness. The object is described as appearing, grail-like, at its own will rather than the will of the listener, in this case the will of Will. Will first hears the music as he sleeps on the morning of his eleventh birthday, the day he comes into his power as an Old One:

> He was woken by music. It beckoned him, lilting and insistent; delicate music, played by delicate instruments that he could not identify, with one rippling, bell-like phrase running through it in a gold thread of delight [and] the deepest enchantment of all his dreams and imaginings. (Cooper, 1973: 20)

As Will wakes the music 'begins to fade': 'He sat up ... and reached his arm out to the air, as if he could bring it back. Later he hears the music again, 'the same phrase':

> He swung round vainly searching for it in the air, as if he might see it somewhere like a flickering light. 'Where are you?' It had gone again. (Cooper, 1973: 21)

Whatever the musical object of *The Dark is Rising*, it is not at Will's command. It is the object that summons, like the magical horn that summons the children in *Prince Caspian* (Lewis, 2005: 317–18), or beckons, as the bell-like music beckons Will. Will reaches out his arm for it 'as if he could bring it back'. Of course he cannot. You cannot take hold of a sound even if the instrument is in your hands and, in any case, Will cannot locate it; the sound is acousmatic, having no visible bearer. Will swings round, 'vainly searching for it in the air, as if he might see it somewhere like a flickering light'.

The acousmatic sound permeates fantasy fiction, always bringing with it that exquisite frisson of the *unheimlich*. In Alan Garner's *Elidor*, for instance, a fiddler plays, now in one place then immediately in another, impossibly distant:

> 'There's the fiddle again!' said Roland. It was distant, as before ... 'But I can't see the old man. ... He was by the lamppost a second ago, and it's miles to the houses. We couldn't hear him and not see him.' [...] Then the music came again. Roland jumped up, but there was no fiddler in sight, and he could not make out which direction the sound was coming from. ... The music faded. (2006b: 10–11)[23]

Will's synaesthetic confusion, his cross-sensual attempt to see or touch a sound is, at one level, his need to assign the music to something visible or tangible, so as to tame it to the status of object. In the field of vision, we assume, objects can be located, named, comprehended, sometimes taken hold of. Touch also offers a handle on the object. Sound, like smell, engages us differently, its presence is amorphous, enveloping, penetrating. Music has had, since ancient times, the reputation of finding its way into 'the inward places of the soul' as Plato asserted in Book 3 of the *Republic* (1994–2009: n.p.). This reputation arose from distinctions made between sight and sound in the ancient world which, in practice, still hold sway. These distinctions privilege the visual.[24] Kathryn Kalinak describes the distinction as a 'model of sensory perception which connected the eye more closely to the mediating structure of consciousness than it did the ear' (Kalinak, 1992: 23). The eye, according to this model, provided a rudimentary ordering of the visual field into separate entities. The ear, for the Greeks, was a void into which sound was poured unmediated (Aristotle, 2002: 177).

Eyes learn to divide the visual field into a series of discrete entities and it is the field of vision which is still privileged to dictate what, in everyday life, we call reality. Our understanding of what an object is, is founded very largely on the evidence of sight, with touch coming on as understudy when sight is unavailable. Sound is less divisible, less amenable to objectification. While the Greek model valorised the eyes over the ears as more objective, that very lack of a mediating structure of organisation allowed to sound privileged access to the emotional life of the hearer (Kalinak, 1992: 22). An acousmatic sound, emanating from nowhere or everywhere, detached from the organising principle of sight, offers itself as an appropriate object for nameless longing. It is less easily tamed to the status of object and therefore to the control of the possessor.

At another level, Will's synaesthesia creates yet another *space between* (between sight and hearing), a cranny where the enchantment I call 'between-ness' can nestle. That enchantment would fail if Will could locate the sound or identify the instruments. For such an equivocal object the senses which lend themselves less to division, like hearing and smell, or a confusion of different senses, keep the object undefined but not imperceptible. Lucy refers, in *The Voyage of the Dawn Treader*, to a 'dim, purple kind of smell' (Lewis, 2005:

513).²⁵ When Dave blows the horn of Owein in Guy Gavriel Kay's *The Summer Tree*, 'the sound was Light' (2006: 342). (Here again is the assertion that one thing *is* another, as Will's music *is* the *space between*.) In *The Darkest Road*, Kay refers to 'a voice so clear [that it blurred] forever, the borders between sound and light' (Kay, 2001: 41).²⁶

Madeleine L'Engle is only marginally a writer of medievalist fantasy fiction, but where it figures most prominently in her books is through music – the harmony of the spheres.²⁷ In *A Wrinkle in Time*, the narrator speaks of Aunt Beast's song as 'a music more tangible than form or sight':

> It had essence and structure. It supported Meg more firmly than the arms of Aunt Beast. It seemed to travel with her, to sweep her aloft in the power of song, so that she was moving in glory among the stars, and for a moment she, too, felt that the words Darkness and Light had no meaning, and only this melody was real. (L'Engle, 2005c: 185)

Aunt Beast, along with her entire species, is blind, and she has no faith in sight: 'We do not know what things *look* like [she says]. We know what things *are* like. It must be a very limiting thing, this seeing' (L'Engle, 2005c: 181).²⁸ Aunt Beast claims knowledge of the essential nature of things, lost to beings entrapped by the specular. This nature is, apparently, not based on the law of non-contradiction; the interdependent opposites, darkness and light, fail here in their task of signification. This most crucial of distinctions in high fantasy, that between the Dark and the Light, is, at this point, meaningless. For Meg, in that moment 'in and out of time', as T. S. Eliot puts it (1968: 44), only the song is real. Everything else is jettisoned.

Finally, Will's music, like Roland's in Garner's *Elidor*, sounds then 'fades' or 'dies', again and again, emphasising the elusiveness of the musical object. Silence is part of the pattern, the part played by absence: '[M]usic, born of silence returns to silence', as Vladimir Jankélévitch has it (2007: 287).²⁹ This predilection for the dying fall in music betrays the Romantic influence on fantasy fiction. Jean Paul wrote: 'It is more than an analogy to call the Romantic the undulating hum of a vibrating string or bell, whose sound waves fade away into ever greater distances and finally are lost in ourselves, and which, although outwardly silent, still sound within' (cited in Hoeckner, c.2002: 54). Intermittence acts as a temporal form of the juxtaposition of opposites, creating another *space between*, like that hush which MacDonald places 'between music and silence', gesturing towards a music to which the words sounding and silent, *as alternatives*, cannot be applied. Having spoken of a music that is both sounding and silent, it is only a short step to the discourse of the music of the spheres or *musica mundana*, where the question of audibility has frequently been canvassed. This is one direction my thoughts have taken in seeking a framework for these enquiries and a lineage for this use of language which undoes its signifying function.

## Discourses of silent music I: The music of the spheres

The music of the spheres has a substantial medieval tradition, drawn from the ancients. But when one reads medieval writings on the music of the spheres, they do not seem to have much to do with these ways of using language or much to do with the experience of making or listening to music. And two things become clear from reading fantasy fiction: first, any framework for discussion of this fiction must take into account music and musical ecstasy, where the listener is taken, rapt away out of time; second, the fantasy novel must attempt to perform (however cursorily or derivatively at times) rather than merely describe, the *space between*, where language fails.[30]

Medieval opinion was divided as to why we do not hear the music of the spheres. Boethius (*c*.477–524) offers 'many reasons' but without expanding (Boethius, 1989: 9). Ugolino of Orvieto (*c*.1380–1457) theorises that possibly we do not hear the spheres because we are so familiar with the sound (Godwin, 1993: 143).[31] For Giorgio Anselmi (before 1386 – between 1440 and 1443), 'the human ear shrinks from hearing the divine voices' (Godwin, 1993: 151). Jacques de Liège (*c*.1260 to after 1330) takes Boethius to mean that harmony more likely referred not to sound but to relative positions and proportions (Godwin, 1993: 130–1). Jacques concludes that to speak of the music of heavenly bodies may be a purely metaphorical expression (Godwin, 1993: 138). But whatever their conclusions, these writers are more concerned with very precise questions of number, ratio, proportion, correspondence, hierarchy and morality than with music played or heard. For Boethius, it is the knowledge of music that matters: 'How much nobler, then, is the study of music as a rational discipline than as composition and performance' (Boethius, 1989: 50). He acknowledged the delight that music brings but explained it in terms that subordinated delight to a cosmic unity:

> For when we hear what is properly and harmoniously united in sound in conjunction with that which is harmoniously coupled and joined together within us and are attracted to it, then we recognize that we ourselves are put together in its likeness. For likeness attracts, whereas unlikeness disgusts and repels. (Boethius, 1989: 2)

The study of music for Boethius, based on Platonic theory, was an ethical matter: '[M]usic is associated not only with speculation but with morality as well' (Boethius, 1989: 2). Musical enjoyment had to be explained in terms other than its own. Music remains wild and must be fenced by morality or some other means. As Roland Barthes noted:

> There is an imaginary in music whose function is to reassure, to constitute the subject hearing it (would it be that music is dangerous – the old Platonic idea? that music is an access to *jouissance*'). (Barthes, 1977: 179)

For those who came after Boethius, number served to silence the troubling flesh implicated in practical music along with its temptations and enjoyments. Here is the author of the ninth-century *Scholica enchiriadis*:

> Music is entirely formed and fashioned after the image of numbers. And thus it is number, by means of fixed and established proportions of notes, that brings about whatever is pleasing to the ear in singing. Whatever pleasure rhythms yield, whether in song or in rhythmic movements of whatever sort, all is the work of number. Notes pass away quickly; numbers, however, though stained by the corporeal matter of voices and moving things [corporea vocum et motuum materia decolorantur], remain. (Cited in Holsinger, 2001: 4)

As shown in Chapter 1, the presence of the body at times also troubles music and musical enjoyment in the work of Tolkien and Lewis. Tolkien in particular, like the author of the *Scholica enchiriadis*, preferred to emphasise music's spiritual aspect, in particular the music of those most spiritual of life forms, the elves. This question of body and spirit is one which plagues ideas and fantasies of medieval music. I return to it in Chapters 3 and 4.

We are more accustomed to the music of the spheres in its poetic or Romantic incarnation than with ancient or medieval theories: William Blake's 'To the Evening Star': 'speak silence with thy glimmering eyes' (1976: 63) or Keats's 'Ode on a Grecian Urn': 'Heard melodies are sweet, but those unheard / Are sweeter' (Keats, 1970: 209). For Lewis and Tolkien too, with their Romantic inheritance, it was a poetic matter, as in Lewis's account of the music of the spheres (1998: 52). Bradford Lee Eden suggests that Tolkien takes over the medieval and ancient understanding of the music of the spheres 'and translates it wholesale into his world' (Eden, 2003: 192–3). True, but he has romanticised it along the way. These medieval men, on the contrary, posited an orderly cosmos, meaningful, purposeful, eternal and non-contradictory. As Boethius said, music was a 'rational discipline', unstained by the instability of human flesh that sins and decays.[32] If sound, produced by a body, was the stain, then the *musica mundana* must be silent. With Joseph Addison (1712), these men cried:

> What though in solemn silence all
> Move round the dark terrestrial ball;
> What though nor real voice nor sound
> Amidst their radiant orbs be found?
> In Reason's ear they all rejoice,
> And utter forth a glorious voice;
> For ever singing as they shine,
> 'The Hand that made us is divine'.
> (Addison, 1975: 443)

I do not believe, however, that the reasonable cosmos was ever a matter of dry certitude. If it had been, the author of the *Scholica enchiriadis* might not have been so insistent on the triumph of unchanging number over the uncertain, untrustworthy, pain-ridden flesh. Like Tolkien and Lewis (and perhaps Addison) he wrote the triumph of God's eternity he ardently desired as an act of faith. Like theirs, his writing has the sound of a voice crying in a wilderness that threatened to overwhelm him, a chaos of the body unorganised by the Word.

There is an echo of this cry in a book entitled *The Music of the Spheres*, by Jamie James. When, says the author, after a 'beautifully performed' opera, audience members speak of a '"sublime ... transcendent" experience' their words arise

> from a deep-seated human need to feel a connection with the Absolute, to transcend the phenomenal world. ... There would seem to be an inextinguishable yearning in the human soul, almost its defining characteristic, to form these connections, to find a meaningful order in the bewildering complexity of the perceptible universe. (J. James, 1995: 18)

In a typical nostalgic turn, James argues that the threads of this connection were once in the hands of all:

> Picture to yourself, if you can, a universe in which everything makes sense. A serene order presides over the earth around you, and the heavens above revolve in sublime harmony. ... It is not simply a matter of faith: the best philosophic and scientific minds have proved that it is so. This is no New Age fantasy but our own world as scientists, philosophers, and artists knew it until the advent of the Industrial Revolution and its companion in the arts, the Romantic movement. Those ideals are gone forever. (J. James, 1995: 3)

James's vision of the 'sublime harmony' of the cosmos of the past is an instance of Eliade's 'nostalgia for paradise' which we explored in Chapter 1. James also echoes the nostalgia of Lewis and Tolkien for the supposed certitudes of the old Christian West and its classical inheritance; it is an echo that links this tradition of fantasy with the nostalgia for harmony expressed as music. Order and certainty, the harmonious universe 'in which everything makes sense' is projected into the past of 'gone forever'. But the confident voice of certainty for which they yearned suggests instead the presence of negated uncertainties.

The necessity for certitude in medieval writings of the *musica mundana* and their successors banished the lively tension of oxymoron in favour of the half-life of metaphor where one constituent of the oppositional pair is killed off by making it a metaphor for the other – '*one word for another*' as Lacan puts it in 'The Agency of the Letter in the Unconscious' (Lacan, 1977d: 157; emphasis in original) – although Addison seems to be consoling himself for the loss of something different, his reiterated 'what though' pulling against the triumph of Reason and the reasonable God of the Enlightenment.

Lewis and Tolkien both wrote of music that creates. Their creation music provides an illustration of the warring elements in their fantasy fiction between the romantic and the reasonable, between mystery and explication or justification, and of the way music gets caught in the crossfire. As I have suggested, it is a difficulty inherent in writing Christian fantasy which some of their successors, like Jones and Cooper, did not inherit. They were freed from the necessity to resolve theological issues like the goodness of God or the tension between predestination and free will. Tolkien's and Lewis's Creation music belong on the reasonable side with Addison; the poetic is added on. Creation presents God in his least romantic manifestation. Tolkien's 'Ainulindalë' (the first book of the *Silmarillion*) is the clearest case. It is rare, in Tolkien's fiction, for the Christian apologist to take over proceedings but he does here:

> Ilúvatar (God) declares to the Ainur (the Holy Ones)[33] a mighty theme, unfolding to them things greater and more wonderful than he had yet revealed. ... Then Ilúvitar said to them: 'Of the theme that I have declared to you, I will now that ye make in harmony together a Great Music.' (Tolkien, 1991: 15)

This the Ainur do, but Melkor, the greatest of them, has his own ideas and introduces them into the music, causing discord. Twice Melkor interrupts and on each occasion Ilúvatar derives from the discord a new theme. On the third occasion Ilúvatar stops the music and shows the Ainur the universe their music has created, or at least a preview of it. Ilúvatar proclaims to the assembled Ainur,

> Behold your Music! This is your minstrelsy; and each of you shall find contained herein, amid the design that I set before, all those things which it may seem that he himself devised or added. And thou, Melkor, wilt discover all the secret thoughts of thy mind, and wilt perceive that they are but a part of the whole and tributary to its glory. (Tolkien, 1991: 18)

He has earlier told Melkor that

> no theme may be played that hath not its uttermost source in me, nor can any alter the music in my despite. For he that attempteth this shall prove but mine instrument in the devising of things more wonderful, which he himself hath not imagined. (Tolkien, 1991: 17–18)

This could be read as an extended metaphor (as the music of the spheres can often be), deployed here to justify the presence of suffering and evil in the world via concepts of harmony and dissonance. Ilúvatar allows free will in the Ainur and works with the dissonant consequences 'in the devising of things more wonderful'. Music is made the means to justify the ways of God to man, but unconvincingly.[34] I find Tolkien's God as unappealing as Milton's. The Ainulindalë is not really to do with music. In this Tolkien follows Plotinus:

> What is evil in the single soul will stand a good thing in the universal system; what in the unit offends nature will serve nature in the total event – and still remains the weak and wrong tone it is, though its sounding takes nothing from the worth of the whole. (Godwin, 1987: 21)

For both Plotinus and Tolkien the music is bypassed by the metaphor in the urge to communicate everything necessary for correct theological understanding. No room is left for anything unknown, inexpressible or ungraspable.

In the creation of Narnia, Aslan appears in his most positive form. It is not initially so. Creation begins in absolute darkness with an acousmatic voice that sends shivers of awe through the children. For Digory (in *The Magician's Nephew*), 'it was, beyond comparison, the most beautiful noise he had ever heard. It was so beautiful he could hardly bear it' (Lewis, 2005: 61). Here is an instance of the tendencies we have been exploring, the oxymoronic (alluding to the unbearable aspect of *jouissance*) and the acousmatic. But then creation gets under way and Aslan appears in the clear light of the newly created day. It becomes more difficult to present him as mysterious and awesome when he is out in the open, although Lewis does his best. In *The Magician's Nephew*, the lion, still nameless, is 'huge, shaggy and bright' (Lewis, 2005: 62); luminosity is the visual counterpart of the musical and, like the musical, 'the luminous is numinous', as Edwyn Bevan has it (cited in Downing, 2005: 67).[35]

Nevertheless, explanation is Lewis's strongest urge here and overtakes awe. When Aslan starts singing a different music for each act of creation the mystery and awe are undermined. There is 'a gentle, rippling music' for the grass (Lewis, 2005: 64), 'deep, prolonged notes' for 'a line of dark firs' (65), 'a rapid series of lighter notes' for primroses (65). Things get programmatic and a Disney-like scenario takes off, reminiscent of Mickey's antics in 'The Sorcerer's Apprentice' sequence from *Fantasia*, or *Fantasia*'s version of Beethoven's sixth symphony (Disney, 1940). The simple one-to-one correspondence between creative song and created thing becomes increasingly banal. Again, nothing is left unsaid. Aslan in the flesh, song and all, is like Tolkien's far-off island. Once it is fully revealed the magic is destroyed (Tolkien, 1995: 333).

Lewis longed to combine his orthodoxy with his desire. He longed for a desire that would not be quenched by finding its object. In his writings as a medievalist, he described a 'medieval model', or *Weltanschauung*, that allowed such a union. He is describing the difference between the cold and empty universe which dwarfs the modern like an 'ironic comment' and the cosmos of 'a man of the Middle Ages. He did not think that the spaces he looked up at were silent, or dark or empty' (Lewis, 1998: 52). They were 'bright and resonant [and] inhabited' with spheres, Intelligences, and angels (53). This is his harmonious cosmos, with all its inhabitants moving joyfully along their appointed paths in their desire for God, their 'thirst delighted yet not quenched' (Lewis, 1967: 119).[36]

In this phrase, Lewis describes a desire that finds its object but is still not sated. Lewis's medieval model included two attributes, order and desire, at first glance unlikely bedfellows. Serenely hierarchical, it was built on a passion for order, 'the tranquil, indefatigable, exultant energy of passionately systematic minds bringing huge masses of heterogeneous material into unity' (Lewis, 1967: 10).[37] But this harmony is not achieved by '"the army of unalterable law" [as for Meredith's Lucifer] but rather the revelry of insatiable love' (1967: 119). Desire is the other pole of Lewis's medieval model, except, he insisted, order and desire, law and love were not poles apart. The medieval man (it is always a man) is 'passionately systematic'. Lewis wanted a universe in which desire is a passionate dedication to a wild God,[38] which yet runs steady as a rock. Wildness is a privileged term for Lewis, provided it belongs solely to God. The wildness of human desire is one of its most troubling aspects to orthodoxy and morality. In a letter Goethe wrote: 'Love roves on every path, / Fidelity stays home alone' (Goethe n.p., n.d.); my translation). How to combine the two? Here that troubling wildness is transposed onto its object, God. The heavenly beings are not wild, although they are presented as ecstatic. God is enough of a magnet to keep them faithful. They do not falter in their endless circumnavigation and we can follow their example. Lewis's harmony of the spheres was another attempt to theorise a desire that found its right mark and was not tempted to stray. For both Lewis and Tolkien, in moments when orthodoxy prevails in their writing, music ceases to indicate the unsayable because everything must be spelt out and music becomes instead only a way of saying it.[39] There is, however, a second tradition of silent music, shadowing the first, into which the contradictory strain in fantasy fiction falls more aptly. This second discourse is found in the apophatic tradition, a discourse devoted to unsaying or 'saying away' which does not, like metaphor, abandon the first for the second oppositional term but keeps the two endlessly in play.

### Discourses of silent music II: The *coincidentia oppositorum*

The performance of the juxtaposition of oppositions, named by Nicholas of Cusa the *coincidentia oppositorum*, is found in his 1440 work, *De docta ignorantia* (1981). This juxtaposition begins with the aporia or impasse of transcendence, according to Michael Sells, whose book, *Mystical Languages of Unsaying*, I am paraphrasing here. The transcendent is beyond names, but in order to make that claim I must name it, generating the aporia that 'the subject of the statement must be named in order to affirm that it is beyond names' (Sells, 1994: 2). Wittgenstein proposed in his *Tractatus* (2010: 90): 'Whereof one cannot speak, thereof one must be silent'. But apophasis is a discourse which performs a kind of silence. Apophatic discourse consists of first saying, then unsaying, allowing neither proposition to remain in possession of the field: 'It is in the tension between the two propositions that the discourse becomes meaningful' (Sells, 1994: 3).[40] Mystics use this language in a disontological attempt, 'to avoid reifying the transcendent as an "entity" or "being" or "thing"' (Sells, 1994: 6). The attempt is to make language transreferential (1994: 8), keeping open the place of the referent. This is the place of the missing object, the *space between* opposing propositions. It is an open referent, the 'no-thing' of John the Scot Eriugena (Sells, 1994: 11), viewed from a different perspective.

The subject is missing too. Sells proposes, speaking of the writings of the thirteenth-century German mystic, Meister Eckhart, that in the mystical union of the soul with God there is neither the soul nor God. In that moment there is no *being*, only union (shades of Eliot's 'you are the music while the music lasts'). This mystical discourse offers one key to the contradictory behaviour of language in Tolkien/Lewis fantasy fiction.[41] This is how one thing can be another. But what becomes of longing without a subject or an object? If union banishes longing at the cost of the obliteration of both subject and object, no wonder we treat it with the respect of distance. This is the perilous *jouissance* of the medieval in the face of which readers retreat to medievalist nostalgia. Tolkien may speak of the perilous realm, fictional heroes may suffer its throes, but readers experience a less disquieting flirtation with this *space between* and its perils.

The fantasies of medievalist nostalgia take good care to guard against the chaos of such a *jouissance*; they invoke a law. In Lacan's view,

> the neurotic ... highlights this exemplary fact that he can only desire in accordance with the law. He cannot for his part sustain, give its status to his desire except as unsatisfied for himself or as impossible. (Lacan, 1962–63: 136)

The nostalgic demands a home-world, a *real* one, but the Lacanian Real is 'absolutely without fissure' – far from homely (Lacan, 1991: 97)! The Real cannot make a world (a whole that is), which is a symbolic and imaginary entity, whether it is our world or a fantasy world. To make a whole one must make a hole – a cut. The home-world of nostalgic fantasy is already symbolised, already mapped, demarcated, domesticated. Lacan talks, in *Ethics* about the domestication of space. Sacred space, in that it is supposed to encompass the real, is heavily domesticated (Lacan, 1997: 118). The gods of Plato's *Phaedo* stay inside the temple, on a leash so to speak, to preserve us from their *unheimlich* aspects. The medieval of nostalgic medievalism may gesture towards a state of non-separation – it 'points out the way', as Fradenburg (1997) has it – but it takes care to stay behind the barrier. Nostalgics abide by the law. They take the circular path of unsatisfiable desire. Ecstasy is not reached by this path, except for the ecstasy of unsatisfied longing.[42]

Music has been extolled as a path to ecstatic union and there is truth in the claim. Musicians and listeners know of the loss of self which comes with musical ecstasy, in the sense that they may become aware that something has taken place in their absence. The music is not heard since there is no one there to hear it. The Romantic idea of absolute music was distinguished by its proponents from lesser music on the basis of ecstatic union as well as on the basis of its detachment from any 'extramusical' components such as the word. 'Absolute' carries both connotations. In relation to the second, E. T. A. Hoffmann proclaims:

> When speaking of music as an independent art, one should always mean instrumental music alone, which, disdaining any aid or admixture of another art, expresses the characteristic nature of art which is only recognizable within music itself. (Cited in Dahlhaus, 1989: 8)

Novalis asserted that '[c]onsonants transform *tone into reverberation* (Schallen)' (cited in Hoeckner, c.2002: 53; emphasis in original). Music is reduced to noise (*Laut*) by a text.[43] On the basis of its disdain for language, the apologists of absolute music claimed for it the power to express the divine beyond words. But music is already itself a kind of language prior to any contamination from the word. Musical signifiers signify as words do. Whether we are speaking of chords, cadences, keys, modes, rhythms, tempi, or even single notes, music shares with language the restriction that each signifier can signify only in relation to other signifiers. The difference between the two – words and music – is on the side of the signified. As Theodor Adorno maintained, musical sounds 'say something, often something human' (2007: 262). But if we ask *what* they say the answer is harder to find. It is precisely the *what* that is missing. Adorno suggests that music says something like: '"This is how it is", the decisive ... confirmation of something that has not been explicitly stated' (Adorno, 2007: 265).[44] The question of meaning in music is still contested but, as Edward Pearsall and Byron Almén have noted, although

> explorations into musical meaning lay claim to embodying the central core of our discipline, justifying its very existence by revealing the source of music's power, by translating its implicit message ... that source is as opaque as it is compelling. (E. Pearsall and Almén, 2006: 1)

Absolute music, according to its champions, approaches the transcendent by a process of attrition, casting aside all contaminating influences: text, programme, purpose. The body is also cast aside in the process; consonants, in making meaning from sound, are unwelcome reminders of the body whose intimate embraces of throat, lips, tongue and teeth impede the soul's outpouring in song. But though the aim *could perhaps* be considered similar, the means are different from those I have been exploring, both in fantasy fiction and in the discourse of unsaying. The discourse of absolute music is a discourse of a beyond rather than an exploitation of a between. It does not recognise the intimacy of the *coincidentia oppositorum*, where the transcendent cannot subsist except in the presence of its intimate other: immanence. It is single-minded, single-meaninged, at least in its aim. Like the Sublime of Edmund Burke and Kant and the Holy of Rudolf Otto, the discourse of absolute music opts for transcendence (a break) at the expense of immanence.

Thus, like the discourse of the *musica mundana*, the discourse of absolute music maintains itself as a discourse of reason. The discourses of unsaying turn words to their own undoing, rather than discarding them in the interests of a purity which has no value here. Nothing is discarded here, nothing left behind; nothing is trash. These discourses repeatedly attempt to name, knowing they will fail. Adorno says it well:

> What [music] has to say is simultaneously revealed and concealed. Its Idea is the divine Name which has been given shape. ... It is the human attempt, doomed as ever, to name the Name, not to communicate meanings. (Adorno, 2007: 263)

Music shapes the *space between*, which Adorno called the divine Name. Lacan, in his *Ethics* seminar, called it the emptiness (or empty fullness) of *das Ding*, the term he used at that time for the extimate, the strangeness at the heart.[45] 'All art', he said, 'is characterised by a certain mode of organization around this emptiness' (Lacan, 1997: 130). The three terms of my enquiry: music, medievalism and nostalgia, all circle the *space between* inhabited by this emptiness. Fantasy fiction plays with music and the medieval, linked by the service they provide as joint indicators of the *jouissance* of 'no-thing'. It plays too with nostalgic desire, creating a screen which displays readers' fantasies, while protecting them from the fatal consequences of falling into the emptiness behind the fantasy.

Nonetheless there is ecstasy. It cannot be attained, but it happens. Ecstasy may be retrospectively interpreted by way of a fantasy but it is something entirely different. When people say they are transported by medieval music they may be telling the truth. But if one asked what they meant or where they were transported to, they would have to start fantasising in order to say anything about it. Chapter 3 aims to say something of these listeners' fantasies.

## Notes

1 Cooper, like Diana Wynne Jones, attended lectures given by Lewis and Tolkien at Oxford (Marcus, 2006: 42).
2 Tom Shippey offers two instances of temporal distortion associated with music which Tolkien might have drawn on for Lothlórien. One is the ballad of 'Thomas the Rhymer', who spends three nights in music and dancing in Elfland and returns to find that everyone he knew is dead (Child, 1965: 1:325). The other is the Danish ballad 'Elf-hill' where, 'when the elf-maiden sings: "The swift stream then stood still, that before had been running"' (Shippey, 2011: 89–90).
3 An instance of the infinite instant is found in Diana Wynne Jones's *A Sudden Wild Magic*, where a wild magic possesses Zillah, and 'the instant, and the knowledge, extended infinitely' (1994: 401). Like Bataille's, Zillah's knowledge is unknown: 'The restraints of knowledge harmed this wild power. In order to use it, Zillah could not know what it was' (401).
4 See Atterbery, *Strategies of Fantasy*, on temporal manipulation in fantasy fiction (c.1992: 55–6). See also Verlyn Flieger's (1997) *A Question of Time*, on Tolkien's concern with time.
5 As Carolyn Dinshaw points out, such 'Rip van Winkle' narratives have their roots in the medieval past. Chapter 1 of her book *How Soon is Now?* is devoted to some of these 'asynchrony' stories, like the story of the monk who ventured into the woods, heard the singing of a bird and returned to his monastery to find that three hundred years had elapsed since he left (Dinshaw, 2012: 49–54).
6 William Morris (1898) gave the title *The Sundering Flood* to his novel of parted lovers.
7 See the concept of anamnesis in Plato's *Meno* and *Phaedo*, where to learn is to remember what one knew as a disembodied soul, 'for searching and learning are, as a whole, recollection' (Plato, 2002: 71, 113).

8   See Sarah Randles's 'transformation of [the Middle Ages] from a historical category to a nostalgic fantasy' (2008: 168).
9   Anne McCaffrey wrote of another chilling *between* in *Dragonflight* (first published 1969): 'Accustomed as he was to the sting of the profound cold, to the awesome utter lack of light and sound, F'lar still found the sensations unnerving' (1978: 62).
10  See Lacan's 'ultimate real' in which 'the subject is lost for a moment, blown up' (1991: 176).
11  See Lewis's 'unsatisfied desire which is itself more desirable than any other satisfaction' (1955a: 17–18).
12  Compare, in Cooper's *The Grey King*, 'delicate music that was *achingly familiar and yet strange*, gone as soon as it was heard' (2000b: 62; my emphasis), and 'a voice ... *both sweet and terrible*' (106; my emphasis). Guy Gavriel Kay refers, in *The Darkest Road*, to 'a voice so clear [that it blurred] forever, the borders between sound and light, between music and the spoken word' (Kay, 2001: 41). In *Fire and Hemlock* (2000b), Diana Wynne Jones devotes an entire book to a logic of oxymoron or paradox in which music is central (see particularly 2000b: 376).
13  See also the law of the excluded middle, as in Aristotle's *Metaphysics*, 4.4 (1952: 525–6).
14  Compare Roland Barthes on 'adjectival criticism (or 'predicative interpretation') in music (1977: 179): 'There is an imaginary in music whose function is to reassure, to constitute the subject hearing it (would it be that music is dangerous – the old Platonic idea? that music is an access to *jouissance*, to loss, as numerous ethnographic and popular examples would tend to show?) and this imaginary immediately comes to language via the adjective' (1977: 179–80).
15  The bells are not insignificant, however. Berthold Hoeckner cites Romantic Jean Paul on the bell's special qualities: 'The bell ... is "calling the romantic spirits" because its sound reverberates the longest' (Hoeckner, c.2002: 56). The Romantics considered music as the superior art because it resolved 'future and past into the present [resulting in] the unlimited expansion of time within a single instant of the temporal continuum' (55). This is the collapse of chronological temporality to which fantasy fiction alludes.
16  Barbara Cassin calls *Sehnsucht* 'an open nostalgia that never "returns" to itself ... a nonidentifiable, nonmathematizable infinite that flows but never stops' (Cassin, 2016: 26). Such an open-ended definition might seem too vague for orthodox Christianity.
17  Lewis wrote to Arthur Greeves on 7 March 1916 (he was then eighteen) that he had 'had a great literary experience this week'. The book he had discovered was MacDonald's *Phantastes* (Lewis, 1988: 47).

18  See the section on Hell in Lewis's *The Problem of Pain* (2009: 76–83).
19  See Book 5 of *The Golden Ass* (Apuleius, 1998).
20  Lewis's Space trilogy, of which *That Hideous Strength* is the third book, was written for adults, and he gives freer rein to his more hideous imaginings here than he permitted himself in the Narnia Chronicles.
21  As Farah Mendlesohn notes, 'fantasy desperately wants to make [the universe] moral' (2005: xv).
22  See Charles Butler's discussion of this moral landscape (C. Butler, 2006: 220–2).
23  Compare Shakespeare in *The Tempest*, act 1, scene 2: 'Where should this music be? i' the air or the earth?' (1964: 10–11).
24  See Dugan and Farina on the privileging of the visual over the 'intimate senses', touch, taste and smell (2012: 373–4).
25  Intersense metaphor was a common literary trope among the Romantic poets (O'Malley, 1957: 398).
26  See Gino Casagrande's (2004) 'Synaesthesia and Dante' for a discussion of synaesthesia in medieval writings.
27  In *Many Waters*, 'Yalith raised her head and sang, a wordless melody, achingly lovely. Above her the stars and the moon sang with her [...] [T]he harmony of the spheres and the dance of the galaxies interwove in radiance' (L'Engle, 2005a: 224–5). See also in *A Swiftly Tilting Planet* (L'Engle, 2005b: 67).
28  Compare Terry Pratchett's Granny Aching, in *A Hat Full of Sky* 'Taint what a horse *looks* like ... it's what a horse *be*.' (2004: 342).
29  See Eliot's 'Burnt Norton': 'Words move, music moves / Only in time; but that which is only living / Can only die. Words, after speech, reach / Into the silence. Only by the form, the pattern / Can words or music reach / The stillness' (1968: 19).
30  The performance can become a little perfunctory at times, even in the better authors, and if the better fantasy fiction gestures towards the space between, the worse can only be said to gesture towards a previous gesture, as Christopher Paolini, like many others, gestures towards Tolkien with a nod towards the Song of Solomon: '[Queen Islanzadí, an elf] was beautiful and terrible, like a frightful goddess of war' (Paolini, 2008: 83).
31  This was Lewis's favourite theory (1998: 52).
32  Nonetheless, as Bruce Holsinger notes: 'For a civilisation ever alert to the perils of carnality, the human body represents nevertheless the very ground of musical experience' (2001: 1). See this valuable book for an extended discussion of the body in medieval musical life.

33 Stratford Caldecott suggests that Tolkien's Ainulindalë may have been inspired by Job 38:7: 'Where were you ... when the morning stars sang together, and all the sons of God made a joyful melody' (cited in Caldecott, 2003: 74).
34 See Flieger (2002), especially chapter 3; Eden (2003); chapter 4 of Caldecott (2003); and Jensen (2010) for more extended discussions of the Ainulindalë.
35 See Flieger: 'For Tolkien, as for medieval man, light and music are conjoined elements manifest in the music of the spheres, the singing of the stars' (2002: 59). Music, like light, evokes the numinous.
36 That imperishable desire must be humanity's oldest dream. See Augustine in his *Confessions*: '[T]here is an embrace that no satiety comes to sunder. This is what I love when I love my God' (1998: 6: 8); and Shakespeare in *Antony and Cleopatra*, act 2, scene 2: 'Other women cloy / The appetites they feed, but she makes hungry / Where most she satisfies' (Shakespeare, 1960: 60).
37 Lewis, at least in his academic hat, did not offer this Model as bearing ultimate truth: 'No Model is a catalogue of ultimate realities' (Lewis, 1967: 222). Nor does he recommend a return to the 'Medieval Model' (222).
38 Aslan is always described as wild. For instance, in *The Last Battle*: '"Do you think I keep him in my wallet, fools?" said Tirian. "Who am I that I could make Aslan appear at my bidding? He's not a tame lion"' (Lewis, 2005: 707).
39 Bradford Lee Eden, in 'Strains of Elvish Song', writes on 'the influence of English Victorian fiction on Tolkien's writing style, particularly in relation to musical-literary symbolism' (2010b: 86). Musical symbolism, however, is, in the context of this chapter, a way of saying something rather than an indication of the unsayable. Fantasy writers after Tolkien and Lewis took the music of the spheres 'to illustrate harmony', as Martha Sammons points out (1988: 142).
40 It is 'the tension between the two propositions' that makes me prefer the term apophasis to 'negative theology', which seems to imply a focus on the purely negative. That term itself, therefore (as opposed to writings which go by that name) leaves no room for a 'between'.
41 See Darielle Richards, who observes that Tolkien, in his receptivity, falls into the medieval tradition of 'the *via negativa*, a method of perception through deep contemplation and inner sight that looks to the guiding truths of "not this' and "not that"' (Richards, 2010: 65).
42 See Gilles Deleuze and Félix Guattari in *A Thousand Plateaus*: 'There is, in fact, a joy that is immanent to desire as though desire were filled by itself and its contemplations' (Deleuze and Guattari, 1987: 172).

43 Tolkien would not have agreed. He delighted in the music of speech, remarking that, as a philologist, he 'got a large part of any aesthetic pleasure that I am capable of from the *form* of words' (Tolkien, 1995: 172; emphasis in original). See John R. Holmes's (2010) paper, '"Inside a Song"', on the music of philology in Tolkien's work.

44 See Aaron Copland's very similar statement: 'The whole problem can be stated simply by asking, "Is there a meaning to music?" My answer to that would be, "Yes." And "Can you state in so many words what the meaning is?" My answer to that would be, "No." Therein lies the difficulty' (Copland, 1993: loc. 479).

45 'Fullness and emptiness', says Lacan, were brought into a world that knew them not by the 'fabricated signifier' of the potter's vase (1997: 120).

# 3

# The lost world inside a song: From the book to the record

> Like the features on a cameo
> I wanted the beloved voices
> to remain a keepsake, forever cherished,
> repeating the musical
> dream of an hour all too brief;
> time wishes to flee, I master it.
> (Charles Cros, 'Inscription', *Le collier
> de griffes*, cited in Weiss, 2002: 71)

My aim in this chapter is to explore the links between the representations of music in high fantasy discussed in Chapter 2, and music produced, marketed and received as medieval. The chapter follows those links back and forth between the two. The same thread of nostalgia which in previous chapters I have associated with the medieval, can also be found in the discourses of producers, musicians and listeners in the sphere of medieval music. As before, my main focus is on the medieval fantasies that emerge in these discourses. Some listeners, like the readers of fantasy fiction, are seeking, in these musical reinventions of the Middle Ages, a voice for their fantasies of a lost and longed-for world, more real, more luminous than mundane reality.[1] In this quest they are ably assisted by those who make and sell the records.

Tolkien and Lewis did not invent medievalism. Nor did medieval music recording await publication of their novels.[2] But their medieval fantasies have inflected the way in which medieval music has been recorded, marketed and received since the publication of their work. The enchantments of music and the medieval, conjoined in fantasy fiction, morph into 'medieval music' in the world of performance and recording; that is, 'medieval music' sometimes becomes the name given to music that gives access to the medieval fantasy. The signifiers rearrange themselves, with 'medieval' taking up an adjectival role in relation to 'music', describing the musical experience it promises. The same tropes appear in both: the enchantment, the being taken out of oneself in some way, the inability to describe the experience, the loss of time. Overall, there is a sense of being acted upon by the music in some transforming way, analogous to the temporal distortions in fantasy fiction discussed in Chapter 2.

In music, of course, the fantasy is differently produced and differently received than in literature. We hear and are profoundly affected by what we hear. As Plato understood, music makes its way into 'the inward places of the soul' (*Republic*, 1994–2009, BK II) or, as psycho-neurologists might prefer to say, into the inward places of the brain.[3] But I am attempting to take the pulse of the medieval fantasy which can only be related through speech, not by what can be observed of the impulses of the brain. Fantasy is a discursive construction. In particular, this chapter pays attention to the musical voice – a very particular mode of communication. The singing voice offers another kind of *in between*, between language and melody and between language and the body, that happens nowhere else in music. Roland Barthes observes in his essay 'The Grain of the Voice':

> It is this displacement [of the fringe of contact between music and language] that I want to outline [with regard] to a part of vocal music (*lied* or *melodie*): the very precise space (genre) of *the encounter between a language and a voice*. I shall straightaway give a name to this signifier: the *grain of the voice when the latter is in a dual posture, a dual production – of language and music*. (Barthes, 1977: 181; emphasis in original)

Later on in the essay he puts it this way: 'The "grain" is the body in the voice' (188). Lacan speaks of this encounter in his theorising of the voice as *objet (petit) a*, but in a way which reverses the trajectory, naming the drives 'the echo in the body of the fact that there is a saying' (Lacan, 1975–76: 10). That echo is created by the structure of a language. The drive Lacan names 'invocatory' relates to the voice. Both formulations are true – if language cannot escape the body, neither can the body free itself from the echo of saying.

The structures of language structure us. I return to this question later in the chapter.

Like the book, the recording guides its listeners to a particular reception by a series of 'paratextual' or 'paramusical' means, expanding outwards from the music.[4] At the first level, listeners are placed for reception by what is on the record, its choice of material and the arrangement of the music – in two senses, its musical arrangement and its temporal arrangement on the recording – working together to create an artistic and an emotional effect. At another level, reception is guided by the lyrics and any explanatory material or statement of intent offered by the musicians; at yet another, by the visual cues provided by the overall presentation of the cover and booklet, the illustrations, photographs, fonts. Beyond the recording lie the many writings surrounding it, academic and commercial, which combine to guide reception; and beyond again, and in conversation with these writings, are the listeners' responses. I read this conversation as a sequential form of collaboration between producers and consumers in which each appears to respond to a perceived suggestion from the other. On the economic level it could be called supply and demand considered as a dynamic interaction, with each creating and recreating the other. In this dynamic sense, the medieval fantasy is shared, reinscribed and reaffirmed in each exchange, although of course it also evolves in the process.

As argued in the Introduction, I have chosen to focus on recordings rather than performances, partly because they support repeated hearings, fostering a growing familiarity with the music. A recording can, over many hearings – if it hits the mark – become beloved, like a well-known face or a familiar room. I am speaking here of CDs and their predecessors, cassettes and long-playing records. While Spotify, YouTube and MP3s share the capacity to present the album as a whole, they do not offer the same visual cues which add to the album experience in other ways. Some listeners still value the ownership of a physical object they can hold in their hand.[5]

The longer time frame is also important because it allows the telling arrangement of material. Most medieval pieces are short in comparison with a Classical or Romantic symphony, for example. How they are organised on a recording influences the way they are heard and the way they tug the heartstrings. The power to assemble the material tellingly gives greater scope to tell a story, draw together a theme, create an atmosphere. These structures overlay the music with an imaginary and discursive framework, providing guidelines for fantasy.

In some cases this power has now been lost. Tracks can now be bought or listened to one by one online, subverting any attempts on the part of musicians and directors to arrange their material so as to produce an overall effect. Their scope is now, as in the past, limited to what can be made of a single piece. Another reason for my choice of recordings over performances is that they generate online discussion, particularly among listeners. The marketing strategies of online CD sellers like Amazon.com allow listeners to share their responses to recordings with prospective customers by posting online reviews; these reviews form the basis of this part of my research. Reviewers sometimes write under a pseudonym, but where this is not the case I have invented one for them. YouTube is also a valuable source for listener reviews and, in addition, a forum for conversation and argument between viewers.

I have, on the whole, privileged customer reviews over YouTube conversations, because these reviews favour personal responses over arguments. Buying a CD represents a commitment to a recording and the musicians. There is a more intimate relation between an owner and their CD than there is to a listener who tunes in to YouTube. One instance of this is that customer reviewers refer to playing a beloved CD over and over again.[6]

The other reason for focusing on recorded music is that the non-visual recording shares an important characteristic with the book. It funnels reception by limiting the perceptual channels. Although CDs provide visual cues for the listener in the booklet, these cues have an ambiguous relationship to the music. Gregory Whitehead remarked that radio bodies are nobodies (1992: 253). The specular is blocked for the listener; recorded voices are acousmatic. What we get to know is the voice.[7] The voice itself has a body but it is one which rarely matches the visual body offered on the cover or in the booklet and cannot be completely assumed by it. It is not owned. We might find words to describe the body of the voice: warm or icy, thick or thin, transparent or solid, creamy or astringent, luminous or dark, glossy or matte; we might give it a colour, a flavour, a texture, but these characteristics cannot be completely assimilated to the visual, taste or tactile register. While it blocks the visual pathway, the recorded voice nonetheless gives too much, rather than too little, to be grasped. It exceeds sensual boundaries and overwhelms. As in the fantasy novel (for instance, where, in Lewis's *The Voyage of the Dawn Treader*, Lucy describes a 'dim, purple kind of smell'), there is a synaesthetic effect, although it is not a simple one-to-one translation; the heard voice in the listener's fantasy falls between perceptual categories and cannot be apportioned to any one sense.

Certain musical traits and vocal qualities are instantly recognisable to listeners as medieval whether or not there is evidence of any kind for their use in medieval performance practice. Some aspects of medieval music, for instance melody, can, to some extent, be recovered from the notation. For others, such as rhythm and instrumentation (two of the most hotly disputed areas in medieval musicology and performance), the evidence is much less decisive. Performers and directors closer to the flamboyant end of the recording spectrum exploit 'medieval' traits for their archaic and/or exotic otherness, for instance: drones, unusual rhythms, a lack of vocal and instrumental vibrato, unusual and/or sexually ambiguous vocal timbres and registers like the countertenor, exotic instruments – also exploited for their visual effect – played so as to emphasise their raw, 'primitive' timbres and shimmering sound bath effects. Musical elements are freely adapted from other cultures, for instance Morocco (Haines, 2001: 371) and Bulgaria (Yri, 2008a: 53) or simply derived from generic 'world music' gestures (Yri, 2008a: 55). Groups have sometimes 'layered "exotic" tracks against various forms of spiritual chant' (Yri, 2008a: 55). A selection of these strategies can be found on recordings by popular groups like the Mediæval Bæbes, Dead Can Dance and Enigma, and by scholarly groups like Thomas Binkley's Studio der Frühen Musik and Joel Cohen's Boston Camerata. Other musicologists and directors at the scholarly end are no less subject to nostalgia in another form, that of the purity of the authentic reconstruction. I return to this nostalgia in Chapter 4.

How these musical characteristics and tendencies come to be lumped together as medieval takes us back to the significations which the term 'medieval' has accumulated and their relevance for an understanding of nostalgic desire. Since this study is most concerned with *what is said*, the chief focus here is on how the interlocking discourses of musicology, fantasy fiction, promotional material, reviews and so on themselves construct music as medieval. The similarity between the language of producers and consumers of medieval music and the language of medieval fantasy fiction suggests that the discursive power of the signifier 'medieval' overrides musical considerations for both musicians and listeners. 'The music suggests to us what we want it to suggest', as Daniel Leech-Wilkinson argues (2000: 307). It is also the case that we make and interpret the music according to the significations we already ascribe to the medieval. Just as no music is inherently nostalgic, for us no music can be inherently medieval. We cannot completely reconstruct it from the documentary evidence; we have only a plethora of inventions.[8]

Certain recording artists and their backers have benefited by promoting their music along lines reminiscent of the medievalism of high fantasy: the same promise, of refinding a lost world through song, is made. In the next section these ideas are illustrated in a few of the evaluations and responses offered in promotional writing and customer reviews for the music named medieval.

### 'Angels singing in French': Recordings and responses

Recording artists may have been prompted by the enormous popularity of medievalist fantasy fiction and encouraged by the fact that many authors, Tolkien and Lewis first and foremost, had done some of their work for them by presenting music to readers as the magical key which unlocks the door to a lost fairy tale world. A similar narrative unfolds in publicity provided by the groups. Lisa Gerrard, band member of the medieval/Goth-influenced Dead Can Dance, asks: 'What on earth is music for anyway, but a way to transcend the everyday common world' (cited in Yri, 2008a: 3). Different music produces different fantasies, but a proportion of groups favour recordings which match the Tolkien/Lewis magical medieval fantasy. Katharine Blake, founder of the popular medieval music group the Mediæval Bæbes, assures prospective customers: 'My analogy is that listening to the music is like reading a fairy story. ... Your mind gets taken to a special otherworldly place – a strange place of serenity, magic, and beauty. ... This music is very uplifting and serene and tranquil' (cited in Bessman, 1998: 12).⁹ The Bæbes's Facebook biography also stresses the 'storybook' aspect of their own beginnings:

> The Mediaeval Baebes exquisite storybook opened its pages in 1996 when a group of friends broke into a North London cemetery and sang together, clad in flowing white gowns and crowns of ivy. (Mediæval Bæbes, 2021)

Phil Fox, the director of product management at Virgin Records, noted the economic value of the perceived serenity of medieval music, drawing an analogy between the Bæbes and the earlier successes of Gregorian chant: 'Knowing the success garnered a few years ago by the Benedictine Monks, we feel that there's consumer interest in this type of music' (cited in Bessman, 1998: 12). The Bæbes add an extra ingredient to the Gregorian mix, however: the womanly art of seduction. Their self-promotion stresses the erotic aspect of the listening experience. For instance, a 2005 interview with the Bæbes begins:

> 'The theme of our latest album *Mirabilis* is enchantment', purrs Katharine Blake. 'It's about strange creatures who seduce men and women into their faery world. Just like the Baebes – we're seducing the listener into our world. And I can guarantee they'll never be quite the same again.' (*Mirabilis* Release Notes, 2005: 1)

Seduction is the keynote of the band's attraction, as Melvyn Willin notes: 'Blake founded [an] all girl group who would perform medieval music in a modern way and make use of their allure and charm in the process' (Willin, 2012: loc. 2868), although, as Blake's words above suggest, it is seduction of a light-hearted, playful kind.

Some of those who listen to medieval music employ similar narrative tropes to Blake's, usually couched in terms of what happened when the recording was played.¹⁰ As in the artist and production descriptions, listeners too allude to transportation by music, claiming that they are indeed finding access to otherworlds via their favourite medieval recordings; that they, like Sam in *The Lord of the Rings* (*LOTR*), are finding a lost world inside a song. This trend can be observed in response to all sixteen musical groups included in the dataset described in the Appendix, representing 10 per cent of comments. For example, one Amazon customer reviewer says of the group Anonymous 4's album *1000: A Mass for the End of Time*:

> What followed during the listening of this CD, was a deeply meditative state as I let the music, so beautiful words cannot describe, transport me into a deeper consciousness. ('Sweetie', 2002)[11]

There is that notion of the indescribable again, as we saw it in Chapter 2, for instance in Tolkien's description of Faërie as that which 'cannot be caught in a web of words; for it is one of its qualities to be indescribable, though not imperceptible' (Tolkien, 1966: 39). This state *is* nonetheless described further on by the reviewer as a 'serene place' in another 'dimension' from the everyday ('Sweetie', 2002). Like Tolkien, twenty-five listener responses also invoked the notion of the indescribable (0.5 per cent). Words are offered by such listeners as a kind of code for what cannot be said.

As 'Sweetie's review demonstrates, the language of transportation to another world can be found at the scholarly end of the recording spectrum, although not as frequently as in the popular domain.[12] The scholarly Gothic Voices' recording of music by Hildegard of Bingen, *A Feather on the Breath of God*, found similar responses. Hildegard brings this language out in her listeners, particularly this well-loved recording. 'Isala' admits: 'This album is so beautiful it hurts' ('Isala', 2004). For 'Otherworld',

> I still remember picking this up in 1982, playing it (on a record player!) and hearing Emma Kirkby for the first time, I was immediately drawn in to another World. Hear it once, and you simply will be changed, by the work of this incredibly gifted Master, and a true Heroine of her time. Nothing more I could say will describe this; simply give this a listen. ('Otherworld', 2008)

For this listener, as for Sweetie, words are not enough. Hildegard's music is transforming as well as transporting. As Katharine Blake declared in her interview, the listener will 'never be quite the same again'. *The Mirror of Narcissus*, another Gothic Voices album, received the following customer review:

> This album is so beautiful; it takes you to a place that one might mistake for heaven. You will think that you are listening to angels singing in French when you hear it. ('Angels singing', 1999)

Angels and other divine or heavenly beings are frequent visitors in these kinds of responses.[13] They are singing again in Tokaji's response to the Baebes's *Mirabilis*, also the indescribable, the pain inflicted by the beautiful and the transcendence of the mundane:

> The Mediæval Bæbes are the only group I get truly excited talking about, and this album is the 1st one from them to truly transcend the typical and mundane associations with the term Mediæval, which they started with the album Undrentide … There are two songs on this album which are indescribable in their ability to be beautiful to the point of heart-wrenching; Temptasyon and Lhiannan Shee. Rarely have I been literally moved to tears by music, especially in this day and age. I can only imagine the angels of heaven being more moving. (Tokaji, n.d)

This is clearly not the mundane Middle Ages of history.

While these kinds of responses can be found across all the musical groups, the majority of listener responses do not speak the language of instant transportation to heaven or some unspecified otherworld via medieval music. Reviews of scholarly recordings, in particular, are more likely to be based on technical knowledge than on a personal response. Here is a typical example from a customer reviewer of the Hilliard Ensemble's *Motets: Guillaume de Machaut*:

> Frankly, this disc sounds very little like Machaut and very much like the Hilliard Ensemble … To be sure, it's lovely singing, and it is certainly well recorded (though ECM's penchant for 9" reverb does seem quite silly), but the wash of sound favored by the Hilliard Ensemble is very much out of place here, I think (much better in the legitimately choral works of the late Renaissance). The tempi are too slow, the articulation is too smooth, and performance practice too Anglicized. ('amc654', 2004)

Sometimes listeners argue over the lyrics, again more frequently on YouTube than on customer reviews. The tone of many such reviews is contentious, the emphasis on point scoring. These listeners and viewers are less prone to baring their souls or their fantasies. The group of listeners I am concerned with in this chapter is smaller. It consists of those who try to give an account of their own listening experience rather than, or as well as, an appraisal of the performance. The register is personal rather than critical, although standardised and contained within a few repeated expressions. The Mediæval

Bæbes bring this personal note out in some of their listeners. Their promotional material is an open invitation to it. Judging by the tone of these reviews, most of their listeners do not have the musical know-how of listeners like 'amc654'. It seems probable that such knowledge might have the effect of forbidding expression of a personal response for many, at least in public.

In this chapter I have chosen to focus mainly on the Bæbes, partly because their music fosters nostalgic, 'otherworldly' responses and partly because they are a women's group and offer me the chance to explore further the feminine associations of the medieval fantasy. Another reason is that, for the Bæbes, any link with medieval sources is tenuous. They write most of their own music and, unlike their scholarly counterparts, evidently feel no obligation to conform, either to the notated music available or to scholarly notions of musical authenticity. Thus, their own idea of medieval music is given free rein. Every performance of medieval music necessarily involves a degree of invention. Where the Bæbes differ from more scholarly approaches is in their complete dismissal of the musical evidence. Evidently it does not deliver the medieval experience they wish to convey, one determined by the needs of the present and often, judging by the comments, an escape from ordinary life. Without these restrictions the Bæbes can produce – and allow to their listeners – an unfettered musical fantasy of the medieval.

For performers at the popular end of the spectrum, attempts at authentic reconstruction are sometimes perceived as counter-productive. 'We don't pretend to be authentic', says Bæbes director Katharine Blake dismissively (*Mirabilis* Release Notes, 2005). Authenticity is also considered an encumbrance in some of the reviews, where the term 'medieval purists' has a pejorative ring. 'SylverOne' says of the Bæbes' *Mirabilis*:

> I know this is not for the medieval purists, it does not have the icy precision of the anonymous 4 and the Hilliard ensemble. I have cd's of both ensembles, but the baebes find their way to my cd player more often, they bring such life to this music. ('SylverOne', 2006)

Listeners like this are in search of a different kind of authenticity.[14] It is the live spirit that transports, 'SylverOne' (2006) suggests, rather than the dead letter of the purists. Perhaps in this case authenticity is whatever can evoke something of the listener's fantasy.

One reviewer of the Bæbes' 1999 *Worldes Blysse* album, 'Lulublu', writes: 'And while these songs may not be completely faithful to the medieval rendering of music, the spirit is true, and for me that is all that matters' ('Lulublu', 2001).

In spirit, the Bæbes are more medieval than those icy purists. This is not 'mundane' but 'true' medieval music, as another *Worldes Blysse* listener insists: it is 'haunting melodies, true medieval sounding music (with memorable hooks not mundane medieval music you forget 2 minutes after listening to it' ('Michael', 2003). As Andrew Elliot observes in relation to medieval film, in the medieval imaginary accuracy and authenticity are not synonymous (Elliot 2011: loc. 3115). In fact, for these listeners, the reverse is the case – accuracy or attempted accuracy (the mundane) is *in*authentic. In one sense the signifier 'medieval' and its fantasies override the musical text, but not in any sense that invalidates the listener's response. It is just that in their attempts to relate that response words must be found, and these are the words at hand, prompted by the promoters, other listeners and any prior acquaintance the listener may have with the medieval.[15] The true spirit of the medieval is whatever it is possible to say, in the currency on offer, of something haunting, mysterious, otherworldly, the reverse of the mundane. In this process of familiarisation, the medieval fantasy might be expected to wear thin, to sound stale and impoverished, but in fact its very familiarity may be a mark of its attraction. I discuss the joys of repetition experienced by listeners and readers further on in the chapter.

The nature of the spirit of the medieval for 'Lulublu' is intimated in their review of *Worldes Blysse*:

> [T]his women's chorus has a spirit that weaves itself into your consciousness. ... [O]ne experiences ... the heavy despair of the days of darkness ... and yearning for release into a true heaven. ('Lulublu', 2001)

This response marks a difference from those above, however. This is not the serene place in another dimension than the everyday described by 'Sweetie'. It is instead the place where one longs for it. *Worldes Blysse*, the Bæbes's second and most popular album, released in 1999, sets medieval lyrics of almost unmitigated gloom, mostly dealing with the pain, misery and transience of human life, often in terms evoking disgust.[16] Human misery and Christ's sacrifice for our sake are expressed on the booklet cover by a kind of spiral of thorns in which the Bæbes sit, looking sober.[17] The first track, 'Kinderly',[18] is a good example:[19]

> Kinderly is now my coming
> Into this werld with teres and cry
> Litel and povere is min having
> Britel and sone I falle from hi
> Scharp and strong is my deying
> I ne woth whider schal I
> Foul and stinkande is my roting
> On me, Jhesu, you have mercy!

(My arrival here is natural into this world with tears and crying; what I have is not much, and poor at that. Frail and all too quickly I have fallen from on high. My death is sharp and severe, I do not know where I am going, foul and stinking, I rot, O Jesus, have mercy on me!). (Mediæval Bæbes, 1999b)

The music, written by Katharine Blake, is in B Aeolian or natural minor mode, sounding sombre to modern ears with a minor third and minor seventh. It has a driving rhythm enforced by ominous drumbeats and rhythmic clapping. The voices are young, not classically trained, fresh and innocent-sounding. Like singers of both popular and folk music they subdue vibrato. In line with many of Blake's compositions, the rhythms are oddly irregular, perhaps to provide a taste of exotic unfamiliarity, as the unfamiliar melodic mode does also. As the song progresses, other voices enter in canon, both with the melody and a fifth below.[20] Driven by the percussion, the voices chase each other along with a satisfying sense of urgency. As a whole, the song works effectively to suggest the harshness and brevity of life and the agony of death described by the lyric, but without any strong sense of engagement with it. 'Kinderly' does not bear any relation to any notated medieval music but, as with all their recordings, that is not the point. As a fantasy of the medieval it works well enough. In Andrew Elliot's words, it has 'the right "feel" to it' for these listeners (Elliot, 2011: loc. 3112).

Listeners to *Worldes Blysse* do not seem appalled or disgusted at lyrics designed to put the fear of God into their medieval readers or auditors (if, in fact, they are able to understand them; the texts and translations in the booklet are virtually unreadable, as the writing is very small and the font difficult to decipher). Talk of agonising death and decay, worms and hellfire does not trouble their enjoyment – rather it appears to add extra spice to it. For instance, Amazon reviewer 'Eerie' finds there is 'a wonderfully eerie, dark and yet radiant quality to these tunes!' ('Eerie', 1999). (Note the oxymoronic flavour, with its suggestion of something unsayable.) In another response: 'The vocals are enchanting, theatrical, whimsical, heavenly and wantonly pagan simultaneously' ('Enchanted', 2006).[21] Like the Bæbes on the CD booklet cover, untroubled by their thorny bower, these listeners seem inoculated from the horror of the human condition evoked in the lyrics. Judging by these responses it's all just part of the fun – a smorgasbord of emotion, titillating but only mildly disturbing. As in the high fantasy we have been exploring, these oxymoronic gestures – 'dark yet radiant', 'heavenly and wantonly pagan simultaneously' – indicate a troubling *space between* but keep their distance from it. And yet, as some listeners insist, the Bæbes offer the 'true' medieval in spirit. Something rings true for them. These responses are not made inauthentic by distance. It is like crying at the cinema or weeping over the death of celebrities; the safety of distance is what allows emotion to be expressed – displaced yet still genuine.

The second track on *Worldes Blysse* transmutes the transience and pain of life into the register of hopeless desire. The Bæbes's title for the track is 'All Turns to Yesterday'.[22] The lyrics are illustrated in the booklet by two hands holding the thorny spiral on what looks like a marble tomb, intimating perhaps that it is the thorns of hopeless desire that pierce deepest. The lyrics describe a game in which children try to catch shadows on a candlelit wall. The solo voice which begins the song has a particularly young and guileless quality which sits oddly with the lyric voice of an adult speaking about the games of children. Part of its attraction is that sense one also has with child singers that they sing more than they know. These are the last six lines:

> And whom they catchen it best wolde wene
> Sannest it shet out of her sight
> The shadewe catchen they ne might
> For no lines that they couthe lay
> This shadewe I may likne aright
> To this world and yesterday.

(And when they most expect to catch it, it shoots most quickly out of sight. This shadow never shall be caught in any trap they lay, this shadow in the likeness of this world and yesterday). (Mediæval Bæbes, 1999a)

Again, the attractive melody, by Blake, has an archaic sound: C hexatonic, mixolydian but without the D, that is, CEFGAB♭. The flattened seventh, the missing second and, again, the randomly changing rhythms, all contribute to a strangeness that could be heard as medieval but with enough of the familiar to render the strangeness acceptable. The song begins with a rising fifth (C–G), a typical move in the troubadour repertoire, similar to the opening phrase of the troubadour *canso* 'Reis glorios', which the Bæbes sing as 'Alba' to the original melody on track 7 of the same album. There is a simple harmony emphasising fourths and fifths, another sign of the Bæbes's brand of medieval. The canon is employed again, below and above the melody, this time producing a shadowing effect that mimics the shadows of the lyrics.

'All Turns to Yesterday' captures another side of the medieval fantasy, not bliss but hopeless yearning. Some listeners claim to be transported to heaven, others instead inhabit 'the heavy despair of the days of darkness', yearning for the day of release 'into a true heaven' procured by Christ's sacrifice. This is a similar dichotomy to that encountered in fantasy fiction, between those, like Arthur (and Frodo), who set sail for the blessed isle and those, like Bedivere (and Sam), whose fate it is to be left weeping on the shore. But both the ecstasy and the longing reported in listener reviews are fantasies.[23] The difference is in where one places oneself in the fantasy. Ecstasy itself is not so easily spoken, or at least, once it is spoken it is no longer ecstasy, as argued in Chapter 2. In ecstasy no one is there to speak. Words give voice to something mysterious but, in the process, banish it.

Moreover, the pain of longing cannot be entirely distinguished from its enjoyments, as some of the listener comments make clear. That ambiguous ache of longing litters the pages of medieval lyric, as C. S. Lewis knew when he spoke of an 'unsatisfied desire which is itself more desirable than any other satisfaction' (Lewis, 1955a: 17–18). Listeners are aware of this; it is what draws them to the medieval as it drew Lewis and as he in turn drew many more. It can be found, for instance, in the Chastelain de Couci's *chanson* 'L'an que rose ne fueille': 'It is absolutely right that I grieve, since I desire my suffering, and I love more than ever what I cannot enjoy and know I shall never reach' and 'Lady, I have no torment that is not nonetheless a joy' (Chastelain de Couci, 1964: 72). The oxymoron puts it in a nutshell. There is torment in the joy and joy in the torment.

This spirit of yearning which medieval music evokes for listeners sustains desire pleasurably rather than satisfying it. I referred in Chapter 2 of nostalgia's circularity, the desire for desire. In Lacan's terms, it 'attains its satisfaction without attaining its aim' (Lacan, 1981: 179). It is not satisfied as a need like hunger can be satisfied, however, since it is 'a constant force' (165). 'It has no day or night, no spring or autumn, no rise and fall' (165), 'its aim is simply this return into circuit' (179).[24] Listeners demonstrate one aspect of desire's return into circuit, often describing the joys of returning to their favourite medieval music CDs.

### Repetition and renunciation

It appears that familiarity is one of the pleasures of the medieval fantasy, for instance in this review by 'Haunted'. The album is *It'll End in Tears* by This Mortal Coil, a band on the fringes of Goth rock which is mentioned by a Bæbes reviewer as compatible listening:

> A Beautiful Album, So Beautiful It Makes Me Cry, This album is more beautiful than anything I've ever heard. I never actually cry when I listen to this, but I cry on the inside. ... My favorite track on the album is Dreams Made Flesh. It's a haunting otherworldly track that I can't help but listen to it a few times in a row. Buy this album. ('Haunted', 2004)

What do we make of this? The reviewer 'cries on the inside' yet subjects themself to this ordeal 'a few times in a row'. On the one hand there is a satisfaction in the distress, since they keep returning to it. On the other, one could maintain that there is a *failure* of satisfaction, since they return – something is missing, something remains out of reach and will not be captured. The paradox is that if it were captured it would cease to be desirable.

The joyful torment of listeners who keep returning to those CDs which cause tears to flow is familiar to readers of fantasy fiction. It is the same response transposed from the book to the record – the response that oxymoron signals, when words are not enough and demonstrate their failure by refusing their usual function of signification. For instance, at the end of Alan Garner's *Moon of Gomrath* (2006c: 212–13), Susan loses her heart's desire, 'Celemon', a huntress who is a 'shining one':[25] 'It was as though she was waking from a dream of a long yearning fulfilled to the cold morning of a world too empty to bear.'[26] Yet there is 'joy and anguish in her heart'. Colin, her brother, hears the sound of a mysterious horn 'so beautiful that he never found rest again'. Most famously, in *LOTR*, Tolkien brings in oxymoron on the field of Cormallen, and, as so often when words fail, music is invoked:

> And [the minstrel] sang to them … until their hearts, wounded with sweet words, overflowed, and the joy was like swords, and they passed in thought to regions where pain and delight flow together and tears are the very wine of blessedness. (Tolkien, 1993: 933)[27]

In one respect listeners do not follow the example of fictional heroes; heroes may not return but listeners do. In the listener reviews the emphasis is often on repetition, as the 'Haunted' review indicates.[28] The reviewer, 'Sublime', instructs other listeners to try Gothic Voices' *Feather on the Breath of God*:

> Put the CD on, kick off your shoes, put your feet up and lie back in a comfortable chair, close your eyes and unwind to the soothing sounds of Gothic Voices performing a masterful and sensitive rendition of Hildegard's ethereal and melodious music … and suddenly you'll find that life doesn't seem so bad after all. ('Sublime', 2017)[29]

For 'Need to relax': 'It's another one to add to the collection and it's great, if you are just relaxing with a glass of wine this is the music you need' ('Need to relax', 2013).

Some readers also do not emulate the behaviour of their heroes. A glance at *LOTR* reader reviews on Amazon.com turns up a similar tendency to repetition; they do not renounce their favourite books. 'alpha_grrl' calls *LOTR* 'my literary security blanket'; this reader continues:

The Hobbit and The Lord of the Rings trilogy have been my 'go to' books for longer than I can remember. ... When I haven't got anything else to read, or if I'm feeling down, I pick up one of these volumes and everything is forgotten. ('alpha_grrl', 2007)

Another reviewer, 'First Book', says:

> Everyone has a 'first book' that captivated their heart and took them where they had never gone before. Just like a first kiss or a first love, it is something that you always remember. For me, it was the Lord of the Rings. I think I've read the series from start to finish over a dozen times and each time I find something new I hadn't seen before, and the delight starts all over again. ('First Book', n.d.)

These reviewers love to dream of perilous quests over and over again, finding their comfort in the hero's discomfort. They do not mention the law of diminishing returns as a danger in repetition – the danger that one will reach the end of the object's shelf-life as desirable. In this register of wonder and delight which privileges freshness, perhaps that may not be said, although it may be suggested in the review: 'each time I find something new I hadn't seen before, and the delight starts all over again' ('First Book', n.d.). The reviewer may not wish to admit to delighting precisely in the repetition of the same. This always finding 'something new' sounds like a fantasy of loyal desire, reminiscent of the impossible 'thirst delighted yet not quenched' which Lewis finds in the medieval cosmos (Lewis, 1967: 119).

Repetition is a satisfaction denied to the heroes of fantasy fiction. To some extent it is denied by the dictates of narrative. Here there is no question of returning. For a story to take place it must be driven on by the metonymy of desire. The object must remain out of reach either in the future or in the past; if found it must be lost again. Courtly love, born in that suspension between torment and joy that medieval lyric supports, must adapt to the needs of narrative. But for the narrative to remain courtly the object must neither be replaced nor allowed to fall from its sublime state. For Tolkien and Lewis, courtly love wears Christian dress, and a crypto-Christian sense of duty provides the device whereby the object of desire is relinquished and the story can move on. One follows the quest whatever the cost. For Tolkien's heroes to remain in Lórien would be selfishly to abandon the quest, a breaking of vows and a failure in submission to duty. For them, such delights as Lórien are granted to the quester by chance – really by the will of an unseen deity who watches over all. The hero does not take them for himself. In this literature longing is governed by the principle of displacement, not repetition, but it still functions. The object of desire can be juggled back and forth, placed in the past or in the future to suit the narrative.

In this manner, the hero can retain the object in its sublime state as well by renouncing it as by never attaining it. Renunciation, in this context, carries unmistakably the bitter-sweet taste of nostalgia. Legolas attempts, unsuccessfully, to comfort Gimli on their departure from Lórien with this thought:

> [Y]our loss you suffer of your own free will ... and the least reward that you shall have is that the memory of Lothlórien shall remain ever clear and unstained in your heart, and shall neither fade nor grow stale. (Tolkien, 1993: 369)

To which Gimli replies that 'all such comfort is cold. Memory is not what the heart desires' (Tolkien, 1993: 369). For Legolas, to renounce Lórien is to retain it eternally; for the more down-to-earth Gimli, apparently not. The elf's desire is more courtly and more spiritual than the dwarf's.

Listener reviewers, conversely, make no reference to a higher will; they acknowledge nothing that might prevent their returning time after time. Why should they? As unrepentant, unheroic consumers they busily pursue their own pleasures, preparing the scene with practical measures. 'Bibliovore', another expert adviser, instructs listeners on how to get in the mood for *Worldes Blysse*. Listeners should

> [g]et some headphones. Light a couple candles. Pour yourself a nice glass of wine. Then fall into a dozen magnificent voices singing tales of beauty, sorrow, fear, and love. ('Bibliovore', 2002)

And yet the pleasure that listeners arrange is their own ravishment and deprivation. 'Bibliovore' must 'fall' rather than actively jump into listening enjoyment. Even listeners, it seems, need to position themselves as passive recipients of a gift. The Other is in charge because they have manoeuvred it into that position; the fantasy would not work otherwise. Reviewer 'Rainbow Sphinx' alludes to this paradox in the following, tongue-in-cheek, review:

I experienced the most beautiful vision a fortnight ago. I perceived eight lovely maidens dancing and singing in an enchanted grove. Prancing and gliding in the light of a full moon, they moved back and forth between the standing stones scattered here and there around a grassy clearing. At first I surmised they must be wanton maidens from a nearby village, but as I moved closer, working my way through the encroaching brush along a seldom traveled path I discerned them to be more than just pagan women at play. Incredibly beautiful they were with an inner glow about them that made me think them to be Sidhe folk awaiting the arrival of the Fairy Queen. Growing ever more excited, I was just steps away from entering into their magical ring when suddenly the music stopped and the maidens and landscape disappeared into the shadows. Opening my eyes, I found myself alone reclining on the den couch. The room was still, the time just past the witching hour. I walked over to the stereo cabinet and removed 'Mirabilis' by the Mediaeval Baebes from the CD player and placed it back inside its jewel case. Proceeding down the hallway to the bedroom I thought I heard a fairy voice off in the distance but couldn't be certain. Oh well, maybe tomorrow night. ('Rainbow Sphinx', 2006)

'Rainbow Sphinx' knows what they are doing with their carefully crafted fantasy, knows the old stories of enchantment and thwarted desire well and is playing along.[30] (Note the archaism in their use of anastrophe, '[i]ncredibly beautiful they were'.)[31] The fantasy may still work despite the knowing tone, but any enjoyment it conferred would hold no surprises. Like the contributors to the Urban Dictionary (see Chapter 2) 'Rainbow Sphinx' can enjoy the pleasant ache of unsatisfied desire while simultaneously sending it up.

Listeners, like the readers of medieval fantasies, have correctly identified the medieval as the place to go for what haunts them, the desire for desire. Like the lover of the Chastelain de Couci's song (Chastelain de Couci, 1964: 72), they do not want their demands met, because that satisfaction would inevitably return them to the world of the despised mundane; the precious object would fall from grace, become tarnished by familiarity, 'fading and growing stale', to paraphrase Legolas. The otherworld must remain other in order to cater to their desire for the lost object. Repetition maintains the tormenting joy of longing, whether the always missing *objet a* is placed in the unattainable future or the lost past. If in the future, it evokes a yearning for the inaccessible; if in the past, nostalgia for the forever lost.

## Later days for the Bæbes

Times have changed for the Bæbes. In more recent years their popularity has waned. Judging by the Amazon listener responses for *Of Kings and Angels* (2013) the comments, while still enthusiastic, were fewer and, more importantly, no longer employed the language of 'otherworldly' enchantment which their earlier albums sometimes evoked, perhaps unsurprisingly for a collection of Christmas carols. Their 2019 compilation of nursery songs, *A Pocketful of Posies*, received only one rating on Amazon, 4 out of 5, and no customer reviews. It remains to be seen how their latest album, *Prayers of the Rosary*, recorded December 2020, goes down with listeners over time. Blake offers a very different narrative for this new album, describing how she:

> composed original plainsong settings of these iconic Latin prayers and arranged them against a meditative backdrop of local field recordings, archaic and exotic instrumentation and spectral vocal textures. Steeped in the ceremony and mysteries of the Catholic tradition, this album echoes the full spectrum of religious experience, from terror to transcendence, from the sinful to the celestial. (K. Blake, 2020)

Gone is the cheekily seductive tone, the vamped-up Victorian atmosphere. This recording is making stronger claims, both in its religious content and flavour and its more serious tone. There is a deliberate attempt to cater to the mystical/spiritual end of town, whether Christian or pagan with the references to Glastonbury, stone circles, ley lines and the rosary itself:

> Other [tracks] are subtly interwoven with the gossamer threads of the natural world, the web of life captured in field recordings at Glastonbury's Chalice Well, Avebury's stone circle and other sacred sites along the St Michael's ley line. Yet others evoke the hushed mysteries of a hallowed inner sanctum – eerie, almost unsettling chants with eastern flourishes suggestive of ancient rites that predated and influenced the Rosary. (A. Jones, 2020)

Of the very few listener responses I have found so far for *Prayers of the Rosary* were these two, attached to a 'Make Weird Music' YouTube interview with Katharine Blake and the Mediæval Bæbes (Garone, 2020), which included excerpts from the album:

So beautiful and meditative for the mind. l wonder why they chose this music as their new album. ('Meditative', 2020)

This music is warm, calming and feeds the soul. As a woman of faith this music is very spiritual. Very beautiful record and voice. Thank you for sharing. ('Woman of faith', 2020)[32]

These listeners are responding to the recording's rather different style with a vocabulary which reflects its generally serious tone, more in line with the responses to those more scholarly recordings reviewed: 'meditative', 'warm', 'calming', 'soul', 'spiritual'.[33]

## The voice as objet (petit) a

The medieval lost world sought by listeners brings into relief the function of the voice in desire. For Lacan, the lost object in question is an effect of the process by which the speaking subject arrives as already subject to the signifier, the process by which desire is produced. The object can never be found because it came into existence as already lost. *Objet a* is the impossible object around which the drives circle. Lacan adds the voice and the gaze to Freud's list of partial objects of the drive (Lacan, 1981: 168), naming the drive relating to the voice 'the invocatory drive' (180). Its erogenous zone is the ear, its partial object the voice, and the verb associated with it 'to hear', although we also feel music throughout our bodies. It is the most important drive, says Lacan, in that the ear 'cannot be closed [and] it is because of this that there is a response in the body to what I called the voice' (Lacan, 1975–76: 10). As in the reviews cited previously, something calls to the listener; we are seduced by ear.

The object voice in Lacan's theory is not a sonorous voice. According to Jacques-Alain Miller it is as inaudible as it is invisible:

> [T]he voice as an object *a* does not at all belong to the sonorous register. ... [T]he objects called *a* are tuned to the subject of the signifier only if they lose all substantiality, i.e. only on the condition that they are centered by an emptiness. (Miller, 2001: 96)

In fact, as he sternly concludes: '[I]f we sing and listen to singers ... it is in order to silence what deserves to be called the voice as object little *a*' (Miller, 2001: 104).

Mladen Dolar nuances this view in a way which is closer to the mark. To quote again: '[M]usic evokes the object voice and obfuscates it; it fetishises it, but it also opens the gap that cannot be filled' (2006: 31). Where do we locate this gap in music? At the level of discourse, the gap can be thought of as between the body and signification. The voice is the necessary vehicle for signification, yet it does not itself signify, as Dolar points out (2006: 20). In its sonorous capacity it is surplus to signification which relies on pure difference, as Saussure observes: '[I]n language there are only differences *without positive terms*' (1974: 120; emphasis in original). He explains: 'Phonemes are characterized not ... by their own positive quality but simply by the fact that they are distinct' (Saussure, 1974: 119). Nor is the voice part of the body, although it proceeds from it. Body and language share it between them, yet it belongs to neither, suggests Dolar (2006: 73), and this, he maintains, 'is the topology of *objet petit a*' (73). *Objet a* inhabits a *space between*, is a *space between*, the space we are becoming familiar with in its role as the 'middle' in Middle Ages. Music adds another dimension, another *space between*. When a melody is attached to words, signification is further exceeded by an alluring surplus.

Listeners perhaps imagine an Eden, uncorrupted by the signifier, to which the singing voice can carry us. For Lacan, however, such an idea would always need to be seen as retroactive. Dolar observes: 'The voice as the bearer of a deeper sense ... is a structural illusion, the core of a fantasy that the singing voice might ... restore the loss that we suffered by the assumption of the symbolic order' (2006: 31). Dolar calls this fantasy a 'deceptive promise'. It is the promise I have been speaking of – the promise of a return to the lost home, when everything was *really* real, not yet destroyed by the advent of the signifier. The medieval can represent this primordial 'time' in so far as it evokes for us not a history but a prehistory. The 'dark age' remains a dark continent. As Michel Zink observes, we are always searching, in medieval artefacts, for what was there '*before* what we already know or ... think we already know' (Zink, 1998: 13).[34] We relish the archaic, the tantalisingly fragmentary; we are ineluctably drawn towards whatever appears to gesture backwards to a lost wholeness, towards our origin. That origin may in turn associate to the life before birth enclosed within the mother's womb. The 'deceptive promise' is very often a feminine promise. When

Katharine Blake warns her listeners they'll never be quite the same again, she's tapping into an ancient fantasy surrounding the woman's voice, one voice in particular, for whose voice is at the core of the fantasy if not Mother's? The timeless 'dark age' associates here to the darkness of the womb, a *space between* without time.

### 'Music is a woman'

Kaja Silverman has spoken of the cultural fantasy of the maternal voice as 'the image of a child held within the ... sphere of the mother's voice' (Silverman, 1988: 72). This sphere is an aspect of the lost world, another form of the medieval as *space between*, the point of origin surrounded by the mother's body. It is an image provoking both longing and fear; a 'sonorous womb' or 'murmuring house' for Guy Rosolato, a 'pleasurable milieu that surrounds [and] sustains [the child]' (Rosolato, 1974: 81). For Michel Chion, however, it is an 'umbilical web', an image he acknowledges is horrifying in its 'evocation of spiders' (Chion, 1999: 61). It is simultaneously a haven and a trap. We long for mother to enfold us again but return is forbidden and spectres of punishment arise. Mother's music may be felt as a seductive snare.

Lacan invokes Freud's *das Ding* (the Thing) to speak of this haven which is also a trap. To quote again: '[T]here is no Sovereign Good –... the Sovereign Good, which is *das Ding*, which is the mother, is also the object of incest, is a forbidden good, and ... there is no other good' (Lacan, 1997: 70). Such ambivalence plagues the voice which produces both words and music. If Father is the Word, then Mother finds herself cast as the music. Rosolato has brought this association to bear on notions of harmony and, by extension, the *musica mundana*: 'It is therefore the entire dramatization of separated bodies and their reunion which harmony supports' (Rosolato, cited in Gorbman, 1987: 63).[35] If Mother's music might be a seductive snare, Lewis and Tolkien, in their creation music, strove to expel that threat by giving music back to the Father.

This ambivalence towards the feminine figure is very familiar to students of the medieval songs of courtly love, a point Lacan considers in his *Ethics* seminar. He speaks there of the beloved Lady of troubadour lyric as the semblance of *das Ding*. She is not *das Ding*, although she can be 'raised to [its] dignity' (Lacan, 1997: 117–18), Lacan asserts, provided she remains out of reach. *Das Ding* is that which is, 'by its very nature alien' (1997: 52). Unlike an object it cannot be said to have attributes (52). It contains no reflections by which we can identify ourselves with reference to it (112). Although no mother is *das Ding*, mothers, and by extension all women, bear the mixture of love and hostility that this association with the alien *das Ding* produces.

It is this Thing, for Lacan, 'that ... the drive aims for in sublimation. That is to say', he continues, 'that what man demands ... is to be deprived of something real' (1997: 150).[36] *Das Ding* is too real to bear, which is why the Lady must remain at a distance. The lover of troubadour or trouvère song is never quite sure about this Lady of the courtly love song. Like mother she knows him through and through, but he does not know her at all. Her intentions towards him remain obscure, so he can never entirely trust her. These divine qualities are also associated by Chion with the *acousmêtre*, the voice with no visible bearer (Chion, 1999: 19) whose powers are 'usually malevolent' (23). The mother may be the original *acousmêtre*, given that, according to scientists, a baby can hear its mother's voice while still in the womb. Perhaps that maternal power is, at times, overwhelming (Chion, 1999: 23).

*LOTR*'s Galadriel evokes this same uncertainty in the travellers, and possesses the same ambiguous potency. As a semblance of *das Ding*, even when she is judged to be 'good', she is terrifying. In Aragorn's words, '[t]here is in her and in this land no evil' (Tolkien, 1993: 349), yet most of the travellers feel invaded by her attention. It is Sam who gives the most honest account: 'I felt as if I hadn't got nothing on, and I didn't like it. She seemed to be looking inside me' (348). Lacan maintains that the subject 'cannot stand the extreme good that *das Ding* may bring him' and will go to any lengths to avoid it (1997: 73). When you get too close pleasure becomes pain. That is what the fantasy avoids.

Voice plays a part in Galadriel's ambiguous potency, for she, like the singers on a recording, is an *acousmêtre*. In the scene Sam is describing, Galadriel speaks to each member of the fellowship with a voice which does not proceed from her lips but is heard in their minds, offering them a choice 'between a shadow full of fear that lay ahead, and something that he greatly desired' (Tolkien, 1993:

349). As those virtuously bound to a quest, of course they resist her temptations, but she troubles them. Boromir in particular, already obsessed with the ring, is not 'too sure of this Elvish Lady and her purposes' (Tolkien, 1993: 349). Because after all the bad may be beautiful, like the beautiful but evil enchantress in C. S. Lewis's *The Silver Chair*. It is she who enchants the young prince and keeps him locked up, helpless and bemused, for ten years underground partly through the power of her enchanting voice, surely a 'uterine darkness' like that described by Chion (1999: 61). Whether you call her evil or good, *das Ding* is too close for comfort. She is that 'terrible good' which the 'Christian myth makers', as Tolkien, Lewis and others have been called, introduce to readers. In *The Lion, the Witch and the Wardrobe*, the narrator insists: 'People … sometimes think that a thing cannot be good and terrible at the same time. If the children had ever thought so, they were cured of it now' (Lewis, 2005: 168).

Rolland Hein traces the Christian lineage of the fiction of Tolkien and Lewis in *Christian Mythmakers*, beginning with Dante and passing through John Bunyan, George MacDonald and G. K Chesterton, among others. He offers a Christian reading of the 'terrible good' in MacDonald's *At the Back of the North Wind* (Hein, 2002: 93–4). It is a reading which seeks to neutralise the ambiguity of *das Ding*: 'God is so ordering life that good may come out of evil' (93). North Wind, who brings destruction in her wake, 'portrays the divinely appointed presence of adversity in life, the "evil" that issues in good for those who receive her in the right spirit' (93). Here the threat of the feminine has been safely barricaded between inverted commas.

*Das Ding* is what one will go to any lengths to avoid, yet one is drawn to her like the moth to the flame. She is empty but not necessarily insubstantial. That is part of her horror, like the man who wasn't there in the little rhyme my parents used to recite:

> As I was going up the stair
> I met a man who wasn't there.
> He wasn't there again today,
> I wish that he would go away.

In Chapter 2 I quoted Lacan on the emptiness of *das Ding*: 'All art is characterized by a certain mode of organization around this emptiness' (Lacan, 1997: 130). It may be possible for emptiness to have substance but, like Chaos, no form, reminiscent of Kristeva's 'woman's time':

> The massive presence of a monumental temporality, without cleavage or escape, which has so little to do with linear time (which passes) that the very word 'temporality' hardly fits: All-encompassing and infinite like imaginary space. (Kristeva, 1981: 16)

It is hard not to hear in this the terror of the imprisoning womb which repels as it beckons. Here music threatens to overstep the mark between the listener's pleasure and a far more dangerous enjoyment. If you recall the distinction made in Chapter 2 between desire as sustained by enjoyment and desire as a limit to enjoyment, it now becomes clear that Lacan is speaking of two kinds of enjoyment; music can provide both.

## Two kinds of musical enjoyment

The first, more familiar, enjoyment, the pleasurable pain of yearning, keeps its distance from *das Ding*. The pleasure principle regulates the appropriate distance and it is not *das Ding* but its 'pleasurable associations' with which one dallies (Lacan, 1997: 53). Fantasies like the one recounted by reviewer 'Rainbow Sphinx' seem to fall into this category of a tamed, practised pleasure, often invoked but containing no unwelcome shocks.

In the second enjoyment, an implied painful *jouissance un*limited by the pleasure principle, we are on more dangerous ground. This sounds like the Real. As with *das Ding* there is a traumatic element to the Real, which Lacan names 'this something faced with which all words cease and all categories fail' (Lacan, 1991: 164). Cosy fantasies like that of 'Rainbow Sphinx' do not survive here. No fantasies survive this onslaught, but an association with the feminine remains in the speaking of it. Lacan associates the Real in this passage with three disturbing images; all are linked, directly or indirectly to the *space between* of the maternal body: 'the abyss of the feminine organ from which all life emerges', the 'gulf of the mouth, in which everything is swallowed up', and 'the image of death in which everything comes to its end' (Lacan, 1991: 164). In such an ecstatic *jouissance* the subject would, at least for the moment, cease to exist.

Music can carry the listener beyond the boundaries set by the pleasure principle, and for this reason lawmakers of all kinds have sought to regulate or prohibit certain kinds of music. When they do so, they sometimes refer to such music's feminising or enfeebling qualities. A man who listens to too much music, Plato insists, is in serious trouble. A little music softens and tempers his spirit,

> but if he does not break the enchantment, the next stage is that it melts and runs, till the spirit has quite run out of him and his mental guts … are entirely removed, and he has become what Homer calls 'a feeble fighter'. (Plato, 1994–2009: 154)

The feeble fighter is unmanned.

The Bæbes trade on this troubling ambiguity associating the feminine with the enfeebling enchantments of music. In the 2005 interview already mentioned, singer Marie Findley remarks: 'In 'Temptasyon' [the third track on the album *Mirabilis*] I imagine someone being enchanted by angel voices', but she adds, in the next breath, 'we're like sirens luring someone away with strange sounds' (*Mirabilis* Release Notes, 2005). It is a curious juxtaposition – angels and sirens – with no apparent sense of dissonance, despite the fact that angels call us to our heavenly home while sirens lure us to our death. In this context the track title, 'Temptasyon', is suggestive, the suggestion being that we may be tempted to risk destruction for our listening pleasures or even that part of the enjoyment is in flirting with the risk. What militates against the sense of threat is the Bæbes's air of laying it on a little too thickly to be taken seriously. They are always on the edge of self-parody. Their trade is in flirtation with danger. It is hard to imagine their music precipitating a more profound dislocation.

Listeners and musicians sometimes do more than flirt, however. Michel Poizat quotes opera lovers who fall apart at a certain point in the music:

> I could listen to that aria ten times a day; it tears me apart, sends me into an ecstasy of sorrow. I have lost my Eurydice … That music drives me mad: it sweeps me away, my soul craves this kind of pain. (Julie de Lespinasse, cited in Poizat, 1992: 5)

Poizat calls this 'an ecstatic gratification in the lost object, the feeling of its recovery, but never without the pain of remembering its loss' (Poizat, 1992: 5). George MacDonald spoke of birdsong that 'sounded like a welcome already overshadowed with the coming farewell' (2000b: 67). In each case two events, an appearance and a disappearance, are collapsed into one. Eurydice is an apt figure to evoke such a response, since, as Judith Butler observes, she is lost in the moment of finding her. It is our gaze that causes her to vanish (J. Butler, 2006: vi–viii). Perhaps when she appears we are no longer there to see, like the listener who falls into the music and is lost. This simultaneous appearing and disappearing seems to be what Poizat is getting at. This is no longer the territory of nostalgia. Nostalgia is what provides a safeguard against the listener's disappearance. It is also useful to remember Eurydice in this context, since Orpheus, that legendary singer, opened the portals of her otherworld with song.

An Irish musician recounts an experience at a jam session:

> I would call [music] a dangerous art ... Paddy had gone to a place in the music ... I'm now beginning to tremble as I talk about this because what happened that day I will never forget. He had gone into a place that was deeper and beyond what was happening ... Paddy Keenan had gone to some place where ... if they went further you mightn't be able to come back in one piece ... come back to earth. (Fitzgerald and McHugh, 2007)

These experiences, the second, less smoothly articulated account more than the first, seem more profound and more dangerous than those described by the Bæbes's fans. Perhaps the fantasy of the medieval, at least as promoted by the Bæbes, pre-empts this fall into a kind of madness, as it does in fantasy fiction (although, as in MacDonald's passage, that fall is indicated). Listeners know too well what to expect. They are too busy manoeuvring the appropriate response to be taken by surprise, or to be *taken* at all.

What does take us beyond ourselves in music, that excess that cannot be made meaning of or represented in any way, is the locus of the voice as *objet a*, the void around which the song spins. In psychoanalytic terms this is the significance of Frodo's inability to capture the song's meaning. To requote Lacan, 'All art is characterised by a certain mode of organization around this emptiness' (1997:

130). When this music is named 'medieval' – the term indicating something more than can be known or spoken – the lure of the singing voice may be joined to the fantasy of a return to a forbidden primordial world, blissful and terrifying, when Mother's voice enveloped us; a 'real' world. There *is* a 'real', but it is Real in the Lacanian sense: paradoxically beyond and before the signifier, produced by signification as its surplus but posited by desire as its origin. The difficulty in *thinking* the Real is the difficulty with origin and with cause in general. If, as Lacan insists, 'there is no metalanguage' (for instance, Lacan, 1966–67: 12) there is no way to think an origin that remains outside language. Nonetheless, although it cannot be thought in spatial or temporal terms (cannot be *thought* at all) its place is in that infinite *between*.

## Notes

1 See Annette Kreutziger-Herr's designation of 'the current construction of the Middle Ages as a desired *beyond* or *other* before our eyes' (Kreutziger-Herr, 2005: 102).
2 In 1904, for instance, according to Harry Haskell, 'the Gramophone Co. sent its engineers to Rome to a congress commemorating the thirteenth centenary of the death of Gregory the Great, traditionally held to be the codifier of the chant repertoire', where they recorded various interpretations of chant (Haskell, 1988: 113). He notes: 'These recordings were recently reissued on Discant Dis 1 and 2' (208).
3 In neuropsychology, now an accepted, even a privileged, strand in the discourse of music reception, the brain sometimes replaces the soul. For a relatively recent review of neurological thinking on music see Daniel J. Levitin and Anna K. Tirovolas (2009).
4 I am drawing here on Gérard Genette's term 'paratext': 'a zone not only of transition but also of *transaction* … an influence on the public, an influence that … is at the service of a better reception for the text and a more pertinent reading of it (more pertinent, of course, in the eyes of the author and his allies)' (Genette, 1997: 2).
5 In March 2018 the journal *Forbes* reported: 'Physical Albums Sell Significantly Better than Digital Ones' (McIntyre, 2018).
6 See Gilad Edelman: 'I find myself listening to full albums over and over and coming to appreciate tracks that I would skip if I were listening on my phone' (Edelman, 2021: n.p.).

7   Allen S. Weiss, in his book *Breathless*, argues that the 'perpetuation of the [recorded] voice beyond the grave radically changed our relation to disembodiment, death, and nostalgia' (2002: xii). But Weiss is speaking of the first century of recording. These days the acousmatic voice of radio or recording is too common in the mainstream West to provoke the uncanny shiver of its earlier years. We are no more likely to be spooked by it than we are to be terrified that having our photograph taken will seize our souls away, although, as argued in Chapter 2, cunningly crafted words in fantasy fiction can make strange the acousmatic sound and re-evoke its frisson. There are exceptions – perhaps the recorded voice of a dead beloved, played at the funeral or heard unexpectedly, or old recordings, bringing back the sense of lost worlds, for instance, the ballad of Stagger Lee sung by Mississippi John Hurt in 1964 (Hurt, 2010).

8   See Leech-Wilkinson (2002: 3) on the inadequacy of the evidence available to determine any coherent performance practice and on the advantages of our ignorance for our desire: 'That we know almost nothing about the sound of medieval music in the middle ages, and never will, is almost an advantage' (Leech-Wilkinson, 2000: 296).

9   Note the reference to fairy stories.

10  In order to investigate and quantify these and other tendencies in listener responses, a large dataset of over eight thousand comments and reviews responding to a range of music that could be classified in some way as medieval was collected and statistically analysed (for the full method and dataset description including artists and albums, see Appendix, pp. 205–8).

11  Customer reviewers write fast and they are not concerned with spelling and grammar. I have silently corrected any typographical mistakes in quotations within the chapter.

12  The concept of transportation to another world is represented in 17.2 per cent of responses in the scholarly group, and 20.1 per cent in the popular group. For explanation of the scholarly and popular categorisations of musical groups, see analysis methodology in Appendix.

13  Such beings can be found in 5.15 per cent of all responses.

14  In the analysed comments, the concept is mentioned more frequently in response to the scholarly rather than the popular groups. See also 'Musical Medievalism and the Harmony of the Spheres' (Dell, 2016) on the question of authenticity for Bæbes's listeners.

15  It is not a matter of accuracy but of authenticity, when employed in its positive sense.

16  The album title was presumably drawn from the thirteenth-century English lyric 'Worldes bliss', which, translated into modern English,

begins: 'Worldly bliss lasts only a short time. / It departs and goes away anon; / The longer I know it the less value I find in it' (translation based on Luria and Hoffman, 1974: 1). Similar lyrics can be found in Section X of Luria and Hoffman (1974: 223–31).

17  The singers up against the thorns ought to be screaming, but they appear quite comfortable in their thorny bower.
18  Should read 'Kindely' (naturally): see Luria and Hoffman (1974: 226).
19  For a live recording of the Bæbes singing 'Kinderly', see Mediæval Bæbes (2009).
20  In a canon, or round, the melody is imitated at a set point after its beginning.
21  Such concepts are echoed in 11.4 per cent of responses to *Worldes Blysse*, compared with 3.7 per cent for the entire dataset, demonstrating that listeners tend to follow and invoke the mood set by the artists in their responses.
22  You can hear the Bæbes singing 'All Turns to Yesterday' at Mediæval Bæbes (2011).
23  This concept of 'longing' or 'yearning' is found in 6.6 per cent of listener responses to the scholarly group, and 6.8 per cent for the popular group.
24  'Drive' is a term used less frequently by Lacan in his later work, although in *Joyce and the Sinthome* he returns to it, naming the drives 'the echo in the body of the fact that there is a saying' (Lacan, 1975–76: 10).
25  Here is the luminous numinous again.
26  Compare Galadriel's luminosity and the 'dreary and cold' world of awakening to her loss.
27  See Edmund Burke's sublime: 'To draw the whole of what has been said into a few distinct points. The passions which belong to self-preservation, turn on pain and danger; they are simply painful when their causes immediately affect us; they are delightful when we have an idea of pain and danger, without being actually in such circumstances; this delight I have not called pleasure, because it turns on pain, and because it is different enough from any idea of positive pleasure. Whatever excites this delight, I call *sublime*' (Burke, 1998: 47; emphasis in original). See also Kant on the 'terrifying sublime' which may be 'accompanied with some dread or even melancholy' (Kant, 2011: 16). Carla A. Arnell (2002: 30) has pointed out C. S. Lewis's indebtedness to Kant's account of the sublime.
28  Similar to 4.2 per cent of other responses analysed.
29  This trend of instructing others on just the right way to listen and experience the music is present in 2.2 per cent of the analysed responses.

30 'Rainbow Sphinx's fantasy is reminiscent of the scene in the Wife of Bath's Tale (ll. 989–96) where the knight stumbles on a group of dancing ladies who vanish at his approach (Chaucer, 1974: 86).
31 The use of archaic or 'olde English' language and grammar is seen in around 1.5 per cent of responses.
32 Now seven responses on YouTube, all positive (2022).
33 These concepts of the music being soothing, calming, warm, meditative, tranquil, relaxing, soulful and spiritual are included in 24.8 per cent of responses to scholarly groups, and 15.9 per cent to the popular category.
34 This concern with what went before has not spared medieval studies, as David Matthews observes: 'As a discipline, it has traditionally been obsessed with origins: the history of textual editing has been dominated by the quest for archetypes, for example, what the author wrote before the scribes got to it' (Matthews, 2015: 168). This has been, and still is to a great extent, just as true for medieval music historians. It has also found its way into medievalist fantasy fiction, as for instance in the scene in Hobbiton where Gandalf deciphers for Frodo the ancient writing on the ring of power (Tolkien, 1993: 49). Tolkien, as a linguist, loved to trace the history of ancient tongues.
35 See Dell (2016a) on the fantasies expressed through the harmony of the spheres.
36 Lacan does not talk much about *das Ding* after the *Ethics* seminar (1959–60), but traces of it remain in his working of the Real and *objet (petit) a*.

# 4

# Exotic sexualities: The countertenor voice in the late twentieth-century medieval music revival

> It is thus not lack of cleanliness or health that causes abjection but what disturbs identity, system, order. What does not respect borders, positions, rules. (Kristeva, 1982: 4)

> If something or someone is neither/nor, but kind of both, not quite either, if something is in the middle of either/or, if it is ambiguous, given the available classification of things, if it is mestiza, if it threatens by its very ambiguity the orderliness of the system, of schematized reality, if given its ambiguity in the univocal ordering it is anomalous, deviant, can it be tamed through separation? (Lugones, 1994: 467)

The idea of the medieval has exercised a powerful hold over the imagination of late twentieth- and early twenty-first-century readers, viewers and listeners, functioning for many as a promised escape route to a fantasy world. Chapter 3 explored the seductions of the feminine voice at the popular end of the medieval music recording spectrum. This chapter investigates the exploitation of one kind of masculine voice in medieval music recording in the 1970s, 1980s and 1990s, the countertenor voice, with the connotations it carried, for some, of gender ambiguity and of a mysterious and forbidden sexual knowledge, power and enjoyment.[1] This ambiguity of the countertenor has constituted a different and – again, for some in the early music world – more unsettling form of the medieval *space between*. The medieval, identified only by its place in the middle between positive terms, has always presented the risk of ambiguity.

The fantasy surrounding the countertenor worked, not just at the level of what he did or what he had or hadn't got but also at the level of what he meant, what he *was* – his identity. The observer's uncertainty morphed into the countertenor's 'secret' and was incorporated into the fantasy. The phenomenon and the conversations I speak of took place principally in England and the USA, at a time when medieval music was attracting a good deal of interest, both academic and popular. Many recordings were being made and reviews and journal articles written. In this scene the figure of the countertenor became a magnet for some of the anxieties surrounding the already ambiguous 'medieval'.

Ambiguity is at the heart of medievalist nostalgia. It is part of the paradoxical lure of the 'medieval', the place in the middle which I call the *space between* – an unnamed space between named ages, the classical age and the Renaissance, inviting fantasies and giving rise to nostalgia. The 'medieval' period, John Ganim has suggested, is 'that foreign land in which we are always at home', as mentioned earlier (Ganim, 2005: 107). It is, piquantly, both homely and exotic.[2] This 'medieval' has always presented the risk of impurity. Ambiguity itself can be experienced as a kind of impurity. One might feel anxiety, finding oneself in that disturbing *space between*. It is the *space between* itself, the state of ambiguity, which disturbs. Humanity craves certainty.

This chapter also investigates the 'resistance', an opposing fantasy which has tried to banish ambiguity, and with it the body, in an attempt to re-create a pure, authentic medieval in music. Nostalgia often invokes a past age *without* the troubling complications of the present; the solo countertenor in medieval music has represented a particularly troubling complication. In this chapter the main focus is the discourse of musicologists, music critics and music historians, along with their close collaborators, musicians and directors at the scholarly end of the spectrum. Sometimes they are the same people. An examination of these discourses and the fantasies they uncover allows an investigation into one of the most significant sites of tension and anxiety in musical medievalism – that of purity, sometimes sheltering in the guise of 'authenticity'. The countertenor may represent a contamination of that yearned-for purity which the medieval symbolises for some. In the next section I outline some of the evidence offered by interested parties in the late twentieth-century medieval music scene.

## 'Something akin to a countertenor voice': Evidence and interpretation

The evidence offered for falsetto singing in medieval performance practice is, in fact, comparatively slight, often ambiguous, sometimes little more than a romantic impression. Peter Giles, for instance, a countertenor, author and vocal teacher, has written a *History and Technique of the Counter-tenor* which begins with a grand claim: 'As we will see, there is considerable evidence to suggest that falsettists' art formed many of the main tonal colourings of early Medieval music' (Giles, 1994: 3). But much of his evidence rests merely on vague references to Eastern influences via the crusades and the Moorish invasion of Spain.[3] Giles also associates falsetto singing, perplexingly, with the cult of Marianism among the troubadours: 'It is easy to connect [Marianism] with the use of falsetto by these male singers' (4). He continues with a romantic odyssey narrative: 'As the wandering singers moved freely round France and Italy, falsetto art was taken through Europe' (4). Wandering minstrels are a sure-fire hit for romance, not to mention the scent of the glamorous otherness of the Orient.[4]

Evidence of a different kind can be found in musical treatises like John of Garland's (1270–1320) *Introductio musice*. John employs a terminology of three vocal registers, chest, throat and head (John of Garland, 1991). According to V. E. Negus *et al.* (2001):

> Possibly, when such 13th-century writers as Johannes de Garlandia and Jerome of Moravia distinguished between chest-, throat-, and head-registers (*pectoris*, *guttoris*, *capitis*), the last of these indicated second-mode phonation, later known as 'falsetto', a term common in Italy by the mid-16th century.

Another kind of evidence for falsetto singing is based on what Roger Bowers called a 'fixed range-relationship' between voices singing polyphony, from which the range (on average two octaves, up to the second half of the fifteenth century) can be established. Therefore,

Bowers argues, '[f]or polyphonic performance ... the choirs ... could offer only two basic timbres of voice – something akin to a countertenor, and a tenor/baritone' (Bowers, 1980: 22). Much of the evidence offered by scholars comes in the form of prohibitions by churchmen, like this one from a Gilbertine statute from 1134:

> It befits men to sing with a manly voice, and not in a womanish manner or ... with 'false voices', as if imitating the wantonness of minstrels. And therefore we have stipulated that a medium is to be used in the chant. (Cited in Page, 1981: 71)

Bernard of Clairvaux (1090–1153) writes along the same lines:

> The words of the Holy Spirit should not be sung in soft, broken voices in a somewhat womanish manner, but uttered with manly sounds and feelings. Yes indeed, it is seemly for men to sing in manly voices, and not to ape, as it were, the wantonness of actors [or minstrels] with shrill or false voices used in an effeminate manner. (Cited in Giles, c.1994: 13)

The Cistercian Aelred of Rievaulx (1110–67) alludes to what sounds like falsetto, among other vocal crimes: 'Sometimes, manly strength set aside, it is constricted into the shrillness of a woman's voice' (cited in Holsinger, 2001: 160). The anonymous writer of the *Instituta patrum* (c.1200), forbids 'effeminate voices and every counterfeit, ostentation, and novelty of voices' (cited in McGee, 1998: 19). This is a sample of the documentary evidence, from a range of sources but necessarily localised to particular times, places and contexts.[5] What is made clear in these few instances is that sounding like a woman was in itself considered disgraceful. As John Haines observed, in the eyes of medieval authors '[t]he worst that can befall a singing man is that he should sound like a woman' (2010: 46).[6] It is then difficult to see how a countertenor voice could have escaped disapproval, at least in the context of liturgical music.

There is also literary evidence for medieval falsetto singing. Absolon in Chaucer's Miller's Tale plays 'songes on a smal rubible [rebec] / Thereto he song som tyme a loud quynible' (Chaucer, 1974: 49). According to John Caldwell (2014), although 'quinible' is, technically speaking, taken to mean a part above the quatreble, which lies above the treble, it appears, more generally, to refer in English to 'a high-pitched song or voice' (Caldwell, n.p.). Absolon's voice is described as 'gentil and smal' (Chaucer, 1974: 50), 'smal' meaning thin, as it does also for the Pardoner, who has a voice 'as smal as hath a goot' (23). But we have already been told that Absolon sings 'quynible', as we have been told that the Pardoner takes the higher line of the love-song to which the Somonour 'bar ... a stif burdoun' (23).

There was considerable disagreement among the interested parties about how to interpret this evidence, although the overall tone of their comments is guarded; for the most part they were careful to limit their claims. Giles is an exception to the rule in his lack of academic caution. Roger Bowers cited the Gilbertine statute quoted here as evidence of a medieval countertenor (Bowers, 1980: 22), noting that the prohibitions were only issued in 'certain of the more austere religious orders [and that] no such prohibitions were ever imposed on the secular churches (22).

Christopher Page and Andrew Parrott took a different view of the statute. Page is the founder and past director of the renowned medieval music group, Gothic Voices, and a highly influential voice in the medieval music scene. Andrew Parrott is the conductor of the Taverner Choir, Consort and Players, also a recognised authority on early music matters. In his 1986 study, *Voices and Instruments of the Middle Ages*, Page put forward the view that the high style songs of the troubadours and trouvères of the twelfth century were performed 'by solo voice alone' (Page, 1986: 134). Coming from such a respected figure, this blessing on the a cappella movement had almost the force of an imprimatur (Page, 1981: 71). Page quibbled over the Gilbertine statute's translation: 'virilis' might not mean 'manly', 'in more femineo' might refer not to the pitch, but to the manner of singing (1981: 71). Parrott argued that if the typical two-octave range for polyphony is assumed to be down a fourth from Bowers's estimate, then basses could be used, excluding the need for countertenors (Parrot, in Page, 1981: 72).

David Fallows was less grudging towards Bowers's argument in his much later (1998) article: 'it is easy enough to demonstrate that the highest voice of early 15th-century three-voice sacred polyphony was normally sung by men in a "falsetto" register' (Fallows, 1998: 381). Joseph Dyer (1976) seems to have had no doubts. He offered as evidence a rubric in the Beauvais Festival Office 'that the antiphons are to be intoned "cum falsetto"', though noting the special context, that is, the parodic nature of the *Fête de l'Âne* ('the feast of the donkey'). He also mentioned the theorist Anonymous XI, who deplored the singing of motet tripla in the tenor range (presumably an octave down because no one could sing them in falsetto) (Dyer, 1976: 489). Timothy McGee (1998: 24) suggested that the words of John, Aelred and the *Instituta* may perhaps refer to falsetto singing. Edward Roesner, on the other hand, praised the Sequentia ensemble for their exclusion of the countertenor voice in a recording of the late twelfth- and early thirteenth-century 'lai, planctus and conductus', since it was a vocal type 'not cultivated in this repertory to my knowledge' (Roesner, 1983: 265).

In 1972, Hendrik van der Werf ruefully commented: 'Unfortunately, however, it is almost customary these days to have countertenors sing medieval songs, and the uninitiated listener might come to the unwarranted and undesirable conclusion that all medieval jongleurs were counter-tenors' (Werf, 1972: 340). Parrott clearly preferred the bass/tenor to the tenor/countertenor blend: 'This alternative hypothesis [the bass/tenor blend] is one that I have consistently adopted in performance' (Parrott, 2015: 72). That is one way for a director to exclude the countertenor. Christopher Page took an alternative approach with his vocal ensemble, Gothic Voices: he kept a higher sonority but placed a female alto (Margaret Philpot, later Catherine King) in countertenor range on the top line.

In 1981 Page did concede, grudgingly, that a medieval countertenor voice was 'conceivable', but only because there was not enough evidence to rule it out entirely:

> [N]obody would be prepared to assert the contrary in view of the fragmentary evidence at our disposal. Yet even if it can be demonstrated that one medieval use of *fausetum* undoubtedly *does* mean falsetto, we must keep a very open mind about the liturgical use of a voice which evoked disgust amongst at least some medieval churchmen. (Page, 1981: 72)

This is a strange argument (but one with which Bowers seems to have agreed [1980: 22]), since the prohibitions would have been unnecessary if the practice were not occurring.[7]

In 1988 Page admitted the existence of such a voice less reservedly: 'I believe that the existence of something like the counter-tenor voice must be granted at the outset', but again added caveats and

# Exotic sexualities 147

restrictions: 'However, the mere existence of such voices does not prove that they were used in composed polyphonic music where the total compass used before 1300 never attains 20 notes and is often restricted to ten or even less' (Page 1988: 152). Page might have been happier if the evidence *had* decisively ruled out the countertenor.

Page was probably right to be cautious. So many medieval misdeeds incurred the charge of effeminacy that it is difficult to pin down the particulars. Nonetheless, there is an air of special pleading in his and Parrott's arguments. Parrott concluded his contribution rather waspishly, stating that his ears 'certainly do not miss the sound of the obligatory countertenor' (Parrott, in Page, 1981: 72). There was a degree of animosity towards the countertenor voice from these two scholar/directors who chose to exclude him from their ensembles, owing partly to the context in which their correspondence occurred, but perhaps also to a more visceral distaste.

Behind this correspondence lies a running battle in musicology between proponents of the 'voices and instruments hypothesis' and the 'a cappella hypothesis' in the context of medieval performance practice. The question was simply whether medieval vocal music of various kinds was performed with voices and instruments or with voices only, instruments performing separately.[8] And behind and underpinning this debate is yet another, the furore surrounding the question of authenticity in the performance of early music. Nostalgia clings to the fantasy of the authentic reproduction as a way of recovering a lost age. Those who argued so passionately on correct early music performance practice were revivalists in Tamara Livingston's sense. As she writes:

> [R]evivalists position themselves in opposition to aspects of the contemporary cultural mainstream, align themselves with a particular historical lineage, and offer a cultural alternative in which legitimacy is grounded in reference to authenticity and historical fidelity. (Livingston, 1999: 66)[9]

Most musicologists rested their case, however derived and irrespective of their position, on the bedrock of 'historical fidelity'.

In 1993 Page outlined an approach to early music performance practice in England, guided by the 'scholar-critics' whose 'vigilant eyes' oversaw the results (he did not mention that his own eyes and ears were some of the most vigilant):

This approach gives primacy to facts, to evidence and to sources, so that the line between knowledge and speculation remains clear: it values imagination but tends to marginalize whatever seems fanciful or eccentric; it is deeply wary of any popularizing impulse while remaining committed to the broadest possible dissemination of its characteristic ideas and enthusiasms. (Page, 1993: 459)

In this context the precarious position of the countertenor rested on the evidence. If his medieval existence could not be verified in the strictest sense from contemporary documentation then 'authenticity' decreed his dismissal from the performance of medieval music. But perhaps even if history had justified his presence, other grounds would have been found to banish him, since the perceived ambiguity surrounding his sexuality and gender gave him what might be construed as an intrinsic inauthenticity. Nonetheless, despite the vigilance of the 'authenticists', the countertenor was not banished.

It was by the proponents of the earlier, voices and instruments, hypothesis and their heirs that he was granted admission, although they too believed they were approaching, in the words of Thomas Binkley, an 'elusive original' (cited in Haines, 2004a: 283), but by less literal means.[10] This hypothesis was associated with a more flamboyant and glamorous performing style with greater instrumental accompaniment and plenty of room for improvisation. The later, a cappella, hypothesis favoured a more austere style which was carried through into the performances and recordings of musicologist/directors like Page.

In Page's 'English *a cappella* Renaissance', a 1993 summing-up of the performance practices favoured by reviewers published in *Early Music* from 1979 to 1991, he detected a characteristically English 'school of thought'. He listed a number of practices which were generally opposed in these reviews, for instance 'no. 5' – 'the "Arab" hypothesis' – and 'no. 7', simply '"over-interpretation"' (Page, 1993: 469). All these practices added what he considered spurious elements to the music, unauthorised by medieval sources, evidence of the popularising tendencies which he condemned (Page, 1993: 469). With their range of exotic instruments, the offending groups gave evidence of an unwarranted 'multiculturalism' in medieval music recording (460).[11]

English performances, on the other hand, favoured a straightforward, unadorned style, for instance unaccompanied or simply accompanied vocal performances. That simplicity was the guarantee that nothing extraneous, 'fanciful or eccentric', had been added to the supposed original. It was to the glamour associated with the earlier, voices and instruments, hypothesis that the countertenor owed his acceptance. The exoticism of a high-pitched male voice resonated with exotic fantasies of the medieval. This may partly explain the scepticism and distaste of the hard-line 'authenticists'. For them he brought to mind a spurious medievalism, unblessed by evidence.

One might ask why authenticity, the faithful delivery of the original in performance, mattered so much and still matters for some. For Parrott the question of what modern performers owe to the music of the distant past has, apparently, been difficult to lay to rest. In his continuing preoccupation with authenticity, the countertenor occupied a central, almost emblematic, position. In a 2015 publication entitled *Composers' Intentions?* he returned to the fray, devoting a chapter exclusively to interrogating the 'uncertain pedigree' of the countertenor (Parrott, 2015: x), questioning whether 'any such voice-type was actually cultivated before the 16th century' (46). Here he proffers a fuller account of the same sources and arguments as had been presented in the later decades of the twentieth century. The title of chapter 1, 'Composers' Intentions, Performers' Responsibilities', declares to the reader Parrott's unswerving commitment to the ideal of *Werktreue* – fidelity to the work. Richard Taruskin referred to this assumption of a conflation of the composition with the performance, in a 1984 contribution to *Early Music*: 'Modern performers seem to regard their performances as texts rather than acts' (Taruskin, 1984: 4).

Taruskin took issue with the moral overtones carried by the term 'authenticity' which are evident in Parrott's declaration: 'One simply cannot dissent from the concept when it is defined in this way. One is hardly free to say, "I prefer inauthenticity to authenticity"' (Taruskin, 1988: 137). The authenticity movement has frequently posed questions of authentic performance in moral or pseudo-moral terms, with a degree of deterrent effect. As Ross Duffin wrote: 'Nobody wants to be criticised for being "inauthentic" or worse yet, "musically immoral"' (Duffin, 2000: x). Taruskin's own understanding of authentic practice was drawn from his own convictions (Taruskin, 1984: 12), which he based on 'a constantly evolving style of performance'. This authenticity was never something finally achieved, but what remained present as 'a perpetually self-renewing challenge' (1984: 12).

As these quotations suggest, a high degree of concern, even anxiety, was evident in questions around authenticity, in particular its moral connotations. The word also carried an echo of nostalgia. As Michael Morrow wrote, in a 1978 article in *Early Music*, 'Authenticity can only mean the real thing' and, he lamented, it cannot be achieved (Morrow, 1978: 245). The musical past cannot be revived. The call for authenticity was a *cri de coeur*, as musicologist Gary Tomlinson wrote (1988: 116). When we see angst and contention arising around the idea of authenticity in music and the forces that threaten it, a fantasy may be in play. The authenticity for which interested parties strove was a sign of the nostalgic quest for the unachievable pure origin, in the words of Tomlinson, 'a single, true, certain authenticity' (1988: 115).[12] Medieval music was infected by a nostalgic fantasy of what was lost – something more real than contemporary reality – that shone with the glow of home and an identity associated with it, in this case authentic Englishness.

In the purity of the quest for authenticity – the perfect reconstruction as a return to a pure origin – the ambiguous glamour associated with the countertenor had no place. Ambiguity – the 'mestiza' in Lugones' sense – threatened that purity, especially sexual or gender ambiguity. The lure of purity is precisely that it banishes ambiguity. As John Ganim has written: 'Modern scholarship has sought a certain purity in the Middle Ages, in method as well as in content. The Middle Ages, and the study of it, is perceived as mercifully free of the conflictual issues that haunt the study of contemporary culture' (Ganim, 2005: 5).

In the scholarship surrounding medieval music the countertenor has represented a flaw in the pure body of authentic musical reconstruction and the historicity it claims. The 'uncertain pedigree' of the countertenor, in Parrott's words, gives one the sense of a threatened lineage. When one's ancestry is at stake, what threatens the past also threatens the present. It becomes a question of identity, in this case national identity. The countertenor's flamboyance could be heard as flouting the valued English characteristics of understatement and restraint. And the impurity of the countertenor's 'uncertain pedigree' is intensified by an anxiety surrounding his sexuality and gender.

Exotic sexualities                    151

As I have previously written, England's ancestry in choral singing as a source of national identity is evident in Page's assertion in the 1993 paper cited earlier, that

> Britain has nurtured something [in] the choral singing of cathedral and chapel which is purified and controlled beyond anything possessed by Catholic Europe, which is purged of excessive artifice and rhetoric ... and whose excellence gives Britain a mission – these are among the ideas and were a principal source of English identity since the Act of Union in 1707 and a foundation stone of English identity long before. (Page, 1993: 454)[13]

An interchange in *Early Music* sheds some light on the fantasies of the a cappella party. Page, in the 1993 article cited, claimed the eminence of English singers in the '*a cappella* renaissance'. Here he makes use of 'a fine Middle English word: clanness, or "cleanness"': 'clanness is the quality of something that is pure (like a pearl) or of fine and precise workmanship (like an elaborate goblet)' (Page, 1993: 466).[14] Donald Greig responded to this article a couple of years later, in a piece that brought forward some of the implications of Page's argument. Greig outlined the qualities that characterised the English style as 'clean' and 'clear':

> In reviews of the Tallis Scholars the most common adjectives used to describe the sound include 'pure', 'blend', 'clear' and 'vibrato-free' or 'vibrato-less'. It is evident, particularly in the neologistic tendencies of the last two words and in Page's own recourse to Middle English, that the struggle for appropriate terms for description of this mode of performance marks a series of assumptions about singing. Singing is often 'impure', works towards distinction and difference, is 'unclear', and, crucially, employs vibrato. It is not my concern here to question the various reports or contest the observation that singers sing without vibrato ... What concerns me is the sense that the perception of *a cappella* performance always tends towards a denial of the physical presence of the singers themselves, a sense that there is a perception of the voice as the mark of the denial of the body itself. (Greig, 1995: 141)[15]

In short, '[t]he figure around which all these adjectives cohere and the metaphor they promote and sustain is that of the angel – bodiless, genderless and asexual' (Greig: 1995: 141).

This is an acousmatic voice, but not as in Chapter 2, where it evoked the frisson of perilous enjoyment in fantasy fiction. Here it guards or attempts to guard against the body in the voice, the heard work of the singing body which Roland Barthes termed the 'grain' of the voice (1977: 181). This is a heavenly acousmatism. The 'nimbus of heaven' hung over the medieval for exponents of the pure a cappella style and their audiences, distilling pure spirit from the dross of flesh, as it did for Tolkien (Page, 1993: 468). It would be difficult to imagine Tolkien's slender, ethereal elves, with their clear voices, singing with vibrato. Like the elves of *The Lord of the Rings* who run light-footed over deep snow, English a cappella voices are 'purged of the gross' (Tolkien, 1995: 143). In such fantasies the weary body escapes itself. The soul itself could be understood as an effect of the body's self-loathing. Those listeners in Chapter 3 who heard angels singing on their favourite medieval CDs also fantasised a disembodied singer. The medieval of the a cappella party was desexualised, decorporealised. But, as I have argued in Chapter 1, what is excluded maintains a presence, troubling the calm sea of purity. It is made conspicuous by its absence. Whatever is most strenuously avoided awakens the suspicion that it is the very thing in question.

But there is a second twist. It is interesting to note that Page's Gothic Voices consort do not entirely bear out his own description of the English style, although purity is the keynote in their website publicity: 'Excellence, refinement, purity, spirituality; these are words which constantly recur in notices of Gothic Voices' concerts and recordings' (Rayfield, n.d.). In fact, the Tallis Scholars sound far more ethereal than the Gothic Voices. The nimbus of heaven does not hover over Page's ensemble. No one could call either Margaret Philpot's or Catherine King's voice disembodied or lacking in timbre, and the group sound overall is too complex, the voices too differentiated to allow the ensemble to be called 'bodiless, genderless [or] asexual'. Gothic Voices are not angelic voices.

Was Page excluding his own ensemble from his account or has Donald Greig misinterpreted him? Probably not, although Greig's interpretation does not really account for the sensuousness of three or four perfectly pitched voices singing unaccompanied medieval polyphony. But then, Page's essay does not account for it either. Individual timbres are not 'blended' out of existence in a small a cappella ensemble, yet this is the sonority Page has chosen to work with. Still less are three male and one female voice able to blend in a way which disguises their difference. If Page had wanted a blend he would have managed it better with a countertenor, as the Hilliard Ensemble does, or at least with a less distinctive female voice. It seems, however, that since purity is considered the appropriate sound for a medieval ensemble, listeners will hear it no matter what, as Melanie M. Marshall has suggested:

> [E]ven ensembles that deliberately develop a different female sound are described as sounding pure: as Kirsten Yri has noted, the full-bodied, vibrato-warmed sound of Sequentia's Vox Feminae is just as likely to be described as pure as the head-voice blend of Anonymous 4. (M. Marshall, 2015: 36)

For many traditionalists the 'male alto', following the traditions of the Oxbridge and cathedral choirs, may have been a less confronting figure than the solo countertenor, singing to the brash accompaniment of exotic instruments. Perhaps too, in the light of those traditions, the intrusions of a woman's voice might be more confronting to purity than the properly segregated all-male choir. Donald Greig reminds us that the need to exclude women 'from employment as musicians within the church [was so great as to necessitate] the most drastic expression of the law – the exercise of castration' (Greig 1995: 142). He goes on to suggest that perhaps 'the real *a cappella* renaissance has been the introduction of female voices into this realm' (142).

From this perspective Page looks less of a traditionalist. The history of the debate has many twists and turns. Greig's argument focused on the disturbance which women bring to the performance of sacred music in England and the strategies employed to 'return that difference to neutrality, to in-difference' (Greig, 1995: 143). My argument is focused on the disturbance created by the solo countertenor in medieval music. In each case, however, the body, with its impurities, its differences, its rank materiality, is central to the disturbance.

The body is not, however, disguised in the Gothic Voices. Their sound has flesh and bones in it. Yet it is the 'individualism and subjectivism' inherited from 1960s' interpretations and still lingering in the 1990s that Page and his colleagues attempted to dislodge in favour of the virtues of the English choral tradition, 'countless individual strivings for the best results in conformity to a communal discipline' (Page, 1993: 466). I am not sure what to make of the discrepancy between Page's words and the Gothic Voices sound, unless Page himself, when it came down to his own choices as a director, inclined more to earthly distinctions than to a heavenly blend; or perhaps that it is not possible to disengage the two so completely. If, as he claims, the modern lay-clerk, due to the traditions of his training, might sing as medieval singers sang (Page, 1993: 466),[16] then might it not follow that something of the body intruded for those medieval singers also? Something emerges in the sound that the words deny. The ideology of the a cappella school of thought is not incontestable. The fantasy of purity wavers.

Bruce Holsinger makes this point about the ideology of the *musica mundana*:

> [T]he 'music of the spheres', supposedly an unquestioned dimension of medieval musical thought, was in fact a dazzlingly successful but ultimately contestable *ideology* of music, one that sought to contain the visceral force of music through endlessly reiterated numerical abstraction while relying upon the sonority of the very flesh it explicitly denigrated. (Holsinger, 2001: 9; emphasis in original)

One can hear echoes of the a cappella faction's ideology in this account. For the Christian West these questions of the body, its denial and its unwelcome eruptions in music, do not go away, and when the medieval is invoked they erupt again. The fantasies of the 'voices and instruments' party were more 'off the rack' varieties, less complex and ambiguous, tending towards excess rather than denial – surplus rather than lack.

### The 'voices and instruments' fantasies

The style the 'voices and instruments' ensembles espoused was suffused with the exoticism of the mysterious East, echoes of which can be heard in Giles's words, quoted at the beginning of this chapter. Falsetto singing, along with a range of exciting and alien instruments and an improvisatory style, was supposedly imported into Europe via the crusades and the Moorish invasion of Spain.[17] After the Second World War, this hypothesis found its way into recordings such as Studio der Frühen Musik's *Chansons der Troubadours*, released in 1970.[18] Thomas Binkley, the director, was an American musicologist and, like Page, a lutenist, who tried out his theories in performances and recordings. Binkley distinguished, in medieval music, between a 'northern style' and a 'southern Arabic style' (Haines, 2001: 371). Here the north/south binary, discussed in the Introduction, is employed to distinguish northern austerity from southern flamboyance and excess.

Binkley and the group journeyed to Morocco in the 1960s, where they heard what was called *musiqa andalusiyya*.[19] Binkley contended that this music, especially a genre called *nuba*,[20] had changed little over the eight centuries since 'the time when Arabian culture exerted such a positive influence on Western Europe' (cited in Werf, 1972: 339). The *nuba* supposedly provided a hotline to the truth of medieval performance. But in fact, according to John Haines, the *Chansons der Troubadours* recording shows significant deviations from the Moroccan model, one of which was precisely the use of the countertenor voice. The Moroccan groups used a tenor. As Haines relates, such deviations were justified by the claim that the truth of past music could be gleaned from present-day folk music (Haines, 2004a: 245).[21]

There is some special pleading going on here as well. Groups like Binkley's, by joining the signifiers medieval and 'oriental', created a redoubled otherness. If oriental music didn't use a countertenor then it wasn't oriental enough for them. Similarly, if medieval music didn't use a countertenor then it wasn't medieval enough. Like the Mediæval Bæbes, Binkley's group knew better.[22] These signifiers, yoked together, and the exotic fantasies attached to them, overrode other considerations. As Parrott accused, the countertenor became obligatory in the modern performance of medieval music.

Like some members of the a cappella party, those who welcomed the countertenor appear to have associated his historically ambiguous credentials with a sexual ambiguity seen as un-English; unlike the a cappella faction, they welcomed it. Countertenors demonstrated their ambiguity in different ways. One instance of this in performance was American countertenor Richard Levitt's interpretation of Peire Vidal's 'Baron, de mon dan covit' on Studio der Frühen Musik's *Chansons der Troubadours* (1970). In some strophes he leapt up and down the octave between alto and baritone registers as if enacting his sexual or gender versatility. As well as being a love song (*canso*)

'Baron de mon dan covit' is a *gap*, a humorous boasting song, and Levitt's vocal agility, employed in the most boastful stanzas, could be read as a demonstration of his prowess, martial and sexual. One of these, stanza 4, reads in part: 'And every day my merit rises and increases; / And the king almost dies of envy, / For with ladies I dance and play' (translation Rosenberg, Switten and Le Vot, 1998: 113).[23]

Another instance is the Boston Camerata's *Tristan and Iseult*, recorded in 1987. The recording intersperses the narratives of Gottfried von Strassburg and Thomas de Bretagne with a range of roughly contemporary repertoires. The central musical texts are drawn from the anonymous Vienna MS BN 2742. Tristan was sung by countertenor Henri Ledroit. He appears as a great lover – sensitive, complex and deeply passionate.[24] In sharp contrast, the baritone King Mark (sung by Richard Morrison) is presented on this recording as crude, drunken and ignorant, interested only in sexual conquest and easily fooled by the bed trick in which Brangane is substituted for Iseult. As the narrator, at this point Gottfried von Strassburg, remarks derisively, 'For him, one woman was like another.'[25] Ledroit's luscious countertenor suggests – particularly on track 6, where Tristan wallows in helpless desire after drinking the love potion – his capacity to be overwhelmed by love and perhaps also an androgynous streak which gives him a depth of feeling associated with femininity, far removed from Mark's ignorant and brash masculinity.

Such vocal practices are best understood in the broader context of medievalist fantasies of masculinity. Alternative medieval masculinities include what one could call the aggressive 'alpha' baritone sometimes associated with the troubadour corpus,[26] and the pained, conspicuously self-effacing tenor voices of the English choral tradition.[27] These are merely tendencies, not rigid categories. The recordings noted, with the exception of Gothic Voices, are lavish with exotic instrumentation, endeavouring to create an atmosphere of masculinity appropriate to particular medievalist fantasies, through vocal and instrumental timbre and expression.

At their best, both traditions, the a cappella and the voices and instruments, produced magnificent recordings. The glory of their performances did not rest on the correctness of their hypotheses, although it undoubtedly benefited from their deep and painstaking research. But their work profited still more from the passion, the seriousness of intent that those hypotheses gave their performance. Their theories, or perhaps their medieval fantasies, inspired them.[28] Since the time of these recordings and conversations, solo countertenors have, by and large, departed the serious medieval music recording scene for the Baroque, which allows them far greater scope for virtuosity. Many of them never investigated medieval song as soloists.

### 'Distant relatives of the castrati'?

Why was the countertenor chosen to personify the 'medieval-oriental' other in music? To respond to this question, I turn now to the reception accorded the earliest twentieth-century countertenor to step out of the ranks of the English cathedral altos onto the concert stage, Alfred Deller. In his biography he is quoted on questions which were 'constantly' put to him by the curious: 'The first, which is of a personal, not to say intimate nature, I leave to the imagination' (cited in Hardwick and Hardwick, 1980: 75). What the question was can be ascertained by this anecdote. The composer Michael Tippett sponsored Deller's first appearance in the prestigious National Gallery series, sometime in the 1940s. Tippett had some misgivings about the audience response and decided to introduce Deller:

> I told them that I was very pleased to present Alfred Deller, the possessor of this remarkable countertenor voice, and that I was very pleased to hear from him that he was already training his two sons to sing, too. It seemed to do the trick. There were no murmurs when he started to sing. (Hardwick and Hardwick, 1980: 97)

The inference could not be clearer; the audience had to be reassured that Deller could father sons. Sometimes the question was put more plainly: The countertenor Michael Chance tells the story of a French woman, who, upon hearing Deller sing, exclaimed 'Monsieur, vous êtes eunuque [a eunuch]' – to which Deller, quick off the mark, replied, 'I think you mean "unique" madam' (1999). The reference to castration is also explicit in countertenor James Bowman's impassioned plea: '[P]lease don't confuse castrati with countertenors. Countertenors sing in the falsetto range, which is where our voices feel most relaxed. Singing countertenor felt like my natural form of vocal expression; anyone who talks of "strain" on the voice, or something unnatural, is misguided' (Bowman, 2009). Peter Giles argues in the same vein:

> The fact that we sing at a higher pitch than the other adult male voices does not instantly make us a peculiar breed apart – distant relatives of the castrati. There is no 'mystique'. We are just singers who, for one reason or another, have preferred to develop the upper reaches of our voices. (Giles, 1982: vii)

Countertenors are just ordinary guys! Giles also insists: '[T]his very high *natural* male voice ... is utterly normal and its use is not at all "quirky"' (Giles, 1982: 73; emphasis in original). It is a curious position to take up. On the one hand there is a strongly felt need to rehabilitate the countertenor and distance him from any suspicion of sexual ambiguity. On the other, this ambiguity, as Giles makes clear, is itself the source of his perceived mystique. There is a discernible ambivalence, for instance, in Giles's references to falsetto singing in pop music:

> While the ... pop world has undeniably welcomed the male falsetto, it is, in my opinion, for the wrong reasons! True, we should rejoice that youngsters seem no longer 'hung up' on the *sexuality* of vocal pitch. But surely what they are celebrating, even flaunting, is sexual *ambiguity* for its own purposes. (Giles, 1982: 5; emphasis in original)

The countertenor must be normalised, made sexually unambiguous; he must shake off the legacy of the castrato, but at the risk of losing the mystique which, at least in part, accounted for his success.

Countertenors differ in their response to their perceived sexual ambiguity. Phillippe Jaroussky apparently revels in the mixed reactions he receives from the fans who 'follow him round':

> Most are women in their forties and fifties: 'I seem to awaken their maternal instincts'. When they bring their husbands along, it's often a different story: 'Middle-aged men can find countertenors repulsive, an affront to nature. I love the way we polarise people's reactions.' (Church, 2011)[29]

David Daniels seemed to be trying to have it both ways, keeping the ambiguous allure while still proclaiming his essential masculinity:

> I don't think my voice is feminine though I understand that's probably the easiest way to describe it. Anyone watching me produce the sound

does, I'm sure, pick up on an essentially masculine quality. ... I hear two conflicting things when people talk about my singing, first, what a masculine, powerful sound it is; and second, how beautiful it is, like listening to a soprano or a mezzo. I hope that both are true. (D. Daniels, 1985)

Such pleas by countertenors to be distinguished from castrati actually draw attention to the perceived link between the two, as comments like Jaroussky's make clear. Giles himself made them part of the countertenor's history by devoting sections to them in both books, in the fond hope that 'this brief section on the castrati will have cleared up definitively any lingering misunderstanding of the difference between the counter tenor and the eunuchoid voice' (Giles, 1982: 80). Clearly the distinction has been difficult to press home to audiences and commentators, as Giles's slightly hectoring tone testifies. The (Un)official Countertenor Page online (Betthauser, 1998) also devotes a section to the castrati, as does the 'Castrati and Countertenors' website: 'This page has been established as a source of information on the Castrati singers of the sixteenth, seventeenth and eighteenth centuries, and the modern "countertenors" who strive to recreate their music' (Lee, 2016). Even more galling is this comment by Peter Gammond: 'Countertenors are the ones who are noteworthy for their inability to sound anything like castrati' (Gammond, n.d.). In this reversal it is the countertenors who suffer by the comparison as mere unsuccessful counterfeits of the castrati.

Evidence of the perceived relationship can be found in other quarters, for instance Elizabeth Randell's article for *Opera News* in July 1996. A picture of the castrato Farinelli is juxtaposed by two contemporary countertenors and captioned: 'Eighteenth-century castrato sensation Farinelli, and two of his heirs, countertenors Drew Minter ... and Derek Lee Ragin' (Randell, 1996: 24). In one sense, how can they be anything but heirs when they take over roles written for castrati? For instance, Drew Minter recorded *Arias for Senesino* for Harmonia Mundi, 'featuring music from Handel's *Giulio Cesare*, *Rodelinda* and *Orlando*' (Randell, 1996: 53). Senesino was a famous castrato. Randell also discusses Philip Glass's opera *Akhnaten*. In the opening act, Akhnaten, the title role written for countertenor, 'is revealed naked as a hermaphrodite, with male genitalia and female breasts'. He sings in a voice higher than his wife's (Randell, 1996: 25).

For twentieth- and twenty-first century audiences, it was the notoriety of the castrati which played the largest part in that mixture of fascination and revulsion which greeted the solo countertenor on his return, and perhaps added an element to the distaste of the 'authenticists'. Journalist Heidi Koelz confessed to an 'objectionable' fascination with the countertenor voice: 'In this music [Philippe Jaroussky singing Anfione in Agostino Steffani's *Niobe, Regina di Tebe*] I had found an unexpected pleasure, one still tethered to another time – and one that, to be honest, hadn't lost the tang of its objectionable origins' (Koelz, 2013: 225).

The castrati, those disavowed 'distant relatives', carried the same whiff of oriental barbarity in the imagination as Glass's *Akhnaten*. Giles relates that castrati were employed first in Byzantium: 'The practice spread ... to Europe and continued into Medieval times and beyond' (*c.*1994: 391), a similar narrative to that which he offers for the countertenor. It is his insistent allusions to the East that interest me. Piotr O. Scholz argues that castration was 'not a marginal phenomenon limited to one particular culture' but an almost universal activity (Scholz, 2001: 53). Castration has no peculiarly Eastern flavour, except in fantasies where the exoticism of the Orient, blended with the exoticism of castration, combines the flicker of forbidden enjoyments with the displacement of responsibility, a typical Western move.[30]

Much ink has been spilled on the nature of the allure of the castrati. They were adored by both men and women and reviled in equal measure. Sam Abel suggests that in their English heyday popular discourse focused on their appeal to women, to the perplexity and discomfort of 'normal' men (Abel, 1996: 139). He cites a satirical poem by George Bickham (*c.*1738), in which a woman is heard to lament for the castrato Senesino, the beloved who is 'neither ... Man nor ... Woman [but] a shadow of something, a Sex without Name' (Abel, 1996: 139). According to Fernanda Eberstadt of the *New York Times*, in the eighteenth century '[w]hen Farinelli – whose voice spanned almost three octaves – appeared onstage, an Englishwoman supposedly cried, "One God, one Farinelli!" and others fainted' (Eberstadt, 2010: n.p.). It seems the castrati were the rock stars of their day.

It was in the period of their decline that the castrati were more overtly homosexualised. Then it was the men who were depicted as captivated. In a cartoon from 1825 it is a man who exclaims 'He is quite perfect in his *parts*', to which the woman responds: 'Not quite!' (Abel, 1996: 142). Dorothy Keyser notes that '[t]o baroque society they appear to have been perceived as blank canvases on which either sexual role could be projected ... the ambiguous figure of the castrato was endlessly fascinating' (cited in Dame, 1994: 143). Here is the fantasy of ambiguity again, the polymorphous fantasy of a sexual partner who does not oblige the fantasist to choose. The nameless sex that can be fantasised as neither can also be fantasised as both.

Dame cites Roland Barthes's (1974) work *S/Z* on 'the sex without name': 'In Barthes's vocabulary, the castrato is either the neuter, a negative qualification, as neither man nor woman; or he is positively qualified as a composite, as both man and woman, in fact as androgyne' (Dame, 1994: 141). But it is not either-or for Barthes. The ambiguity itself is ambiguous, not just an ambiguity between man and woman but between both and neither, as Dame's citation from *S/Z* makes clear (141). Barthes's comment is that Zambinella, the castrato in Balzac's *Sarrasine*, is 'the blind and mobile flaw in this [symbolic] field; he moves back and forth between active and passive; castrated, he castrates' (Barthes, 1974: 36). The field in question 'is not that of the biological sexes; it is that of castration: *castrating/castrated, active/passive*' (36; emphasis in original). Barthes' characterisation is reminiscent of a self-portrait by photographer Robert Mapplethorpe with a bull-whip inserted into his anus (1978). He is holding the whip; *penetrated, he penetrates*. In this image the opposition active/passive cannot be maintained. Mapplethorpe's mastery is complete but it is self-mastery (to employ a deviant usage of the term). He is the lion-tamer and the lion, supremely dangerous as both. He snarls around at the viewer, like a lion disturbed over his kill. The point is that Barthes's Zambinella, in his alternation, cannot be squarely categorised as both sexes or as neither.

The names of famous castrati were associated with lurid sexual scandals. Anne Rice's novel *Cry to Heaven* explores, says Abel, 'the transgressive nature of the castrato's sexuality':

> The castrated singer, his transgression permanently imprinted on his body, is released from the restrictive sexual norms of society. ... Cut off from sexual normality, the castrato teases his audience, saying, 'In my bold deviance I have access to sexual secrets about which normal bodies can only dream.' (Abel, 1996: 131)

Citing Joseph Roach (1989), Abel argues that the body of the castrato 'became a site for the display of sexual ambiguity and free play. The sexual power of the castrati ... arose from their marginality as neither male nor female' (Abel, 1996: 136). My sense is that the castrato's ambiguity, which, to some extent, the countertenor has inherited, chimes with the ambiguity of the 'medieval', the unnamed age in the middle with its acquired oriental overtones. Perhaps, in fantasy, a slippage between those two ambiguities creates an enhanced field for erotic reveries.

Onstage the focus shifts. Here the castrati sang 'with extreme virtuosity but little if any emotion', according to Pietro Francesco Tosi (*Observations*, published 1723), himself a castrato (cited in Giles, *c*.1994: 394). One of the last castrati, Domenico Mustafa (1829–1912), says Giles, taught his students 'Sinus Tone Production [to] achieve the eerie, sexless, disembodied notes which were [his] specialty' (*c*.1994: 396). Paul Henry Lang spoke of the castrato as an 'impersonal instrument' (cited in Freitas, 2003: 196). 'Unemotional', 'sexless', 'eerie', 'disembodied', 'impersonal', 'inhuman', 'instrumental', 'angelic': these are the adjectives in play; a truly acousmatic voice, therefore, dissociated from a bearer.[31]

These adjectives are oddly reminiscent of those used to describe the sound of English singers of the a cappella school. It is strange to find the same qualities applied to the castrato. To return to Donald Greig's account of the English a cappella sound:

> 'Vibrato-free' is a term that marks the denial of the body in the voice ...; the voice is (impossibly!) not produced at all, but emanates, as it were, from the space above the vocal chords, from the throat or head alone. 'Clear' – as synonyms such as 'unblemished'. 'transparent' and 'cleansed' suggest – is concerned with images of non-materiality, or of materiality purged to a degree that negates the terrestrial and corporeal. 'Blend' is concerned with reduction ... of many to ... one, non-identifiable source ... 'Pure' connotes images of innocence, of virginity, of the non-corporeal production of sound. The figure around which all these adjectives cohere and the metaphor they promote and sustain is that of the angel. (Greig, 1995: 141)

The vocal style of the English a cappella groups was also, like the castrato's, considered unemotional. Emotion smacks too much of the body. Page remarks that where European critics complained of the English style, it was on the grounds that it was phlegmatic;

he cites one Spanish critic who deplored an English performance as 'lacking in "temperamento mediterráneo, de color, de entusiasmo"' (Page: 1993: 461). 'White' is a term sometimes applied to the vibrato-less voice. Certainly, the colours of a voice without vibrato are more subtle.

In my work as a singing teacher, I have noticed that some of the singers who chose early music repertoire were those who wished to avoid passion in their singing. It is noticeable too that when passion wells up into the song the voice may move into its vibrato, the beat of the body. That is often where a singer's voice is unmistakeably his or hers, where it releases what is specifically its own, but, paradoxically, also where it can carry the listener beyond any question of ownership, because vibrato may take the voice beyond the intentions of the singer to interpret the music. The body cannot be entirely owned. It is bound to operate according to its own physical make-up and cannot be entirely repressed. And, like the speaking voice, the singing voice is affected by the singer's emotions. In this respect the voice is of the Real.

The similarities between the English a cappella ensembles and the castrato, as reported by observers, are so close as to resemble two sides of the same coin. This similarity suggests that the fantasies associated with each are not as dissimilar as they first appeared. Both contain the ambiguity – the confusion of categories – that the disembodied voice brings with it, but while the fantasies associated with the English a cappella style come down on the side of *neither*, fantasies of the castrato come down on the side of *both*. The first emphasises lack (as disembodiment), the second, excess. This is an incomplete distinction, however, because both lack and excess challenge the sanctity of categories in the same way. They will not allow the set to close.

It appears, therefore, that the 'angelic', 'sexless' purity encouraged by the authenticists has a roundabout affinity with sex, gender and the body after all. My own experience bears this out. When I first became aware of the early music revival in the 1970s, I was struck by what appeared, to my ignorant ears, to be a form of vocal cross-dressing, a little like the boy dressed up as a girl dressed up as a boy who appears in some of Shakespeare's comedies. At the same time as I heard men singing (as I then thought) like women, I was hearing women who sounded as if they were attempting to remove any marks of femaleness and even of adulthood from their voices. To my ears they sounded like boys. I was left with the impression that to be in that scene a woman had to sound like a boy and a man had to sound like a woman, but in each case, not quite. They did not meet at the androgynous centre of a sexual spectrum. If that were so their voices would have sounded more alike. That image of a centre is inert, whereas my sense was of something dynamic. The impression of a border crossing remained – a sense of drag. I have since learned to appreciate the special qualities of the countertenor voice and also the subtle timbres of the vibrato-free, or almost vibrato-free, female voice. But there is nothing asexual in these gender crossings, in whichever direction they go. Both contain that frisson of the *unheimlich* produced by the both and neither, the uncategorisable. It is another version of the *in between* which continues to appear in the course of these investigations.

As well as the qualities mentioned, the castrato voice had tremendous power, attested by many observers. Charles Burney gives an account of a nightly contest onstage between the famous castrato Farinelli and a trumpeter who accompanied him. Farinelli wins with ease after an amazing display of virtuosity and endurance. Here we are offered a different kind of odyssey narrative: what the castrato's body has lost is recaptured in his voice (Abel, 1996: 130). Abel, again speaking of Rice's novel, writes: 'To portray heroic and powerful sexuality, the singer had to become less than a man' (Abel, 1996: 131). He sings the potency he lacks. Tolkien's elf Legolas comes to mind (see Chapter 3) who, by renouncing, retained what he lost. Roland Barthes makes this point: '[A]s though, by selective hypertrophy, sexual density were obliged to abandon the rest of the body and lodge in the throat' (Barthes, 1974: 109). That is the odyssey granted the castrato by observers and historians, made poignant by his sacrifice.

Another quality associated with the castrato voice was its penetration. Charles Burney recounted the amazing vocal cure effected on King Philip V of Spain in 1737 by Farinelli's voice (Burney, cited in King, 2006: 563). Thomas King notes that '[p]ost-Cartesian theory held that music cured melancholia by its mechanical vibration of the body machine [and that] the particular efficacy of the castrato's voice was its power to penetrate' (King, 2006: 563). Again, the castrato supposedly undergoes an exchange of phallic potency between genitals and voice. His is a cosmic potency diffused as vibrations through the receiver's entire body, as it was for Balzac's Sarrasine, who, listening to the castrato Zambinella, 'seemed to hear through every pore' (Barthes, 1974: 237).

But *what* has the castrato lost? Roger Freitas complains of writers who 'while recognizing that European castration normally involved only the removal of the testicles … have written about castrati as if they had also lost all their phallic significance' (2003: 199). He quotes Beth Kowalski-Wallace in this context: '[T]he existence of the castrato forces the issue of the significance of the non-phallus' (cited in Freitas, 2003: 199).[32] But it is not simply a matter of loss, as Freitas suggests; far from it. He blames misreadings of Lacan for this confusion, but Kowalski-Wallace has read Lacan better than Freitas. Freitas speaks of approaches like hers as viewing the castrato simply as 'void' (Freitas, 2003: 199), but for Lacan the phallus becomes significant in its absence. It is the phallus that the woman does *not* have that matters (Lacan, 1977a: 289), because by its inscription of absence it inaugurates the possibility of language. In his *Object Relation Seminar* Lacan observes: '[T]he contrasting couple of presence and absence, the plus-minus connotation gives us the first element of a symbolic order' (2020: 60). It is a symbolic phallus, derived from anatomical differences between men and women but raised to a different level.

This phallus, he continues, in the same seminar,

> is a symbolic phallus, in so far as it's in its very nature to present in exchange as an absence, as an absence that functions as such. Indeed, everything that can be tralatitious[33] in symbolic exchange is always something that is as much absence as presence. It is made in such a way that it has a sort of fundamental alternation, which means that, having appeared at one point, it disappears then to reappear at another. In other words, it circulates, leaving behind it the sign of its absence at the point from which it came. (Lacan, 2020: 161–2)

This passage captures something of the castrato's symbolic (non) phallus. It plays the game of language and suffers the same affliction. It circulates, 'leaving behind it the sign of its absence at the point from which it comes'. Its absence (from where it belongs) is a presence and, conversely, its presence (in the voice) is infected with the absence by which it is achieved. Language always exceeds the terms of its binary agreement, carrying traces of its past transactions along with it.[34] An alternation and, consequently, a fundamental uncertainty are produced.

This uncertainty is the castrato's vaunted secret; it is *we* who are forever uncertain as to what he is, what he *means*, since meaning is so entangled with sexual difference. He cannot be categorised, and thus he becomes a site for fantasies of 'sexual secrets about which normal bodies can only dream'.[35] It is in this alternation (noted by Barthes) that we can find something of the castrato's seductive powers offstage and on. He became for the seduced what Lacan calls a fetish character. Lacan, drawing on Freud, argues that the fetish object 'represent[s] the phallus qua absent, [the] symbolic phallus' (Lacan, 2020: 146)

Some anecdotes of the castrati suggest something reminiscent of the alternation described by Lacan. Casanova, for instance, wrote of a meeting with a castrato in his memoir.

> An abbé with an attractive face walked in. At the appearance of his hips, I took him for a girl in disguise, and I said so to the abbé Gama; but the latter told me that it was Beppino della Mamana, a famous *castrato*. The abbé called him over, and told him, laughing, that I had taken him for a girl. The impudent creature, looking fixedly at me, told me that if I liked he would prove that I was right, or that I was wrong. (cited in Hardwick and Hardwick, 1980: 86)[36]

Lacan speaks of such a magical alternation with reference to fetishism, a term he associates with *fée* ('fairy'; *féerie* is enchantment). Lacan is relating the story of Jacques Cazotte's novel *Le diable amoureux*. The devil, here a 'fetish character' for Lacan,

> becomes [for the narrator] a charming young man, and, then, a charming young woman. Furthermore, until the end they intermingle with total ambiguity. This beloved protagonist ... becomes for a while the stunning source of the narrator's every happiness, ... the properly magical satisfaction of everything which he may wish for. (Lacan, 2020: 161–2)[37]

If it is granted that the castrato offered the world something like this gratifying fantasy, then the question remains: to what extent does his heir, the countertenor, offer the same fantasy? With him the questions are different but related. One asks of the castrato his 'forbidden secrets': what he is, what he means, what he offers and what he enjoys, and one fantasises the answers. For the countertenor the uncertainty arises at a different point; his 'secret' is different: listeners ask of the countertenor (not necessarily out loud) first if he *is* castrated (as Deller was asked), and perhaps, if not, why he sings in a register still unusual for adult Western males and associated, in the West, with both femininity and castration. This is something like the second question put to Deller: when (I think a 'why' is covertly included) did he decide to become a countertenor? (Hardwick and Hardwick, 1980: 74). That is to ask a question about his enjoyment.

Things have changed in recent decades. The countertenor voice becomes, as we acclimatise to it, less alien and therefore less potent as a site for fantasy. The timbre has changed, too. It is less eerie, less acousmatic, more human and more idiosyncratic. We can hear a vocal agent; a body is present, one gendered less ambiguously masculine than the 'sexless', angelic or demonic instrument of the past. Masculinity expands to (almost) contain it; the ambiguity is no longer perfect. But there was until recently (and is, even now, for some), still room for the transgressive fantasies that even an imperfect ambiguity generates. Jaroussky's mixed reception bears witness to that.

The same questions are still being asked and will probably continue to be. Witness this response to Andreas Scholl's 'Habañera' from *Carmen* on YouTube (Scholl, 2013):

> Scholl's not gay. Whereas some countertenors are 'proud of being gay,' Scholl is not one of them. He is happily married to a woman and is a father. He grew up singing as a boy soprano in church and simply continued singing that way when he got older. Nothing to do with his sexual orientation. It's best not to make assumptions. (rmm413c, n.d.)

A glance at other comments on the site suggests that, since some listeners are so keen to emphasise their own unconcern, there might be some grounds for concern. Consider, for instance, these vehement responses to earlier postings on the same site: 'Who cares gay or not, his voice is crystal clear and arias are there to sing.

... Why travesty??? Music does not have gender, and this aria is written for high voice, so what is the problem?'; and 'why all these comments? if you are gay you can sing better maybe???or if you are married to a woman your voice sounds better??? Stupid discussions.'

These more recent postings, the first reminiscent of Tippett's attempts to reassure Deller's audience back in the 1940s, suggest that not much has changed. If negation is the hallmark of repression, as Freud argued (see Chapter 1), and the repressed is the desire for what is enjoyable but prohibited, such desires still operate. As before, anxieties about the countertenor's sexuality are so entangled with matters of musical taste and savoir faire that it is difficult to separate them, but musical matters can serve to mask sexual anxieties. If a commentator alludes in any way to the brute fact that the Habañera is a woman's song (and not just any woman but Carmen, that most seductive of songstresses), they risk condemnation both as a musical ignoramus and as harbouring anti-gay sentiments or, conversely, expressing an inappropriately sexual enthusiasm for Scholl's performance. The only safe course is to concentrate solely on the singer's skill and to deny all interest in his sexuality – a difficult matter when Carmen is doing her utmost to highlight it. There are some less savvy comments, including those which provoked these rebuttals, for instance: 'It's so wrong it's right', and this one: 'Is this a tranny Carmen?' Not everyone is anxious and perhaps anonymity allows the expression of politically incorrect comments, but some commentators seem unwilling to risk the reputations, even of their internet avatars.[38]

Scholl's Habañera is a more overt provocation to musical or political correctness than anything heard at the scholarly end of the medieval music recording spectrum. Nonetheless, the countertenor's widespread presence, representation and reception in the performance of medieval music in the late twentieth century suggests that such fantasies are still interwoven, for many, with nostalgic fantasies of the medieval with its 'oriental' undertow, and that these fantasies combine to create an atmosphere of forbidden enjoyments available to the listener. Like the castrato, the countertenor can still, for some, be imagined as saying: 'In my bold deviance I have access to sexual secrets about which normal bodies can only dream' (Abel, 1996: 13).

## Notes

1 Some parts of this chapter build on my research (2016b), 'The Medieval Voice'. Aspects of the discussion on authenticity in medieval music also share some ground with Dell (2019b): 'A Single, True, Certain Authenticity'.
2 See also Renée Trilling: 'Because of its dialectical structure, nostalgia can point both to a place of absolute alterity and a place that we recognise as our lost home' (2011: 220).
3 David Munrow made a similar point (perfectly true) in the liner notes of *Music of the Crusades* (1971): 'The returning Crusaders brought back with them some of the Saracen instruments, new to Europe' (cited in Haines, 2004a: 248).
4 Edward Said's 'haunting memories' bring to mind some of the contradictions of nostalgia in its post-colonial guise; in Renato Rosaldo's words, the 'mood of nostalgia [which] makes racial domination appear innocent and pure' (Rosaldo, 1989: 107). Rosaldo continues: 'Curiously enough, agents of colonialism – officials, constabulary officers, missionaries, and other figures ... often display nostalgia for the colonized culture as it was "traditionally" (that is, when they first encountered it). The peculiarity of their yearning, of course, is that agents of colonialism long for the very forms of life they intentionally altered or destroyed' (107–8).
5 For a detailed account of such prohibitions see Simon Ravens (2014: 14–37); and also Andrew Parrott (2015: 46–121).
6 See Haines's section in *Medieval Song*, entitled 'Women's Song' (2010: 44–50).
7 See Ravens (2014) on the difficulties of assessing the evidence of prohibitions and the either/or logic employed by both those who accepted the presence of a voice 'akin to a countertenor' in medieval music and those who denied it. Ravens considers that '"yes or no" answers to such complex questions are simplifications'. He adds that 'In the ongoing battle to establish or discount the place of the falsettist in northern Europe during the Middle Ages ... the unwitting words of these clerics have been dragged into both front lines' (Ravens, 2014: 20–1). As he is intimating, neither side has been completely disinterested.
8 See chapters 1 and 2 in Leech-Wilkinson (2002).
9 See Livingston's account of the authenticity debates in her essay on music revivals, where she notes certain ideologies shared by music revivals in general, one being a preoccupation with authenticity (1999: 76–7). See also Elizabeth Randell Upton's essay (2012) 'Concepts of Authenticity' on the similarities between the early music and folk revivals

170  Fantasies of music in nostalgic medievalism

of the twentieth century. John Haines has also, in a 2014 publication, commented on 'just how closely related are the revivals of early music and of folk music' (2014b: 84).

10  Binkley adopted what Howard Mayer Brown called an 'ethno-musicological approach … rather than relying solely on written documentation from medieval Europe' (Brown, 1988: 49).

11  See also my essay (Dell, 2019b), 'A Single, True, Certain Authenticity', for an account of the wars waged around authenticity in the early music scene of the 1970s and 1980s.

12  See also Leech-Wilkinson (2000; 2002); and Haines (2004a; 2004b).

13  See also Dell (2019b).

14  See also Dell (2019b).

15  See Yri (2008b: 9) on the kind of voice production that results in a disembodied sound.

16  See also Page (1993: 454): '[W]e proceed to the theory that, in certain respects [English singers performing medieval and renaissance polyphony a cappella] represent a particularly convincing postulate about the performing priorities of the original singers'. See also where Page claims that 'medieval singers regarded an a cappella performance as ideal for their most serious and worthwhile songs – the High Style lyrics of the troubadours and troubadours' (459).

17  John Haines notes nineteenth-century versions of Orientalism in accounts of medieval music; for instance, in Walter Scott's *Ivanhoe*, 'wild barbaric music … of Eastern origin' is played at a tournament (Scott, 1819: 81). Rebecca's Palestinian songs were 'strangely sweet' (Scott, 1819: 311).

18  The hypothesis was current in musicology in the 1930s. Orientalism was an ingredient in the work of Arnold Schering and Marius Schneider, musicologists of the 1930s supporting the voices and instruments hypothesis. See Leech-Wilkinson (2002: 64–6). By the end of the 1950s, the oriental approach had already taken off with the New York Pro Musica's *Play of Daniel*, using exotic Arabian percussion instruments (Haines, 2001: 370).

19  In this they were following in the footsteps of Arnold Dolmetsch, who, with his family-ensemble, made the journey to Morocco in the late 1920s, as John Haines relates (2014a: 77).

20  The *nuba* was 'a monophonic setting of several poems with instrumental interludes' (Haines, 2001: 372).

21  See also Haines's 'Antiquarian Nostalgia': 'Folk music, as [musical antiquarians] saw it, transmitted orally what written sources could not: the early music of the West in its most primitive and naïve form, untainted by the literacy of modern print' (Haines, 2014b: 90). See also Elizabeth Randell Upton: 'To some extent, musical revivals of

pre-Classical music function as a kind of temporal exoticism exchanging imaginative travel in time for travel in space in the minds of listeners' (2012: n.p.).
22 See Yri, however, who saw Binkley's Arabic interpretations of European music as arising from painstaking research rather than mere glamorising Orientalism (2010: 279).
23 For a recording of Levitt singing 'Baron, de mon dan covit', see Studio der Frühen Musik (2013).
24 This lai (Arthurian so-called), 'La u jou fui dedans la mer' (Anon., Vienna, BN 2542, lai 16), is the second song on track 6 of the CD (Boston Camerata, 1987) and can be heard on a YouTube extract (Boston Camerata, 2011a).
25 King Mark (Richard Morrison) sings 'Bache bene venies' (*Carmina Burana* 200) (Boston Camerata, 1987: track 9) with a male chorus in a drinking bout before retiring to bed on his wedding night, supposedly with Iseult, really with Brangane. It is the second song (starting 3:07) on a YouTube extract (Boston Camerata, 2011b).
26 Martin Best provides a good example. He sings Marcabru's 'Pax in nomine domini', available from YouTube (Martin Best Mediaeval Ensemble, 2015), originally recorded 1983; see also the Clemencic Consort's 'Ich was ein chint so wolgetan' (*Carmina Burana* 185), available from YouTube (Clemencic Consort, 2011), originally recorded 1974.
27 One example is English tenor Rogers Covey-Crump, singing 'Fins cuers enamourée' by Wibers Kaukesel on the Gothic Voices' album *Songs of the Trouvères* (1995: track 17), and 'Tuit mi penser' by Guillaume de Machaut on the Gothic Voices album *Mirror of Narcissus* (1987: track 4).
28 European groups, for instance the vocal and instrumental ensembles Alla Francesca and Ensemble Gilles Binchois, evidently have not felt the need to stick rigidly to the dichotomy produced by anglophone theory. They sing faultless a cappella polyphony but also allow themselves some licence in the areas forbidden by the a cappella purists: a range of instruments, instrumental improvisation and some vocal and instrumental arrangements of fourteenth-century polyphony.
29 See also Andreas Scholl's comment on a 2010 'gender-bending' concert with Jaroussky consisting of 'doing things we're not supposed to do' (Service, 2012: n.p.). The two were engaged on a programme of Purcell duets with Jaroussky's Ensemble Artaserse.
30 Muhammad 'specifically condemned castration' in Islam, although his directive seems not to have been fully obeyed: see Patterson (1982: 316).

31 Deller offered an interesting coda to these remarks, suggesting a similar impersonality on the part of the singer: 'I am not Alfred Deller, singer, performing a song; but Alfred Deller being used, if you like, to communicate with the listener' (cited in Hardwick and Hardwick, 1980: 119). There is, however, perhaps an element of this impersonality or loss of self in any remarkable performance, as discussed in Chapter 3.

32 Freitas cites Roland Barthes and Joseph Roach in the same context.

33 'Tralatitious' means 'having a character, force, or significance transferred or derived from something extraneous' (Merriam-Webster, 2022: s.v. tralatitious).

34 Compare with Derrida: '[T]he meaning of meaning ... is infinite implication, the indefinite referral of signifier to signifier ... [I]ts force is a certain pure and infinite equivocality which gives signified meaning no ... rest but engages it in its own economy so that it always signifies again and differs' (Derrida, 2005: 29).

35 For Lacan, the phallus, although it is what allows signification, has no signified of its own; it is what he terms, following Saul Kripke, a 'rigid designator', a pure signifier which does not signify anything.

36 Other translations of the same passage give the last phrase differently: 'he will serve me as a boy or a girl, whichever I choose' (André, 2006: 29). I have preferred the first, possibly euphemistic, account, because it reflects more of that radical uncertainty, that alternation of presence and absence, than the second, more straightforward assertion. The first addresses the very being of the castrato. It carries a flavour of paradox, of an almost magical alternation between boy and girl. The second, more mundanely, merely outlines the services he will provide.

37 In the 1994 film *Farinelli*, directed by Gérard Corbiau, Farinelli's 'voice' is constructed from the voices of a countertenor and a soprano, electronically fused. The castrato's perfect ambiguity is achieved by high tech!

38 These comments on Scholl's Habañera on YouTube are no longer accessible, although the recording is (Scholl, 2013). A similar dispute arises in response to a YouTube video of Edson Cordeiro singing Habañera from *Carmen* (Cordeiro, 2009). See in particular the heated exchange between 'Behoth77' and 'baritonebynight'.

# 5

# The call of the mother: Music for myth and fantasy in two Arthurian films

This chapter examines music in two pieces of Arthurian cinema: John Boorman's film, *Excalibur* (1981) and the television miniseries *Mists of Avalon* (2001, hereafter *Mists*), directed by Uli Edel. Both present aspects of the Arthurian myth. *Excalibur*, written by Boorman, presents a version of the traditional story, partly based on Thomas Malory's *Le Morte d'Arthur*. Boorman gives prominence to mythic aspects of the Arthuriad, such as that 'the land and the king are one'. *Mists* alters the perspective to that of the various women connected with the story: Morgaine (as narrator and character), Igraine, Morgause and Viviane. *Mists* also highlights the tussle between paganism (mainly feminine) and Christianity (mainly masculine) in the midst of which the story is set.

Medievalist film, like the medievalist fantasy novel, supports the fantasy that somewhere or somewhen lies the blissful home from which we have been so cruelly torn and to which we long to return. In this chapter the ambiguous *space between* represents a kind of womb. Nostalgic fantasies of non-separation, a harmonious time or place at peace and in tune with nature, abounded in the New Age and have not waned in the present. These two screen shows, and their music, played a role in fostering fantasies like these.[1] But such fantasies could also take a terrifying turn. This chapter throws a light on the tensions lurking beneath the nostalgic surface – the horror that accompanies fantasies of return.

The fantasy of return to the mother is, as I have argued in earlier chapters, an attempt to evade what Julia Kristeva calls the 'castration' that language imposes on the speaking being. For Kristeva, this 'castration' by language is the imaginary construction of a radical operation which constitutes the symbolic field and all beings inscribed therein. This operation constitutes ... language as a separation from a presumed state of nature. (Kristeva, 1981: 23)

The assumption of a previous state of perfect attunement with nature (the garden of Eden fantasy) from which we have fallen, and for which we long, is the foundational fantasy of many films. *Avatar* (2009), mentioned in Chapter 1, is a prime example of the cinematic fantasy of an unfallen Edenic home where the inhabitants are completely at one, both with other beings and with the planet itself.[2] These impossible amalgams of animal and speaking being are truly at home as we humans can never be. For humanity, with its damaged instincts, the proper functioning of those instincts is an aspect of the longing for Paradise: the capacity to truly inhabit nature, to know as the animals know, what to do and how to be in the world. Paradise is in the foreground of *Avatar*; its theme song, 'I see you', carries the line: 'Your life shines the way into paradise' (Cameron, 2009).

The music of film supports the paradisal fantasy scenario in its own particular way. Claudia Gorbman, in *Unheard Music*, observes that film music 'lessens defences against the fantasy structures to which [film] narrative provides access [increasing] the spectator's susceptibility to suggestion' (Gorbman, 1987: 5). Theodor Adorno and Hanns Eisler take a darker view. For them, film music acts as a kind of drug in its 'intoxicating, harmfully irrational function' (Adorno and Eisler, 2005: 15). Film music can manipulate us in this way because it works unnoticed, hence *Unheard Melodies*, Gorbman's title, adapted from Keats: film music is unheard. Musicologists like Gorbman write so as to make it heard for the purposes of analysis.[3] She describes in her introduction how, after a moment of lucidity when the soundtrack enters the 'foreground of consciousness',

> we drop off, become re-invested in the story again. Then the music is 'working' once more, masking its own insistence and sawing away in the backfield of consciousness. (Gorbman, 1987: 1)

This movement of music to the backfield of consciousness occurs in both *Mists* and *Excalibur*, but in the Arthurian tradition there is something else at work, something which militates against the lost world fantasy that ensnares the nostalgic. This countering operation could be called myth, and it has its own music, whose presence is particularly evident in *Excalibur*. In Chapter 1, myth appeared as the numinous conveyed in a particular kind of narrative. Here I wish to further refine the idea of myth, and separate it out more definitively from the narrative of fantasy.

Writing on George MacDonald, C. S. Lewis separated the 'mythopoeic art' of which, he said, MacDonald was the master, from the words which tell it (Lewis, 1986: ix). He argued there that myth is not fundamentally a matter of words at all, but of a pattern of events (ix). Lacan says something quite similar in his essay 'The Neurotic's Individual Myth': 'Myth is what provides a discursive form for something that cannot be transmitted through the definition of truth ... It can only express truth – and this, in a mythic mode' (Lacan, 1979: 407). In his seminar of 1960–61, *Transference*, Lacan effectively glosses this remark by saying that what manifests in the Real can only be spoken of as myth (2015: 52). His dictum, that the truth can only be half said, is another way of articulating this. Myth is the only way to express a truth that cannot be fully spoken. For Lewis, what myth expresses via its patterning is 'the real universe, the divine, magical, terrifying and ecstatic reality in which we all live' (Lewis, 1986: xii). For Lacan too there is something of the Real in myth, which he characterises in this way: 'Every myth is related to the inexplicable nature of reality' (Lacan, 2015: 52). There is a kinship evident in their way of writing the Real (to the extent that writing the Real is possible) in its terrifying and ecstatic aspects. The difference is that, for Lewis, the real is meaningful.

Fantasy, unlike myth, cannot function without a narrative. Slavoj Žižek (1998) emphasises this narrative aspect of fantasy, as I have written in the Introduction. He calls fantasy 'the primordial form of narrative which serves to occult some original deadlock', the aporia of Lacan's lost object. To requote:

> [T]he lost quality only emerged at this very moment of its alleged loss. This coincidence of emergence and loss designates the fundamental paradox of the Lacanian object *a*, which emerges as being-lost. Narrativisation occludes this paradox by describing the process in which the object is first given and then gets lost. (Žižek, 1998: 199)

Stuart Tannock provides a similar narrativisation in his definition of nostalgia:

In the rhetoric of nostalgia one inevitably finds three key ideas: first a prelapsarian world …; second, that of a 'lapse' (a cut, a Catastrophe, a separation or sundering, the Fall); and third, that of the present, postlapsarian world (a world felt in some way to be lacking, deficient or oppressive). (Tannock, 1995: 456–7)

There is a fourth component, implicit in the third: a never-relinquished desire to return to a prelapsarian paradise where nothing lacks.

Fantasy's narrative, as Žižek proposes, functions to temporalise the loss endemic to speaking beings so as to hide the 'coincidence of [its] emergence and loss' (1998: 199). The Arthurian story, like Genesis, is exemplary, since it temporalises a primordial loss within a narrative of prelapse, lapse and postlapse. It also promises a return. But in *Excalibur* and *Mists*, in particular *Excalibur*, the fantasy does not entirely occlude the coincidence of emergence and loss, because it must contend with the co-presence of mythic elements which operate within a different temporal landscape.

Žižek, who explores the social and ideological dimensions of fantasy, notes also the prevalence of paranoia in common fantasies of the given and lost object; for instance, the necessary obverse to the 'beatific' notion of the harmonious Nazi *Volksgemeinschaft* is the 'paranoiac obsession with the Jewish plot' (1998: 192). As he explains,

> Those who have alleged to have fully realized the (stabilizing) fantasy, had to have recourse to the (destabilizing), fantasy in order to explain their failure. The foreclosed obverse of the Nazi harmonious *Volksgemeinschaft* returned in the guise of their paranoic obsession with the Jewish plot (1998: 192).

Without the evil machinations of the Jewish plotters there would have been no reason for the Nazi *Volksgemeinschaft* to have failed. Paradise must have its serpent in order to explain the inevitable failures of human dreams of perfect order and harmony (Žižek, 1998: 192). There is no room for ambiguity here – no *between* space. Paranoia cannot tolerate doubt. The fantasy requires someone to hate with impunity, someone it is right to hate. It is one of cinema's greatest and most frequently offered enjoyments, perhaps particularly so in medievalist film, as Nickolas Haydock has pointed out: 'Understood in broad terms, conspiracy is cinémedievalism's defining cliché' (Haydock, 2008: 35). In Chapter 1 we saw that paranoia in

Diana Wynne Jones's 1981 fantasy novel, *The Homeward Bounders*, where evil demons called only *They* and *Them* steal reality from all the worlds in order to play games with them.

Neither *Excalibur* nor *Mists* can be entirely reduced to a conspiracy theory, however, in which blameless innocents are deprived of the precious object by wicked conspirators, although each has its paranoiac tendencies. In *Mists* the masculine hierarchy of the Christian church is most singled out as an object of righteous hatred. In *Excalibur* it is those representatives of ungovernable womanhood, Guenevere and Morgana, who bear the heaviest load of blame. But, in the end, the Arthurian story, like Genesis, is so familiar to us that the end appears inevitable by whatever means it is produced. It is this tendency to subvert the film narrative, more apparent in *Excalibur* than in *Mists*, which moves it into mythic territory.

Boorman makes his own claim to mythic truth in *Excalibur*, as John Aberth notes, citing an interview Boorman made with Harlan Kennedy of American Film: '"I think of the story, the history, as a myth. The film has to do with mythical truth, not historical truth"' (Aberth, 2003: 21). Boorman made the same claim in a more didactic mode to Philip Strick of *Sight and Sound*: '"Listen carefully to the echoes of myth. It has much more to tell us than the petty lies and insignificant truths of recorded history"' (Aberth, 2003: 21). Boorman places myth and history in opposition, defending his contempt for 'the petty lies and insignificant truths of recorded history' since some criticism of historical film is still founded on accusations of inaccuracy. But I am more concerned here with the way the constancy of myth at work in the Arthurian tale undermines the narrative process itself.

In myth, agency is de-emphasised, since myth subverts the idea of cause and effect along with the narrative. There is less temptation to say 'if only' – if only Guenevere had never met Lancelot or if only Morgan had not been so bloody-minded – any more than there is a temptation to say: if only Oedipus had not met his father at the crossroads and killed him. That would feel to us like beginning at the wrong end (the beginning, that is), as if there were any other possible ending when the end is implicit in the beginning. In the films under discussion – again more so *Excalibur* – conspiracy paranoia is reduced by the impression of a tragic necessity endemic to humanity.[4] In this respect the films follow the mythic Arthurian tradition in the sense that I use here: that is, they speak this tragic necessity, always true, and therefore beyond time and narrative.[5]

Myth, like fantasy, allows a speaking, but it is of a different kind. For Lacan, myth 'doesn't explain anything' (1997: 143), unlike fantasy which always seeks to explain the catastrophe in either personal or ideological terms; that is, in narrative terms,

> [the myth] concerns the individual and also the collectivity, but there is no ... opposition between them at the level involved. For it is a matter here of the subject as he suffers from the signifier. (Lacan, 1997: 143)

At this level we are all necessarily in the same boat in so far as we are speaking beings, suffering our subjection to the signifier.

The *necessity* of loss is harmful to desire, which relies upon hope in a future and thus on the narrative means to produce it. To the extent that necessity banishes hope, these two films could more properly be called myths than fantasies. But what *is* occluded in the films is the impossibility of a return. Desire is sustained in both films by the hope of return to the beloved lost home, a hope which fends off knowledge of the impossible, and, to the extent that hope survives the dictates of necessity, the films can be called fantasies. One might say that they contain aspects of both myth and fantasy in uneasy cohabitation and in differing proportions. Both *Excalibur* and *Mists* are set in an animistic Eden, caught in a moment of decline brought about by the forces of Christianity. In each case, to different extents, the mythic aspect of the Arthurian material is weakened by the narrative requirements of fantasy.

## Two Edens

For *Excalibur*, the Edenic time before the decline was the time 'when the world was young and bird and beast and flower were one with man and death was but a dream' (Boorman, 1981). This is the time of the dragon, which 'is everywhere [and] everything ... Its scale is in the bark of trees, its roar is heard in the wind and its forked tongue strikes like ... lightning.' These are Merlin's words. It is through Merlin's power that this time is glimpsed again in Arthur's reign ('You will be the land and the land will be you' he instructs Arthur). It is the fantasy of fusion with the land again, but its reign is momentary. Merlin foresees its failure even as he labours to bring it to birth. Even at the height of Arthur's reign, he tells Morgana (*Excalibur*'s version of Morgan le Fay) that the time of the dragon is already passing, driven out by Christianity, whose music swells triumphantly over their conversation, as if to emphasise his point:

> The days of our kind [the necromancers] are numbered. The one God comes to drive out the many gods, the spirits of wood and stream grow silent. It's the way of things. It's a time for men and their ways. (Boorman, 1981)[6]

Merlin's foresightedness is the perfect vehicle to convey the inevitability of loss: 'It's the way of things.' As Tolkien does at the end of *The Lord of the* Rings (*LOTR*), Boorman's Arthuriad looks forward to another Fall, when magic departs and men are left to blunder along in a world turned ordinary. It is no accident that Arthur's story, like Oedipus's, has a prophet on the scene. For the prophet, the future coexists with present and past; thus chronological time is collapsed and with it the fantasy narrative, so that the emergence and loss of the precious object can be perceived at once.[7] 'Too late', Merlin observes, as he watches Arthur's burgeoning love for Guenevere (Boorman, 1981). For Merlin, and for us, who have our hindsight to confirm his foresight, it has always been too late.[8]

In *Mists* the Edenic time is the time of the Goddess, still preserved in an Avalon under threat. The miniseries, like *Excalibur*, catches it in its last flowering. Avalon, the place, and the old religion of Goddess worship is protected by priestesses, headed by Viviane, Lady of the Lake and high-priestess of Avalon, seconded by a benevolent but ineffectual Merlin. This Merlin is little more than a diplomatic mouthpiece for Viviane's pronouncements. Neither he nor Viviane quite fulfils the function of fully fledged seer, unlike *Excalibur*'s Merlin, who is immortal (Haydock, 2008: 71) and sees as an immortal. He, like T. H. White's Merlin, cannot help but see (White, 1996: 29), whereas the sight of the mortal Viviane is flawed and partial. Her passionate desire to save Avalon blinds her, for instance, to the character of Mordred. whom she unwittingly assists in his destruction of Camelot.

*Mists*' Viviane, Merlin and Morgaine are all too mortal. With typically human self-centredness they ask where they went wrong, like the eponymous protagonist of Steven Barron's TV series *Merlin* (1998). They examine their consciences, at least as death approaches (something no immortal would be in a position to do), contemplating the possibility of other endings if only things had been different. This failure to view prophetically gives *Mists* more of a tendency towards the narrativisation of fantasy than towards the temporal and causal collapse of myth. In *Mists*, myth is psychologised with frequent, urgent justifications for the behaviour of privileged characters. Morgaine acquits Igraine of any wrongdoing in sending her husband Gorlois to his death with these words: 'You are not to blame. You had no choice' (Edel, 2001). Morgaine also exonerates herself in voice-over for her night of love with her brother Arthur in the Beltane ritual since they were both masked and unable to identify each other. She is the innocent victim of Viviane's manipulations. The film employs the logic of the signifier where white can only be white in relation to black; Morgaine can be innocent because Viviane is guilty. It is a narrative of villains and victims. A moral framework, held in place by Morgaine's calm, authoritative voice-over narration, is placed like a grid over what Derek Pearsall called 'the old incoherencies' (2003: 47). *Mists* is a discourse of reason, like those discussed in Chapter 2, with explanations for everything, despite its occasional lip-service to 'destiny'. It is not a discourse where one thing can be another. It is an uneasy blend, however, with the necessity of destiny called in to prop up the explanations provided by Morgaine as spokesperson for the film's ideology. Myth is co-opted for fantasy.

Viviane instructs the young apprentice priestess, Morgaine, another version of Morgan le Fay:

> The Goddess is everything in nature and everything in nature is sacred. Look [they look out over a field of grain], that is her face, listen [a bird calls], that is her voice. She is in everything that is beautiful and everything that is harrowing as well. (Edel, 2001)

In each film the primeval being, dragon or goddess, *is* everything (*Excalibur*'s dragon, like the Goddess, 'is everywhere [and] everything'), although, again in each case, there is an immediate slippage from '*is* everything' to 'is *in* everything'. The first suggests more powerfully an undifferentiated state before the separations inflicted by language, although the impression of undifferentiation is already weakened simply by the naming and thus the personification of 'everything' as Goddess or dragon. In *Mists* differentiation is further implied in Viviane's later words, as she stands before the altar of the Goddess with Morgaine: 'The Goddess holds all things in balance, good and evil, death and rebirth, the predator and the prey' (Edel, 2001). Thus, there is slippage from an unseparated, primordial *state* of nature to a *being* dwelling within nature in the first case, or presiding over nature in the second. Fantasy must have its narrative and no narrative can be sustained by the primordial.

In both films Arthur and other youngsters are guided or manipulated by these magical elders into preserving the paradisal time/place. We, looking back, know that in all possible variants it will be lost, but always leaving behind it the hope of its return. At the end of *Mists*, Morgaine recognises the Goddess in the garb of the Christian Virgin Mary, and prophesises, with a nod to the New Age, that 'future generations may bring her back as we knew her in the glory of Avalon' (Edel, 2001). The New Age was quick to pick up the nod. The prophecy is fulfilled, according to one neo-pagan who writes in a review of *Mists* on Filmtracks.com: 'Thankfully the Goddess is coming back to us in our lifetime to restore love, respect, and common sense' (Filmtracks.com, n.d.). Restoration is also the theme in a poem by Becca Tzigany on the website 'Venus and her Lover', entitled 'Return of Morgaine': 'There gleam again through the mists / Magic groves on the distant shore / Maiden, mother, and crone / Their spells and chants intone / That the four elements be restored' (Tzigany, n.d.). Balance is invoked again, the triple Goddess keeping the elements in order. In *Excalibur*, more traditionally, Arthur tells Perceval that 'one day a king will come and the sword will rise again' (Boorman, 1981). The ship with the four queens signals that the king will always be Arthur, the once and future king who, like Christ, has never truly gone.[9]

Music is one of the most important means by which audiences are cued to the various functions of different scenes and guided in their responses. In the next section I turn to some of the music considered appropriate for these different functions in *Excalibur* and *Mists*.

## Music for myth, music for fantasy

The music in *Excalibur* and *Mists* can be organised, with some differences, according to various functions. First, in both films diegetic or semi-diegetic music accompanies scenes providing light relief from the tensions of the plot. Second, usually with strings predominating, there is music to represent the human dimension of events, the pitiable attempts of human beings caught up in the vast tides of destiny which govern their fate. Audiences are reassured by this music, both that this is the time for compassion and – cued to their response by the music – that they are capable of it. Third, in *Excalibur*, pre-composed music on a grand scale accompanies and establishes mythopoeic or myth-making moments. There is similar music in *Mists*, but, as music composed for the film, it is backgrounded by the action. Last, music creates a miasma around magical or sacred acts, places or events. Here the voice predominates – a woman's voice.

The first function could be called musical décor or, perhaps, medieval lite. This music accompanies backstairs scenes, feasts, dances and comic scenes. Unlike the unheard melodies of Gorbman's title, it is meant to be heard. It cannot do its atmospheric and referential work otherwise. In the liner notes to the soundtrack CD for *Excalibur*, Boorman stated he chose to 'score the film primarily with classical music', Richard Wagner and Carl Orff (T. Jones, 2000). Trevor Jones wrote the new music for the soundtrack but it has a secondary role. He was contracted to 'create the supporting music atmosphere for the film' (T. Jones, 2000). In this function, however, what Jones's medieval music offers us is an atmosphere devoid of significance. By its emphasised unimportance it has the effect of suggesting that there is little in actual medieval life worth representing.[10]

Perceval, arriving at Camelot for the first time, is packed off to the kitchens (T. Jones, 2000: track 9). It is essentially a comic scene. On his way he passes people engaged in all kinds of mysterious activities: cauldrons bubble with unknown ingredients, strange apparatus is glimpsed, but all these activities are offered as everyday occurrences which only Perceval's ignorant eyes find remarkable. He also sees jesters and dwarves (always a comic touch), while quaint medieval music, apparently diegetic (although the source is not located) starts up.[11] It is in this context, which renders the exotic unimportant, that medieval music is 'quoted'. The usual exotic instruments are present: the CD liner notes refer to 'the light music of lute, bells and hammered dulcimer', but reed instruments and recorders are also in evidence. The music is a kind of jumble of themes, sounding more Tudor than medieval, but only cursorily like either.[12] It represents a light-weight, genericised medieval, suitable for light relief. Nothing that sounds even remotely medieval is risked for serious scenes. In those scenes the heavy lifting is done by the classic Hollywood narrative means – the Romantic idiom adjusted for film.

The 'castle dance' cue for *Mists* has a similar function (Holdridge, 2001: track 11). Sandwiched between two serious scenes, it is only really heard for brief seconds while dwarves (again) are seen running upstairs, after which it is practically drowned out. What distinguishes it from the backstairs music in *Excalibur* is that it is scored for bagpipes, tin whistle and bodhrán. This is a Celtic medieval and Lee Holdridge must have felt that Irish folk music was the best way to represent it. The music in and of itself is unimportant, but as a signifier of the 'Celtic' it *is* important. The film, following Marion Zimmer Bradley's novel of the same name, taps into a sizeable audience of neo-pagan viewers, for whom the signifier 'Celtic' has a special valence; in this instance it glorifies an ancient matriarchy oppressed by the emerging Christian patriarchy. Another Irish tune has a similar function (Holdridge, 2001: track 3, 1:48). It is first used for the happy times after Arthur's birth, then for the childish high jinks of Morgaine and Arthur, escaping from their fussy, monkish tutor. It takes a serious turn when they come upon a group of peasants praying to the Goddess for a good crop. One man, looking like an escapee from a Book of Hours, stands stiffly, playing a huge recorder, while another sows seed and a woman pours milk onto the ground, while Morgaine, watching, explains the ritual to her little brother. The intensity and solemnity of their gaze confirms the significance of the scene before them.

Scene 3, 'the sign foretold' (Holdridge, 2001: track 3, 27) is an excellent instance of the second function, the human dimension. The scene in which Igraine and Uther are struck by love begins in E♭ major, with the strings in a warm, swelling, uplifting melody. But their status as pawns of destiny whose love is imposed upon them is evoked by an invasion from the wind section, like a storm brewing, turning the melody into the minor and progressively fragmenting the theme. Fate is intervening in the lives of frail humans, turning their dreams to dust. It appears again (track 4) when Morgaine and Arthur leave home, co-opted into Viviane's plans for Avalon, and again when Morgaine and Arthur part to take up their separate fates. The love theme is ousted as Morgaine is introduced to Viviane's world and musical themes of the Goddess infiltrate the human dimension. Solo wind instruments slide exotically. Avalon is musically evoked as a site of ancient feminine mystical wisdom with an oriental tinge. Viviane's manipulations are now seen as secondary in the broader canvas of the Goddess's will to 'hold all things in balance'. There is a kind of catharsis, a calming effect, in this aural shift. A mythic moment occurs as the tensions within human affairs are suddenly eclipsed within the vast purview of the Goddess. The narrative progresses musically through a complication and interpenetration of themes and functions, stressing now one aspect, now another, and commenting musically on their relation to each other by the development, intertwining and fragmentation of themes and changes in the instrumentation.

These are all classic Hollywood narrative ploys. They exemplify the way music is typically employed for film, for its capacity to guide the viewer's response unobtrusively by means of tried and true musical idioms. Their familiarity is essential; radical change would threaten their representational and evocative function – and bring it out of hiding. This is the major function of music (mainly orchestral) in medieval film, as John Haines observes: 'For the most part, composers of film music keep to the classic Romantic style that had become so strongly identified with the medieval epic' (Haines, 2014a: 76). As he also observes, medieval film music stays clear, on the whole, of 'extant notated music from the Middle Ages', owing its inheritance not to the 'twentieth-century Early Music movement', but to orchestral music which became 'the trademark sound of film' (2014a: 76).[13]

The last two of the musical functions of film music I have identified: the third, instrumental music to establish mythopoeic moments; and the fourth, the woman's voice which calls the listener home, have a particular bearing on questions of myth and fantasy, necessity and desire, and also on nostalgia. In the third (mainly) instrumental music on a grand scale accompanies and helps to create mythopoeic moments. In the fourth, music creates a miasma around magical acts, places or events. Here the voice predominates – a woman's voice, calling to the listener to come home.

*Excalibur* is primarily a 'compilation' score, built on pre-composed music. In the function I call mythopoeic, Wagnerian music bestows a momentousness on the events it accompanies, placing them beyond the personal or ideological into a mythic dimension.[14] The presence of Wagnerian music has an extra significance, since Wagner himself made famous the leitmotif with its mythopoeic power as a primary tool in opera. The leitmotif's role in cinema, derived from Wagner's practice, is equally important.[15] In *Excalibur* we are alerted to the unfolding of an inevitable tragedy. The end is already present in the prologue, signified by the doom-laden tones of Siegfried's funeral march from *Götterdämmerung* (1871). Here the full weight of Wagner's extensive orchestral resources and the signifying power of the major–minor harmonic system are employed to provide a saturation of meaning and significance. The theme begins with kettle drums, building to a climax of fateful consequence via a series of tense, semi-tonal stabs, emphasising each line of the synopsis, finally modulating to a menacing, brass-heavy C minor chord coinciding with the appearance of the title in dazzling, sword-like letters. This leitmotif is repeated at crucial mythopoeic points, such as when the sword changes hands. The prelude to *Tristan and Isolde* is fittingly set for the unfolding of Lancelot and Guenevere's tragic love; Arthur rides into battle to the tune of the much-exploited 'O fortuna' from Carl Orff's *Carmina Burana* (1937). Orff's relentless rhythms suggest vast, surging tides of human destiny, an impression supported by the thirteenth-century lyrics: 'Fate ... is against me, driven on and weighted down, always enslaved ... Fate strikes down the strong man, everyone weep with me' (Orff, 1937:'O fortuna').[16]

The musical sources are not medieval, although they cite the medieval, through more modern eyes, in an inflated, ennobled form.[17] It is as if Arthur and Co. gain mythic density via these citations which feed the idea of the medieval as mythic time. In Chapter 1 I pondered depth, an added dimension, as a marker of the mythic in fiction. Here, since music is a temporal art, depth is gained by repeated citation. Music drawn from medieval sources is not employed; medieval composers could not be expected to have any appreciation of the medieval as it might be coded for us. As for the characters in Henry James's similarly named short story, medieval music might be 'the real thing' but the real thing will not do. It is the wrong 'real thing'. Historical accuracy has no glamour in this context. The artist prefers, as James's narrator comments, 'the represented subject over the real one: the defect of the real one [is] so apt to be a lack of representation' (H. James, 2004: 86). Medieval music does not have the distance required to represent the medieval, since representation of any kind presumes non-identity with the original.[18] Nothing can represent itself. The representation each film provides with its music is, instead, the means it employs to sustain a particular idea of the medieval which suits its creative and ideological ends.

In *Mists*, Mordred confronts Arthur in the last battle. The music here, composed by Lee Holdridge, echoes Wagner. There is the same scoring for brass and percussion, the same doom-laden chords, but functioning rather differently. When heard with the image, this music is less momentous, less mythopoeic, partly because the exploits of men, so central in *Excalibur*, are reduced to a subplot in *Mists*'s re-visioning of the legend. But another difference is that, as music newly composed for the film and harnessed to the narrative, Holdridge's battle theme has no citation value. Citation value accrues over time, like interest, each one creating added value and, in this case, a further guarantee of mythic status. Holdridge's music, with so little time to impress itself on the listener, is much harder to hear, much more easily over-ridden by visual image and narrative momentum. Even for viewers unfamiliar with Wagner, his music overturns the usual balance whereby music is the self-effacing handmaiden of the classical cinematic narrative. Here I must part company with Norris J. Lacy, who argues that

> whether the use of Wagner ... simply sets a mood or instead establishes a complex overlay of themes prefiguring ... passion or death depends quite simply on the viewer's recognition of the music. (Lacy, 2002: 41)

It is not quite so simple. Music composed specifically for film is structurally quite different from music composed in other contexts; as Gorbman explains, it is produced with 'a minimum adherence to musical syntax [and] a maximum flexibility of resources, so that the score can accommodate itself to narrative events' (Gorbman, 1987: 14).[19] This is how music can pass unnoticed under the action.

Ears unfamiliar with Wagner and Orff will still recognise the difference between a musical quotation and music composed for the film.[20] That difference has representational value even when the music is unknown. The compilation score does its representational work differently because, all of a sudden, it *is* heard. It is very hard *not* to hear Wagner. His music, evidently not custom-made for the film, floats free from the image, bestowing a mythic character on the scene. *Excalibur*'s oft-repeated leitmotifs from Wagner and Orff inform us that there is more here than can be garnered from the image or the narrative. At these moments the flow of image/narrative is punctuated by injections of an eternal, collective necessity; fantasy is interrupted by myth.

I call the fourth function of medieval film music 'the calling voice'. Usually it is a wordless call, gesturing towards a time before words had meaning: mother's voice, in fact. The call is acousmatic, a 'sonorous womb', surrounding us with no localised source (Rosolato, 1974: 81). Something of the lure of that call (in its Celtic incarnation) is given words in the group Celtic Woman's song, 'The Call': 'Open your heart / I am calling you / Right from the very start / Your wounded heart was calling, too' (Celtic Woman, 2009). Another, 'Going Home', begins: They say there's a place where dreams have all gone, / They never said where, but I think I know, / It's miles through the night just over the dawn, / On the road that will take me home' (Celtic Woman, 2019).

In *Excalibur*, the call comes as a high, icy coloratura voice which conveys, say the soundtrack liner notes, 'the powers of darkness' (T. Jones, 2000).[21] This cue is often used when the dragon's power is invoked, as in the scene where Uther rides the dragon's breath to his encounter with Igraine and the conception of Arthur. The dragon is the source of all power, since it is itself 'everything', but you wake it at your peril. Merlin warns Morgana, who craves the knowledge of necromancy: '[S]uch knowledge would burn you' (Boorman, 1981).

This cold voice, calling amidst shrill, discordant instruments, aurally represents the peril of such knowledge as the extreme cold that burns, visually represented in the dragon's cave of ice and fire. Both Morgana and Guenevere, like Eve, stretch forth their hand for forbidden knowledge, Guenevere for her unlawful passion for Lancelot, Morgana for the powers of necromancy which she will use to avenge her father's death. Merlin accuses Morgana: 'Perhaps you lust for what you cannot have' (Boorman, 1981). It is such knowledge that ultimately destroys her. This is fantasy as Žižek reads it, revealed by its paranoid fear. It is a masculine fantasy of women who, in their ungovernable lust, transgress the law, bringing the world tumbling down around them.[22] That siren cry spells doom to men and their hard-won achievements, drawing chaos in its wake.[23]

In *Mists* the voice is very different – two voices actually, both belonging to singers of 'Celtic' music with a reputation beyond the film. One is Loreena McKennitt, whose song 'The Mystic's Dream', from a 1994 album, *The Mask and the Mirror*, is quoted throughout the film, for instance during the scene of Morgaine's apprenticeship as a priestess on Avalon.[24] Usually, what we hear in the film is the wordless prelude.[25] The other singer is Aeone, whose voice, also wordless, accompanies Morgaine's first journey to Avalon with Viviane (Holdridge, 2001: track 4, 2:34).[26] With its vocal breaks, and vocal and string slides, this wordless call offers itself as strange yet familiar. Here the cry enacts longing but we also know it as the 'one woman wail', the lamenting woman's wordless keening in many cinematic moments of mourning.[27]

Aeone, together with Holdridge, also wrote a song inspired by the film, 'I Will Remember You Still', which is included on the soundtrack CD (Holdridge, 2001: track 18).[28] McKennitt's song, like *Excalibur*'s quotations from Wagner and Orff, has citation value from its previous incarnations, but the citations valorise not myth but fantasy. The medieval is exploited differently here, not as confirming a collective destiny but as musically evoking an ancient lost home. It stresses the archaic and exotic of fantasy rather than the inevitable and eternal of myth. In *Mists* songs also carry a strong nostalgic yearning, very evident in the texts, for instance: 'my heart is calling', in Loreena McKennitt's 'Mystic's Dream' or 'Carry my voice on the wind' in Aeone's 'I Will Remember You Still'.

In *Mists* also, medieval music is passed over as not medieval enough, lacking the power to represent the film's medieval. This time it is passed over in favour of orientalising and medievalising musical gestures. McKennitt's first wordless, arhythmic cry is in the double harmonic scale, sometimes called Byzantine: semitone – augmented second – semitone – tone – semitone – augmented second – semitone, that is, in C: C, D♭, E, F, G, A♭, B, C. 'Double harmonic' refers to the two augmented seconds, between the 2nd and 3rd and the 6th and 7th pitches. The augmented 2nd sounds foreign and exotic to Western ears. The melody shifts, in a second, male-voiced, chant-like prelude which McKennitt takes up, to a natural minor, which also sounds exotic and is associated with medieval music. The minor 7th is particularly stressed because, like the augmented 2nd, it is unfamiliar.

To a modern Western listener, trained on the more recently developed major–minor harmonic system, the raised 7th is heard as leading up to the tonic. For instance, the online *Britannica* observes:

> This note has a strong leading tendency toward the tonic, or keynote [...] because it is only a half-step away from the tonic, and is thus called the leading note. Because the leading note is a member of the dominant chord, this chord also has a strong pull toward the tonic chord. (*Encyclopædia Britannica*, 2021: s.v. 'leading note')

The leading note is drawn to the tonic. A minor 7th *not* reaching for the tonic sounds, to modern ears, strange, almost wilful (why does it resist the pull of the tonic?) and, in particular, ancient. Its representational value in *Mists* is that of an ancient feminine resistance to the masculine order. It may also represent a kind of stasis, a refusal of movement and change. The first prelude stresses the 'elsewhere' of exotic, the second the 'before' of archaic, together a potent recipe for nostalgic longing. In *Mists* the archaic *is* exotic; the medieval as primordial past *is* another country, but offered to us as home. It is again that strangeness at the heart which inhabits the medieval – in Lacan's term, extimacy.

There is a well-worn path between the medieval, the (feminine) primordial and the exotic/familiar. It is trodden in the *LOTR* films, where the figure of Galadriel, as the enlivening heart of Lothlórien, is musically given as both ancient and mysterious. Here is the account of Doug Adams in *The Music of the Lord of the Rings Films*:

> In style, [the Lothlórien theme] is the most Eastern and exotic of all the Elves' music. This is Lothlórien as a land of mystery, scored with plaintive female chorus and a trickle of monochord, ney, and sarangi. The writing is emotionally unreadable – neither sad, happy, aggressive nor passive, but aloof. This ... creates a melody that, in certain contexts, can be disturbing. When the Company reaches Galadriel's domain, the first coiling phrases of [the theme] become indistinctly

threatening. 'Rivendell is more about learning and knowledge,' says Shore, 'but this is different. This is a more mysterious world of Elves. They could be bad; they could be good – you're really not sure.' (Adams, 2010: 51)[29]

Howard Shore, who composed the score, brings the mysterious and disturbing back again to the medieval: 'The voices [the plaintive female chorus] carry it. This is Middle-earth of thousands of years ago. When I started doing research, I started thinking about Gregorian chants and so on' (Adams, 2010: 51). These associational slippages, between the voices of women, the archaic medieval and the disturbingly ambiguous, are familiar. Even Adams's word 'coiling' has a serpentine sound, reminiscent of the myth of the lamia, a woman who is a serpent from the waist down. The directionless chromaticism and rhythmic instability of the Lothlórien theme leaves the listener disoriented.[30]

In *Mists* the feminine archaic is (supposedly) purged of its threat. 'The Mystic's Dream', like Aeone's song, is brimming with lost-world longing and the half-promise of an eventual return. There is no sense of either a definitive fulfilment or a necessary and final loss. Rather, since 'nostalgia is the desire for desire' (to requote Susan Stewart), there is an ambiguous *tristesse* which keeps its options open with an endlessly repeated 'maybe', half suffering, half enjoying its yearning.

The lyrics of both 'The Mystic's Dream' and 'I Will Remember You Still' reinforce this effect. They have a vague, all-purpose quality. They appear to function as elements in a medieval/Celtic, pro-forma fantasy which can then be fleshed out by the listener according to inclination; fantasies have both a cultural and an individual aspect. The songs contain numerous key words and phrases: 'voiceless song in an ageless night', 'birds in flight are calling there', 'even the distance feels so near' ('Mystic's Dream' lyrics),[31] and 'it's there my heart is longing', 'drifting years', 'draws me far away', 'your lamps will call me home', 'distant shore', 'carry my voice on the wind', 'waters that keep us apart' ('I Will Remember You Still' lyrics). In fact, almost every word carries a note of yearning for a lost, faraway home which calls unceasingly in a 'voiceless song'. The words support a fantasy of the wordless, and, beyond the wordless, a *voiceless* song, something which cannot be signified but which language strives to indicate by oxymoron (as I have argued earlier).

Similar lyrics can be found on the soundtracks of the *Narnia* films, if one allows for a very different religious sensibility which references the eternal rather than the primordial. This home, no doubt in deference to Lewis, is 'out there' waiting, but ahead not behind, onward and upward, demanding both faith and striving. Here are a few samples:

> There's a place out there for us,
> We can be the kings and queens of anything if we believe
> It's written in the stars that shine above
> A world where you and I belong,
> Where faith and love will keep us strong …
> We'll find what we've been waiting for
> We were made for so much more! (Arnold, 2010)

> Oh empty my heart
> I've got to make room for this feeling
> So much bigger than me. (Heap, 2005)

> This is home
> Now I'm finally where I belong …
> I've been searching for a place of my own
> Now I've found it …
> Belief over misery
> I've seen the enemy
> And I won't go back …
> And now after all my searching
> After all my questions
> I'm gonna call it home
> I've got a brand new mindset
> I can finally see the sunset
> I'm gonna call it home. (Switchfoot, 2008)

The same nostalgic impulses are catered for but transformed into a discourse of conversion, a commitment to take up the arduous path home, either predestined for those who believe, 'written in the stars', or called up in an act of willed belief, 'I'm gonna call it home'. No wavering here! No melting back into mother's arms. This voice makes a decision. Temporally speaking, it is difficult to distinguish the primordial from the eternal nostalgias because, as argued in Chapter 2, the temporality of nostalgic desire is circular but forced by the grammar of tense to masquerade as linear, going backwards by going forwards. But eternal nostalgia approves this arrangement.

For Christians the eternal is both origin and eschaton, but time-bound mortals can only reach it on the onward and upward path of effort. The difference in the *Narnia* songs is carried in the signifiers of effort, faith and worship (as against the much more passive language of McKennitt's and Aeone's lyrics): 'We were made for so much more', 'so much bigger than me', 'if we believe, 'belief over misery', 'I've seen the enemy and I won't go back', 'I can finally see the sunset'.[32] Lewis is well represented here.

McKennitt's song has had numerous incarnations; it can be heard on YouTube, accompanying mystical and warrior scenes, and, elsewhere on YouTube, in association with a World of Warcraft character called Arthas. Aeone's song, 'I Will Remember You Still', has also had a life on YouTube, accompanying, among other images, an antlered man enthroned, cowled figures, prehistoric huts and their ruins, excerpts from the film, a Celtic cross, maidens or priestesses in a circle.[33] The images associated with these songs appear to function, like the lyrics, as cues for a fantasy which approaches what cannot be represented or spoken.

Unlike the danger signals issued by the piercing voice of *Excalibur*, the calling voice of *Mists* appears in its warmest, most benign aspect. In both cases the voice calls us to an impossible, pre-Oedipal home before language, but differently inflected and with very different effects. *Excalibur* speaks in the '*name of the father*', that is, in Lacan's terms, that which 'support[s] ... the symbolic function [language], which, from the dawn of history, has identified his person with the figure of the law' (1977b: 67). The name of the father ('nom-du-père') is, in French, homophonous with the 'no' of the father. From the point of view of *Excalibur*'s masculine fantasy of uncontrollable feminine desire, the feminine call amounts to a refusal of the father's 'no'. The voice here represents the anxiety this tempting call evokes and a corresponding hostility towards women. The incestuous home to which this voice calls is one of horror, not a haven but a house of shame, or perhaps both, since it evokes both desire and horror.[34] As Kaja Silverman suggests, fantasies of a return to the maternal voice are always 'charged with either intensely positive or intensely negative affect' (Silverman, 1988: 72). But, as she also remarks, the fantasy is profoundly ambiguous (72). It is intensely positive *and* intensely negative. The positive and negative are intimately related, the horror implicating the desire. This is no human mother but the Mother 'as she occupies the place of *Das Ding*' (Lacan, 1997: 67). As Lacan asserted, '[t]he Sovereign Good, which is *das Ding*, which is the mother, is also the object of incest, is a forbidden good, and ... there is no other good' (1997: 70). These two films bear out, in different ways, Lacan's assertions.

All mothers bear the weight of this association with *das Ding*. David Marshall investigates the horror evoked by the Mother in the 1999 film *The 13th Warrior* by reference to Kristeva's theory of abjection:

> Heavily indebted to Lacan, Kristeva claims that a subject must push the mother and the maternal body away in the process of aligning itself with the symbolic system, which is associated with the Law of the Father. That process, however, creates a simultaneous desire for the primal connection to the maternal and utter revulsion produced by becoming a subject in the symbolic order. (D. Marshall, 2010: 137)

In *Mists* that ambiguous desire/revulsion is masked. Here the call is, in the main, addressed to women. It is the same call, offering a return to a time before the separation imposed by the father's 'no', but with a different valence. Women have not fared well under the father's law and the promise held out of a return to a time before its advent is enticing. The film and its music encourage us to follow Morgaine's example in her adoption of the Goddess as mother: 'Gradually I came to look upon the Goddess as my own Mother and the Mother of the earth itself' (Edel, 2001). This call bids the listener to return to mother's arms and her loving voice, refusing separation. Hélène Cixous has described such a voice, which 'sings from a time before law, before the Symbolic took one's breath away and reappropriated it into language under its authority of separation' (Cixous, 1986: 93).

But, as Kristeva warned, this call is treacherous for women too:

> For a woman the call of the mother ... troubles the Word. It generates hallucinations, voices, 'madness'. Once the moorings of the word, the ego, the superego, begin to slip, life itself can't hang on: death quietly moves in. (1977: 39)

Kristeva voices in this passage the menace in mother's wordless call which, masked in the text of *Mists*, makes its presence felt in the music. The word is invoked (in Morgaine's reassuring voice-over) to sanitise the call.

The Mother's voice makes a seductive call, partly because it offers solace to women in a harsh world ruled by men, partly because it supports a recuperative programme, set out in the prologue. The film begins with Morgaine's announcement in voice-over: 'Most of what you think you know [of the Arthurian legend] is nothing but lies' (Edel, 2001). We are very close to a conspiracy theory here.[35] There has been a cover-up! Christian masculinity has distorted the story, defaming the old religion and demonising women, but the truth will now be told: there was once an ancient, feminine way, more just, more harmonious than patriarchy. It was destroyed but it can return.[36] Allied to this recuperative value is the identificatory power that Goddess-worship offers women, the heady sense of a specifically feminine sacred power and wisdom.

In fact, what *Mists* poses is a law before the law, a pre-symbolic symbolic. This is what happens when we fantasise backwards, since we can only fantasise from within the law, which is the law of language. This is what saves *Mists'* fantasy from the manly fear evoked by the chilling voice in *Excalibur*, a fear of an uncastrated feminine chaos, feminine desires running wild without a good father/ king at the helm and a good phallic sword in his hand. It is, at the same time, the fear of a primordial chaos without the differentiations the law of language imposes. This is a fear that afflicts women as well as men, an instance of the ambivalence of medievalist desires. But for believers in the Goddess like the one quoted, or for those whose disbelief is suspended for the duration of the film, the fear is neutralised. The Goddess will 'restore love, respect, and common sense', good sound law laid down by a sensible mother. 'The Goddess holds all things in balance', as Viviane proclaims (Edel, 2001), distancing the mother Goddess from the terror of *das Ding*.

*Mists* tries to have it both ways: it poses a tamed archaic Mother Goddess, one who is on the one hand 'everything' in an unseparated state, what Kristeva called the 'full, total englobing mother ... with no ... separation ... no castration' (1981: 29) and, on the other, a good, commonsensical lawmaker. No such claims are made for *Excalibur*'s dragon, which is presented as a wild force, utterly lawless and apparently mindless – to be treated with the utmost caution. *Mists* needs its law because without the notion of a pre-patriarchal, just and harmonious law, the series could not achieve its ideological ends. The words and acts of men could not be correctly judged and the record set straight. But it must be mother's law, not father's. Merlin is presented as little more than Viviane's mouthpiece; Arthur is a puppet king who, when he disobeys, is ousted.

It is this last function, the call, which fosters a fantasy viewed in the terms I began with: that it sustains the desire – or a horror which betrays the desire – of a return to a lost, maternal paradise; that it occludes the coincidence of the object's emergence and loss by providing a narrative account of the loss; last, that it operates ideologically, that is, in this context, paranoically, providing a narrative of perpetrators and victims to account for the disaster.

Both films sustain the fantasy of a maternal voice calling us home, but *Mists*, owing to a logical and ideological impasse, tends less towards the sense of necessity that makes a myth. *Mists* attempts to sit on both sides of the symbolic divide, because to acknowledge the necessity of the paradoxical loss which language entails might involve acknowledging the name-of-the-father, if, as Lacan suggests, this name 'support[s] ... the symbolic function [and is associated with] the figure of the law' (Lacan, 1977b: 67). *Mists* associates the symbolic function, not with the paternal *figure* of the law, but with the actual, oppressive laws of the fathers. In the series these laws are expressed in Arthur's betrayal of Avalon and the Mother Goddess, and the subsequent Christian destruction of the old matriarchal religion. This is what creates the impasse for *Mists* – a confusion of the symbolic name-of-the-father with the politics of patriarchy. *Excalibur* also confuses the two, but because of its different positioning there is no impasse. To put it another way, *Excalibur*'s mythopoeic strategies present no obstacle to its fantasy; the film shelters from the fear of mother's unsettling desire behind the barrier of father's symbolic law. Myth is co-opted by fantasy in *Excalibur* as it is in *Mists*.

In the films myth and fantasy evoke different temporalities, myth the eternity of the immortals because it invokes what is always true for humanity (but an eternity viewed from the side of the symbolic). Fantasy can evoke the primordial because it can gesture to a time before a cut or Fall – before the calamity. The medieval is invoked to stand in for each of these temporalities, the eternal and the primordial, and the film music functions to differentiate the two.

One could say that because of their different ideological agendas (their fantasies) – *Excalibur* on the side of the function of a symbolic associated with the father, *Mists* on the side of a maternal, pre-symbolic symbolic – each favours the music that supports these positions, *Excalibur* the mythopoeic, *Mists* the calling voice.

## Notes

1 I use 'screen shows' here as a title to cover both *Excalibur*, the film, and *Mists of Avalon*, the TV series. But for the sake of simplicity I refer to both indiscriminately as films throughout the chapter.
2 See too Philip Pullman's odd twist to the Fall narrative in *His Dark Materials*, in particular the third book, *The Amber Spyglass* (2000), where it is a Fall which liberates humanity from the cruel grip of God and his Church but in such a way that suggests something of a new Eden, where conscious beings will live more in harmony with the natural world. Tolkien's *LOTR*, of course, also laments bitterly the loss of a pre-industrial Eden.
3 See also the work of Kathryn Kalinak (1992) and Anahid Kassabian (2000) for further analyses of the ways in which film music works to guide audience response.
4 As Raúl Ruiz has observed, 'in the stories of King Arthur, characters act without Will; they cannot *not* want what they want' (2009: n.p.).
5 The following response to *Avatar* is an instance of a seductive fantasy of harmony which yet could not disguise the necessities of the 'real world': 'Every time I watched this, tears came in my eyes. Why? Pandora is so much like my deepest dreams. Everything is in harmony. In the real world everything is sad. Guess that's what it's all about: "Sooner or later though, you always have to wake up"' ('tuulari', 2011). 'tuulari' is quoting Jake Sully's words from the film: 'I was a warrior who dreamed he could bring peace ... but sooner or later though, you always have to wake up' (Cameron, 2009).
6 There is a Tennysonian echo here, as in so much nostalgic medievalism. Compare Arthur answering Sir Bedivere from the barge: 'The old order changeth, yielding place to new', from the 'Passing of Arthur' (Tennyson, 1969: 1752).
7 For Nickolas Haydock '[t]he dragon is time itself', but it is the prophet's eternal time in which '[p]ast, present, and future are screened within the crystal cave [of the dragon] like so many reflections in a house of mirrors' (2008: 71).

8  See Haydock: '[Memory] screens what will have been' (2008: 5). See also Arthur Lindley's account of *Excalibur*, in which myth skews temporality: 'Alternatively, the medieval is translated into the eternal present of myth, as in John Boorman's *Excalibur*, in which Arthur as a figure in a Jungian myth ... is necessarily a past, present and future king' (Lindley, 2007: 20).
9  See Kevin J. Harty who refers to self-fulfilling prophecies of the Arthurian tradition: '[T]he medievalist urge is further encouraged by that part of the legend of Arthur which sees him as once and future king ... and contemporary retellings of the legend of Arthur ... only serve ... as self-fulfilling prophecies of the king's postmedieval return' (Harty, 1999: 6). John Aberth cites John Kennedy as a twentieth-century Arthur, whose 'one brief shining moment' was made over as a latter-day Camelot by the '"Camelot School" of sympathetic scholars' (Aberth, 2003: 16). In *Mists*, of course, it is the Goddess who returns. Or who, perhaps, never really went away.
10  Guinevere's dance music offers an important exception, but as it gains in importance as she takes centre stage it loses its medieval qualities.
11  Diegetic music is 'music that (apparently) issues from a source within the narrative' (Gorbman, 1987: 22).
12  Distinctions between the Middle Ages and the Renaissance are not usually observed in music for film or TV. Easily remembered motifs, such as the 'Hey nonny nonny' and 'Down a down' of Tudor England, work for either, as in the supposedly twelfth-century TV miniseries *Pillars of the Earth* (2010), directed by Sergio Mimica-Gezzan.
13  There are a few exceptions to this rule, one of which is Eric Rohmer's *Perceval le Gallois* (1978) (Haines, 2014a: 76).
14  Howard Shore has something a little similar in mind in the score of *LOTR*. According to Jonathon Dean, the Trilogy's education associate, 'Howard Shore has basically, as his mythic motives, the cultures of Middle-earth. That's what he interprets the story as being about' (Adams, 2010: 9). Shore has composed his leitmotifs for peoples rather than for individuals, emphasising the collective nature of myth.
15  Theodor Adorno considered Wagner's system of leitmotifs 'bankrupt', due to an 'allegorical rigidity' which, he believed, has followed it into cinema music. That fate, for him, was enough to damn it: 'The degeneration of the leitmotif is implicit in this: ... it leads directly to cinema music where the sole function of the leitmotiv is to announce heroes or situations so as to help the audience to orientate itself more easily' (Adorno, 2005: 36).
16  Of course, most audience members will not pick this up from the Latin lyrics, but they will pick up a sense of the sublime.

17 See Pugh and Weisl, who cite Orff's *Carmina Burana* (1937) as a '"medieval" touchstone, standing in for "real" medieval music' (Pugh and Weisl, 2013: 103).
18 Pugh and Weisl are getting at something like this when they speak of the 'deeper medievalness of [Carl Orff's] adaptation [of the *Carmina Burana*] than the original' (2013: 103).
19 Adorno and Eisler point out the impossibility of maintaining conventional musical forms in film composition: 'A photographed kiss cannot actually be synchronized with an eight-bar phrase' (Adorno and Eisler, 2005: 8).
20 For instance, on the boards at IMDB, 'johnnywalker2001' asks: 'What music is heard over the opening credits when the word Excalibur first appears? (It's used a lot every time the sword appears in the film, too.) Does anyone know, it's driving me crazy trying to find out!' ('johnnywalker2001', n.d.). This listener doesn't know he's hearing Wagner and will not pick up the Wagnerian references, but he does know it is a quotation and as such has a significance beyond that of the film score.
21 2 The Merlin's spell theme is accessible on YouTube (T. Jones, 2016).
22 See Jacqueline de Weever's account: 'Boorman ... joins the tradition of antifeminist interpretations of *Sir Gawain and the Green Knight*, that woman's power is to be feared because it produces only evil' (Weever, 2002: 59).
23 Susan Aronstein has noted the value of the Arthurian narrative for the American mythopoeic men's movement in its quest for a positive masculine image. Citing Michael Schwalbe and Michael Kimmel, she speaks of a 'crisis in masculinity' 'rooted in the 1960s and reaching its peak in the 1980s and early 1990s' (Aronstein, 2001: 147). The Arthurian legend, especially the quest for the grail, became, in the hands of the movement's promoters, a myth for the recovery of white middle-aged men, 'figuratively' wounded by the demands of feminists and other marginalised groups (147). See also Aronstein's more complex reading of the movement and her discussion of *Excalibur* in chapter 7 of *Hollywood Knights*, in which *Excalibur* and the mythopoeic men's movement were hijacked and ended up as 'poster boys' for the 'neoconservative politics of the 1980s' (Aronstein, 2005: 150).
24 'The Mystic's Dream', accessible on YouTube (McKennitt, 2017).
25 First verse: 'A clouded dream on an earthly night, / Hangs upon the crescent moon; / A voiceless song in an ageless light, / Sings at the coming dawn. / Birds in flight are calling there, / Where the heart moves the stones; / It's there that my heart is calling, / All for the love of you' (Holdridge, 2001).

26 On YouTube (Holdridge, 2012: 2.33).
27 See TV Tropes, 'One-Woman Wail', which offers a number of examples (n.d.). See also Karen Cook's 'Medievalism and Emotions' for a variety of uses of wordless voices in video games (2019: 490–3).
28 On YouTube (Aeone, 2012). First verse lyrics: 'O my love, I stand on a distant shore, The turning tide, Breathes all the mystery of you'. Refrain: 'Mists of Avalon / Cover my heart, / Carry my voice on the wind, / Over the waters that keep us apart, / I will remember you still ... / I will remember you still ...'
29 Howard Shore's Lothlórien theme is available on YouTube (Shore, 2014).
30 See Susan McClary's interpretation of Carmen's 'treacherous undermin[ing] of [José's] diatonic confidence' with her chromatic interventions in the opera *Carmen* (1991: 59).
31 See another McKennitt song, 'Gates of Istanbul', from her CD *An Ancient Muse*: 'Hear there, in that dark blue night / the music calling us home' (McKennitt, 2006: track 2).
32 Also apparent is the monarchism of 'kings and queens'.
33 Website no longer accessible.
34 See also Michel Chion's idea of the 'umbilical web' which 'the voice of the Mother weav[es] around the child' (1999: 61).
35 See again Haydock on conspiracy as 'cinémedievalism's defining cliché' (2008: 35).
36 There is a lively and acrimonious debate on the internet between Christians and neo-pagans about the film, its merits, its supposed obscenity and its historical veracity. See, for instance, filmtracks.com (2001–4).

# Aftermath

Whatever the intentions with which one begins to write it is only in the aftermath, when the writing is finished, that a point is reached where one can see clearly the work that a book is doing. Now that this book is ending it becomes clear that I have always been homing in on a kind of hotspot, a place intensified by the intensity of the engagement of the participants I have studied and of my own engagement; I know it by the heat it generates. This book is the product of an engagement with that hotspot, which I have called the *space between*, a space which music may indicate or into which it may precipitate a fall. To requote Eliot, it is the space where music is 'heard so deeply / That it is not heard at all, but you are the music / While the music lasts' (1968: 44). One cannot know it because when it happens no one is there. In this sense that unknown has directed this investigation of which it is the object – an objectcause. As I have argued, naming the music '*medi*eval', the age in the middle, indicates its placement *between*, guaranteeing that this is indeed the place of that fall.

Each chapter has been marked by some form of ambiguity. As a space between, the *Middle* Ages are named only for their temporal (and, by imaginative association, physical) location, sandwiched between two named entities, the classical age and the Renaissance. These names have a substance of their own. The third is named only by its position relative to the others– a negative framed between two positives – thus an elusive *space between*. This placement has allowed fantasies of a range of contradictory aspects to become attached to the period – sometimes paradisal, sometimes diabolical, sometimes a mixture of the two. And these roads will be different for each one of us. Our choices or our inability to choose mark the difference. Ambivalence is the companion of ambiguity.

Chapter 1 introduced the medieval as an inner space in another sense – that of unconscious desire. The unconscious necessarily produces ambiguity, since it houses those desires repressed by the conscious mind, as in Freud's dictum quoted in Chapter 1: 'It has consequently become a condition for repression that the motive force of unpleasure shall have acquired more strength than the pleasure obtained from satisfaction' (Freud, 1991: 147). The age in the middle suffers from the ambiguity to which any middle (as neither one thing or another) lends itself, and the insecurity produced by ambiguity may be suffered unconsciously.

These ambiguities presented the medieval as dangerous in various ways, capable of blurring or bursting open binaries, as the image of the countertenor threatened in Chapter 4 or the use of oxymoron in fantasy fiction enacted in Chapter 2. In Chapter 3 the *space between* was linked to the mother's body, producing both longing and fear, the 'sonorous womb' as Guy Rosolato termed it (1974: 81) or, in Michel Chion's words (1999: 61), an 'umbilical web', reminiscent of spiders. In Chapter 4 an anxiety around impurity became attached to the countertenor's gender/sexuality, which could not be easily addressed in the context of the academic discourse available to the participants. I suggested that the word 'authenticity' came to stand, in part, for a hoped-for solution to this dilemma. Chapter 5 returned to the linking of the *space between* to the mother's womb and also to a planetary home inhabited by creatures who, as impossible amalgams of animal and human (a version of the Eden dream), are able to live in harmony with their environment as we are not.

In various senses such a blurring of binaries produced the medieval as a non-signifiable space, glimpsed behind the veil drawn over it by fantasy. Thus, it threatened to shatter the hierarchies of categorisation and representation that uphold metaphysical order for humanity. Tolkien and Lewis attempted to bind back this strangeness to its proper place – home – Lewis's 'central region' with God at its heart. God was the safeguard with which they attempted to contain the strangeness of home.

When home is the body, whether our mother's or our own (matter has always referenced the feminine in any case),[1] we are confronted by something more abject than perilous or terrible. Tolkien and Lewis used terms like the 'perilous realm' and the 'terrible good', as discussed in Chapter 3. Such dangers may astound, but they are not unclean, and God is never far away, keeping all things safe and safely masculine, keeping the discomfort of femininity at bay. One instance is Tolkien's description of Aragorn's response to the strange old man met in the forest:

> Aragorn felt a shudder run through him at the sound, a strange cold thrill; and yet it was not fear or terror that he felt: rather it was like the sudden bite of a keen air, or the slap of a cold rain that wakes an uneasy sleeper. (Tolkien, 1993: 483)

The old man, of course, turns out to be Gandalf, returned to Middle Earth in angelic form. Such perils, in spite of the physicality of Tolkien's language, act on the sleeping soul, jolting it awake to new perceptions. They herald its awakening to the divine. This is the numinous in full force. It is fierce and cleansing, almost baptismal, as in Rudolf Otto's description (to reiterate):

> Fear, awe, holy dread
> Fascination, attraction, yearning
> A sense of unspeakable magnitude and majesty
> Energy, urgency, intense dynamism
> Wonder, astonishment, stupefaction
> Mystery, Otherness, incomprehensibility. (Downing, 2005: 65)

You could not call it bowdlerised – it is too strong for that. But it is very clean. What is occluded in the idea of the numinous and in most benign fantasies of the medieval is – always – the poor old body, never clean enough, vulnerable, full of strange lusts, prey to illness, doomed to die. From all this doom the voice can be presented as exempt. Angels may sing, as in the listener comments in Chapter 3, but they do so without calling on the physical apparatus required for song. The only thing we can imagine escaping the body's fate is the voice – built of air, most immaterial of elements, all that separates the living body from the corpse and might therefore outlive it? The voice rises straight and unimpeded to the heavens like the smoke from Abel's sacrifice or, as in Macrobius's account: 'Every soul in this world is allured by musical sound ... for the soul carries with it into the body a memory of the music which it knew in the sky' (Macrobius, 1993: 66). That dream of the bodiless voice is the castle in the air built by the numinous, singing medievalism of the

Tolkien/Lewis tradition and carried into the modern making and reception of medieval song.

Kristeva observed 'It is ... not lack of cleanliness or health that causes abjection but what disturbs identity, system, order' (1982: 4). But it is horror of the abject that constitutes the body *as* unclean. That uncleanness of the musical body was at times so disturbing to medieval minds that it was denied in favour of eternal number, for instance by the author of the *Scholica enchiriadis*: 'Notes pass away quickly; numbers, however, though stained by the corporeal matter of voices and moving things [corporea vocum et motuum materia decolorantur], remain' (cited in Holsinger, 2001: 4). The body is still a disturbance in medieval music. Listeners who hear angels singing on their medieval CDs know, or think they know, what must be excluded for purity, although, as Holsinger has demonstrated, medieval and patristic sources offer a far more varied and contested story.[2]

The modern fever for disembodiment in medieval music is reminiscent of comments by Gilles Deleuze on Francis Bacon's figurative paintings:

> [T]he Figure presses outward, trying to pass and dissolve through the fields. Already we have here the role of the spasm, or of the scream: the entire body trying to escape, to flow out of itself. (Deleuze, 2005: xiii)

And again: 'It is not I who attempt to escape from my body, it is the body that attempts to escape from itself' (2005a: 11).

That 'I', strenuously sustained by the ego, determined to *be* at all costs, is what we name the soul, the breath of life which escapes the body in song, and for good at the hour of our death, Amen. Because surely something must escape! The alternative is appalling to the cleanness of autonomy, the good grammar of subject and object, owned and owner, clearly demarcated with nothing *between*. The pitiful body, desperate to escape itself and achieving it only through the annihilation of death, is an imprisonment like Milton's Satan's, in which 'myself am Hell'.

Desire keeps things clean, as Kristeva observed, marking a decent separation by producing an object which sustains 'I' as subject:

> When I am beset by abjection, the twisted braid of affects and thoughts I call by such a name does not have, properly speaking, a definable

object. The abject is not an ob-ject facing me, which I name or imagine. Nor is it an ob-jest, an otherness ceaselessly fleeing in a systematic quest of desire. (Kristeva, 1982: 1)

This abject

> is something rejected from which one does not part, from which one does not protect oneself as from an object. Imaginary uncanniness and real threat, it beckons to us and ends up engulfing us. (Kristeva, 1982: 4)

That engulfing, in different guises, is both the threat from which medievalist nostalgia preserves the subject and what it fantasises as heart's desire – a more real reality. That very heart of things turns strange at close quarters. This work has led me to that point repeatedly, always unexpectedly, each time astonished again by the rank incompatibility of competing urges in the quest for the medieval evoked by nostalgia, in which music figures so prominently: the urge to go beyond language – the grammar of 'I' and 'thou' – to escape and return home, to become immersed, to fuse with the music, no longer isolated and alone, *and yet* not to die, not to be torn loose from a coherence only made possible by separation. The *between* place, not as troubling ambiguity but as the impossible reconciliation of that paradox is the lure dangled by medievalist nostalgia.

## Notes

1 As in Aristotle's *Generation of Animals*: 'By now it is plain that the contribution which the female makes to generation is the matter used therein' (Aristotle, 2000: 101), or in Isidore of Seville's association of *mater* with *materia*: A mother is so named because something is made from her, for the term 'mother' (mater) is as if the word were 'matter' (materia), but the father is the cause' (Isidore, 2006: 206).
2 Holsinger attributes to the 'powerful legacy of D. W. Robertson Junior and his so-called Exegetical approach to the study of medieval literature and aesthetics' the continuing belief in 'the ubiquitous medieval aspiration to transcend the flesh' (Holsinger, 2001: 28).

# Appendix: Listener response analysis methodology

Listener reviews of, and responses to, the broad category of music they refer to as medieval elicit a number of recurrent tropes, themes and trends, such as the listeners being 'transported to another world' by the music. Such trends draw parallels with high fantasy fiction indicating the influence of this language in listener responses to music which is described as medieval. While there is no assumption that listener responses are sincere, what is important is that the language crafted, and the concepts described, were considered appropriate and relevant expressions in response to these particular musical groups. Such responses are not the norm; rather, they represent a significant minority of the overall corpus of listener responses available online, and are included in Chapter 3 as qualitative data. In order to investigate and quantify these trends, a large dataset of online reviews and comments responding to albums of modern medieval music was collected and analysed.

## Method

1. A total of 14 musical groups were selected for analysis whose music is described, by the artists themselves, in publicity material, or by the listeners as medieval music (see Table 1).
2. Discographies of the selected artists were assessed, with 1–4 albums per artist considered most representative of medieval music chosen for analysis, ensuring a statistically significant dataset of listener responses to 38 albums.
3. A range of websites where music is discussed, including retail sites (Amazon, eBay), streaming sites (YouTube), music review

sites (musicweb.com, rateyourmusic.com, Gramophone.UK etc.) and music discussion/news/discovery sites were identified to ensure a balanced sampling.

4. Identified websites and google search engine results up to page 6 were reviewed with all available comments for the selected albums collected into a spreadsheet documenting: artist, album, website, comment, URL. The following method was applied to prepare the data:
   - Where comments were in a language other than English, translation using translate.google.com was conducted. Where a comment could not be translated, it was excluded.
   - Comments that did not include intelligible text (e.g. emojis only) were excluded.
   - Only top level comments were included, not replies.
5. In order to analyse and compare musical groups stylistically, each album was classified as being from either the 'scholarly' or 'popular' domains, where:
   - **Scholarly groups** carefully conform, either to the notated music evidence available or to the scholarly notion of medieval musical accuracy and authenticity
   
   and
   - **Popular groups** dismiss or disregard the musical evidence with little to no adherence to accurate reconstruction, selection or reinterpretation of specific elements of medieval music in their own style.
6. The dataset of listener responses (n=3375) was then imported into the qualitative analysis software package NVivo and coded for keywords to draw out concepts discussed in Chapter 3.
7. The coded datasets were then manually checked to ensure they represented the intended concept and calculated as percentages.

Table 1 Artists and albums selected for listener response analysis

| Artist | Scholarly / popular | Album | Number of responses |
|---|---|---|---|
| Hilliard Ensemble | Scholarly | Machaut: Motets | 23 |
| | | Pérotin and the ars antiqua, vol. 1 | 9 |
| | | Medieval English Music | 23 |
| | | Power and Dunstaple: Masses and Motets | 12 |
| Gothic Voices | Scholarly | The Mirror of Narcissus – Secular Songs by Guillaume de Machaut | 7 |
| | | A Feather on the Breath of God | 129 |
| | | The Service of Venus and Mars | 10 |
| | | A Laurel for Landini | 9 |
| Mediæval Bæbes | Popular | Worldes Blysse | 71 |
| | | Mirabilis | 90 |
| | | The Rose | 60 |
| This Mortal Coil | Popular | It'll End in Tears | 157 |
| Anonymous 4 | Scholarly | 1000: A Mass for the End of Time | 35 |
| | | The Origin of Fire: Hildegard von Bingen | 57 |
| | | An English Ladymass | 63 |
| Dead Can Dance | Popular | The Serpent's Egg | 126 |
| | | Aion | 160 |
| Enigma | Popular | MCMXC AD. | 542 |
| | | Le Roi Est Mort, Vive Le Roi! | 164 |
| The Boston Camerata | Scholarly | Tristan & Iseult | 7 |
| | | The Sacred Bridge (Jews & Christians in Medieval Europe) | 12 |
| | | Carmina Burana | 7 |
| | | A Medieval Christmas | 29 |

**Table 1** Artists and albums selected for listener response analysis (Continued)

| Artist | Scholarly / popular | Album | Number of responses |
|---|---|---|---|
| Omnia | Popular | Wolf Love | 18 |
| | | Earth Warrior | 134 |
| | | Reflexions | 354 |
| Faun | Popular | Eden | 111 |
| | | Midgard | 181 |
| | | Von den Elben | 350 |
| Corvus Corax | Popular | Viator | 8 |
| | | Swerker | 54 |
| | | Seikilos | 18 |
| Blackmore's Night | Popular | Secret Voyage | 109 |
| | | Shadow of the Moon | 133 |
| Qntal | Popular | Translucida | 20 |
| | | Qntal V: Silver Swan | 21 |
| Trio Mediaeval | Scholarly | Stella Maris | 24 |
| | | Aquilonis | 43 |

# Works cited

Abel, Sam (1996) *Opera in the Flesh: Sexuality in Operatic Performance*. Boulder, CO: Westview Press.
Aberth, John (2003) *A Knight at the Movies: Medieval History on Film*. New York: Routledge.
Adams, Doug (2010) *The Music of the Lord of the Rings Films: A Comprehensive Account of Howard Shore's Scores (Book and Rarities CD)*. Van Nuys, CA: Alfred Music.
Addison, Joseph (1975) 'Ode'. In *The Norton Anthology of Poetry*. Revised edition, 443–4. New York: Norton.
Adorno, Theodor (2005) *In Search of Wagner*. Foreword by Slavoj Žižek. Translated by Rodney Livingstone. London: Verso.
Adorno, Theodor (2007) 'Music and Language: A Fragment' (From *Quasi una fantasia* and *Negative Dialectics*, III.iii.12.). In *On What Cannot Be Said: Apophatic Discourses in Philosophy, Religion, Literature, and the Arts*. Volume 2: *Modern and Contemporary Transformations*, edited by William Franke, 262–70. Notre Dame, IN: University of Notre Dame Press.
Adorno, Theodor, and Hanns Eisler (2005) *Composing for the Films*. New York: Continuum Impacts. Originally published 1947.
Adorno, Theodor, E. Frenkel-Brunswik, D. J. Levinson and R. N. Sanford (2019) *The Authoritarian Personality*. Introduction by Peter E. Gordon. London: Verso. Originally published 1950.
Aeone (2012) '"I Will Remember You Still" by Aeone ["The Mists of Avalon" Theme (with Lyrics)]'. YouTube, 2 June. www.youtube.com/watch?v=OsZxhF7aGjY. Accessed 8 July 2022.
Ahmed, Saladin (2012) 'Is "Game of Thrones" Too White?' *Salon*, 1 April. www.salon.com/2012/04/01/is_game_of_thrones_too_white/. Accessed 24 June 2021.
Ahmed, Sara (2007) 'A Phenomenology of Whiteness'. *Feminist Theory* 8 (2): 149–68.

# Works cited

Alexander, Lloyd (2006) *The High King*. Book 5 of *The Chronicles of Prydain*. New York: Henry Holt.
Alexander, Michael (2007) *Medievalism: The Middle Ages in Modern England*. New Haven, CT: Yale University Press.
Alla Francesca (2001) *Le Roman de la rose*. Opus 111, OP 30303, compact disc.
'alpha_grrl' (2007) Amazon customer review of *The Lord of the Rings*. www.amazon.com/LORD-RINGS-HOBBIT-Boxed-Set/product-reviews/B00PVJ70LW/ref=cm_cr_arp_d_viewopt_kywd?pageNumber=1&filterByKeyword=everything+is+forgotten. Accessed 5 February 2021.
'amc654' (2004) Amazon customer review of Hilliard Ensemble, *Motets: Guillaume de Machaut*. www.amazon.com/Motets-Hilliard-Ensemble/dp/B0001A7D3G/ref=cm_cr_pr_product_top. Accessed 4 January 2021.
Anders, Charlie Jane (2012) 'George R. R. Martin Breaks it down for You about Sex and Violence in Entertainment'. Gizmodo. https://io9.gizmodo.com/george-r-r-martin-breaks-it-down-for-you-about-sex-and-5929401. Accessed 1 January 2021.
Anderson, Walter Truett (1995) 'Four Different Ways to be Absolutely Right'. In *The Truth about Truth: De-confusing and Re-constructing the Postmodern World*, edited by Walter Truett Anderson, 110–16. New York: Putnam.
Anderson, Walter Truett (1996) *The Fontana Postmodernism Reader*. London: Fontana.
André, Naomi (2006) *Voicing Gender: Castrati, Travesti, and the Second Woman in Early-Nineteenth-Century Italian Opera*. Bloomington, IN: Indiana University Press.
'Angels singing' (1999) Amazon customer review of Gothic Voices, *The Mirror of Narcissus*: www.amazon.com/gp/product/B000002ZGV/qid=1137393828/sr=2-1/ref=pd_bbs_b_2_1/103-2919817-8132605?s=classical&v=glance&n=5174. Accessed 15 January 2021.
Apuleius (1998) *The Golden Ass*. Translated, Introduction and Notes by E. J. Kenney. Harmondsworth: Penguin.
Aristotle (1952) *Metaphysics*. Translated by W. D. Ross. In *The Works of Aristotle*, vol. 1, 499–626. Chicago: Encylopaedia Britannica.
Aristotle (2000) *Generation of Animals*. Translated by A. L. Peck. Cambridge, MA: Harvard University Press.
Aristotle (2002) *De Anima*. Translated, Introduction and Notes by Hugh Lawson-Tancred. London: Penguin. Originally published 1986.
Arnell, Carla A. (2002) 'On Beauty, Justice, and the Sublime in C. S. Lewis's "Till We Have Faces"'. *Christianity and Literature* 52 (1): 23–33.
Arnold, David (2010) *The Chronicles of Narnia: The Voyage of the Dawn Treader (Original Motion Picture Soundtrack)*. Sony Classical, 88697811422, compact disc.

Aronstein, Susan (2001) 'The Return of the King: Medievalism and the Politics of Nostalgia in the Mythopoetic Men's Movement'. In *Medievalism and the Quest for the "Real" Middle Ages*, edited by Clare A. Simmons, 144–59. London: Frank Cass.

Aronstein, Susan (2005) *Hollywood Knights: Arthurian Cinema and the Politics of Nostalgia*. New York: Palgrave Macmillan.

Atterbery, Brian (*c*.1992) *Strategies of Fantasy*. Bloomington, IN: Indiana University Press.

Augustine (1998) *Confessions*. Translated by Henry Chadwick. Oxford: Oxford University Press.

Austin, Linda (2003) 'Children of Childhood: Nostalgia and the Romantic Legacy'. *Studies in Romanticism* 42 (1): 75–98.

Austin, Linda (2011) 'The Nostalgic Moment and the Sense of History'. *postmedieval* 2 (2) (Special issue: *The Medievalism of Nostalgia*, edited by Helen Dell, Louise D'Arcens and Andrew Lynch): 127–40.

Balestri, Avellina (2014) 'Did C. S. Lewis Create the Calormenes Characters to Demonize Muslims?' *The Wisdom Daily*. https://thewisdomdaily.com/did-c-s-lewis-create-the-calormenes-characters-to-demonize-muslims/. Accessed 14 August 2021.

Barbaro, Michael (2017) 'The Daily' Transcript: 'Interview with Former White Nationalist Derek Black'. *New York Times* (22 August). www.nytimes.com/2017/08/22/podcasts/the-daily-transcript-derek-black.html.

Barnhouse, Rebecca (2000) *Recasting the Past: The Middle Ages in Young Adult Literature*. Porthouse, NH: Heinemann.

Barrett, Frederick S., K. J. Grimm, R. W. Robins, T. Wildschut, C. Sedikides and P. Janata (2010). 'Music-Evoked Nostalgia: Affect, Memory and Personality.' *Emotion* 10 (3): 390–403.

Barrett-Peacock, Ruth, and Ross Hagen (2019) *Medievalism and Metal Music Studies: Throwing Down the Gauntlet*. Bingley: Emerald Publishing.

Barthes, Roland (1974) *S/Z: An Essay*. Translated by Richard Miller, preface by Richard Howard. New York: Hill & Wang.

Barthes, Roland (1977) 'The Grain of the Voice'. In *Image, Music, Text*. Translated by Stephen Heath, 179–89. London: Fontana Press.

Barthes, Roland (1984) *Responsibility of Forms*. Translated by Richard Howard. Berkeley: University of California Press.

Bataille, Georges (*c*.2001) *The Unfinished System of Nonknowledge*. Edited and introduction by Stuart Kendall, translated by Michelle and Stuart Kendall. Minneapolis, MN: University of Minnesota Press.

Baudrillard, Jean (1983) *Simulations*. Translated by Paul Foss, Paul Patton and Philip Beitchmann. New York: Columbia University Press.

Benjamin, Walter (1970) 'Theses on the Philosophy of History'. In *Illuminations*, edited and introduction by Hannah Arendt, translated by Harry Zohn, 253–64. New York: Harcourt Brace Jovanovich.

Bennett, Alana (2015) 'Reinventing the Past in European Neo-Medieval Music'. In *The Middle Ages in Popular Culture: Medievalism and Genre*, edited by Helen Young, loc. 91–112. Amherst, NY: Cambria. Kindle.

Bernau, Anke, and Bettina Bildhauer, eds (2009) *Medieval Film*. Manchester: Manchester University Press.

Bessman, Jim (1998) 'Virgin's Baebes Get Mediaeval in U.S: A Cappella Act Brings Contemporary Edge to Medieval Music'. *Billboard* (8 August), pp. 12, 17. https://worldradiohistory.com/Archive-All-Music/Billboard/90s/1998/BB-1998-08-08.pdf.

Betthauser, Eric (1998) 'The (Un)official Countertenor Homepage'. www.medieval.org/emfaq/performers/countertenors.html#castrati. Accessed 25 January 2021.

'Bibliovore' (2002) Amazon customer review of Mediæval Bæbes, *Worldes Blysse*. www.amazon.com/gp/product/customer-reviews/B00000JMXJ/ref=cm_rev_next/002-4342554-6800848?ie=UTF8&customer-reviews.sort%5Fby=-SubmissionDate&n=5174&s=music&customer-reviews.start=11. Accessed 27 January 2021.

Biskas, Marios, Wing-Yee Chung, Jacob Juhl, Constantine Sedikides, Tim Wildschut and Erica Hepper (2019) 'A Prologue to Nostalgia: Savouring Creates Nostalgic Memories that Foster Optimism'. *Cognition and Emotion* 33 (3): 417–27.

Blake, Katharine (2020) 'The Making of Prayers of the Rosary'. Bandcamp. https://mediaevalbaebes.bandcamp.com/album/prayers-of-the-rosary. Accessed 6 February 2021.

Blake, William (1976) *The Portable Blake*. Edited by Alfred Kazin. New York: Viking Press.

Blocher, Christoph (2006) 'When Sehnsucht Desire Leads You up the Garden Path'. *Speech Ninth International Woodcarvers Symposium in Brienz on the Theme of Sehnsucht (Desire)*, 10 July. www.ejpd.admin.ch/ejpd/en/home/latest-news/reden—interviews/reden/archiv/reden_christoph_blocher/2006/2006-07-10.html. Accessed 21 October 2014.

Boethius (1989) *Fundamentals of Music*. Translated, introduction and notes by Calvin M. Bower, edited by Claude V. Palisca. New Haven: Yale University Press.

Bonnett, Alistair (2010) *Left in the Past: Radicalism and the Politics of Nostalgia*. London: Continuum.

Boorman, John, dir. (1981) *Excalibur*. Burbank: Warner Bros.

Boston Camerata (1987) *Tristan and Iseult*. Directed by Joel Cohen. Erato CD # 98482, compact disc.

Boston Camerata (2011) 'Tristan & Iseult: 2 – From Ireland to Cornwall; The Love Potion'. YouTube, 27 January. www.YouTube.com/watch?v=XR8_JbJghsA. Accessed 5 February 2021.

Bowers, Jane (1993) 'Women's Music and the Life Cycle'. *International League Women Composers Journal* (October): 14–20.
Bowers, Roger (1980) 'The Performing Pitch of English 15th-century Church Polyphony'. *Early Music* 8 (1): 21–8.
Bowman, James (2009) 'James Bowman on Striking a High Note'. *The Guardian* (26 November). www.theguardian.com/music/2009/nov/26/james-bowman-countertenor-revival. Accessed 15 January 2021.
Boym, Svetlana (2001) *The Future of Nostalgia*. New York: Basic Books.
Bradley, Marion Zimmer (1993) *The Mists of Avalon*. London: Penguin.
Bragg, Melvyn (1985) 'Interview with Francis Bacon'. Documentary, directed by David Hinton. London: *Arena* for London Weekend Television, *The South Bank Show*.
Brown, Howard Mayer (1988) 'Pedantry or Liberation: A Sketch of the Historic Performance Movement'. In *Authenticity and Early Music: A Symposium*, edited by Nicholas Kenyon, 27–56. Oxford: Oxford University Press.
Budner, Stanley (1962). 'Intolerance of Ambiguity as a Personality Variable'. *Journal of Personality* 30 (1): 29–50.
Burke, Edmund (1998). *A Philosophical Enquiry into the Origin of our Ideas of the Sublime and Beautiful*. Edited by Adam Phillips. Oxford: Oxford University Press. Originally published 1757.
Butler, Charles (2006) *Four British Fantasists: Place and Culture in the Children's Fantasies of Penelope Lively, Alan Garner, Diana Wynne Jones, and Susan Cooper*. Lanham, MD: Children's Literature Association and Scarecrow Press.
Butler, Judith (2006) 'Foreword: Bracha's Eurydice'. In *The Matrixial Borderspace*, by Bracha Ettinger, edited by Brian Massumi, vii–xii. Minneapolis, MN: University of Minnesota Press.
Byatt, A. S. (2003) 'Harry Potter and the Childish Adult'. *New York Times* (7 July).
Caldecott, Stratford (2003) *Secret Fire: The Spiritual Vision of J. R. R. Tolkien*. London: Darton Longman & Todd.
Caldwell, John (2014) 'Quinible'. In *Grove Music Online*: Oxford University Press. www.oxfordmusiconline.com. Accessed 15 December 2020.
Cameron, James, dir. (2009) *Avatar*. Los Angeles: 20th Century Fox.
Camille, Michael (1985) 'The Book of Signs: Writing and Visual Difference in Gothic Manuscript Illumination'. *Word and Image* 1 (2): 133–48.
Carlos, Caitlin Vaughn (2020) '"Ramble On": Medievalism as a Nostalgic Practice in Led Zeppelin's Use of J. R. R. Tolkien'. In *The Oxford Handbook of Music and Medievalism*, edited by Stephen C. Meyer and Kirsten Yri, 530–46. Oxford: Oxford University Press.

Carpenter, Humphrey (1977) *J. R. R. Tolkien: A Biography*. London: Allen & Unwin.

Carpenter, Humphrey (2006) *The Inklings: C. S. Lewis, J. R. R. Tolkien and their Friends*. London: HarperCollins.

Carroll, Shiloh (2018) *Medievalism in 'A Song of Ice and Fire' and 'Game of Thrones'*. Cambridge: Brewer.

Casagrande, Gino (2004) 'Synaesthesia and Dante: A Synaesthetic Approach to *Purgatorio* X 55–63'. www.gicas.net/purg.html. Accessed 25 January 2021.

Cassin, Barbara (2016) *Nostalgia: When Are We Ever at Home?* Translated by Pascale-Anne Brault. New York: Fordham University Press.

Celtic Woman (2009) 'Celtic Woman – The Call (Official Video)'. YouTube, 28 November. www.youtube.com/watch?v=XD6RdI1QqCg. Accessed 9 July 2022.

Celtic Woman (2019) 'Celtic Woman | Going Home'. YouTube, 19 April. www.youtube.com/watch?v=zmNvFWFz-7g. Accessed 9 July 2022.

Chance, Jane, ed. (2003) *Tolkien the Medievalist*. New York: Routledge.

Chance, Michael (1999) 'Countertenors'. Interview on *The Southbank Show*. Website no longer accessible.

Chandler, Alice (1970) *A Dream of Order: The Medieval Ideal in Nineteenth-century English Literature*. Lincoln, NE: University of Nebraska Press.

Chastelain de Couci (1964) *Chansons attribuées au Chastelain de Couci fin du xii$^e$–début du xiii$^e$ siècle*. Edited by Alain Lerond. Paris: Presses Universitaires de France.

Chaucer, Geoffrey (1974) *Complete Works of Geoffrey Chaucer*. Edited by F. N. Robinson, 2nd edition. London: Oxford University Press.

Child, Francis James (1965) *The English and Scottish Popular Ballads*. 5 vols. Mineola, NY: Dover.

Chion, Michel (1999) *The Voice in Cinema*. Edited and translated Claudia Gorbman. New York: Columbia University Press.

Church, Michael (2011) 'We Polarise People's Reactions'. *Financial Times* (28 January). www.ft.com/intl/cms/s/2/bb55f17a-2a62-11e0-804 a-00144feab49a.html#axzz400RF0jN1. Accessed 15 December 2020.

Cioran, E. M. (1998) *History and Utopia*. Translated by Richard Howard. Chicago: University of Chicago Press.

Cixous, Hélène (1986) 'Sorties: Out and Out: Attacks/Ways Out/Forays'. In *The Newly Born Woman*, edited by Hélène Cixous and Catherine Clément, translated by Betsy Wing, introduction by Sandra M. Gilbert, 63–132. Minneapolis, MN: University of Minnesota Press.

Clemencic Consort (2011) 'Carmina Burana 24 – Ich was ein chint so wolgetan'. YouTube, 28 September. www.YouTube.com/watch?v=L9lIHmurpyo. Accessed 15 June 2022.

Clute, John (2016 [2007]) '"Fantastika in the World Storm": A Talk'. In *Pardon this Intrusion*. Gateway. Ebook.
Cohen, Jeffrey Jerome (2003) *Medieval Identity Machines*. Minneapolis, MN: University of Minnesota Press.
Cook, Karen M. (2019) 'Medievalism and Emotions in Video Game Music'. *postmedieval* 10 (4): 482–97.
Cooper, Susan (1973) *The Dark is Rising*. Book 2 of *The Dark is Rising* sequence. New York: Aladdin Paperbacks.
Cooper, Susan (2000a) *Silver on the Tree*. Book 5 of *The Dark is Rising* sequence. New York: Aladdin Paperbacks.
Cooper, Susan (2000b) *The Grey King*. Book 4 of *The Dark is Rising* sequence. New York: Aladdin Paperbacks.
Copland, Aaron (1993) *What to Listen for in Music*. New York: New American Library.
Corbiau, Gérard, dir. (1994) *Farinelli il castrato*. Paris: Stéphan Films.
Cordeiro, Edson (2009) 'Carmen Habanera – Live in Brazil'. YouTube, 25 October. www.youtube.com/watch?v=pOJb5CteMpg. Accessed 15 January 2021.
Coveney, Peter (1967) *The Image of Childhood*. Revised edition, introduction by F. R. Leavis. Baltimore: Penguin.
Dahlhaus, Carl (1989) *The Idea of Absolute Music*. Translated by Roger Lustig. Chicago: University of Chicago Press.
Dame, Joke (1994) 'Unveiled Voices: Sexual Difference and the Castrato'. In *Queering the Pitch: The New Gay and Lesbian Musicology*, edited by Philip Brett Elizabeth Wood and Gary C. Thomas, 139–54. New York: Routledge.
Daniels, David (1985) Article no longer accessible.
Daniels, E. B. (1985) 'Nostalgia: Experiencing the Elusive'. In *Descriptions*, edited by Don Ihde and Hugh J. Silverman, 76–90. Albany: State University of New York Press.
D'Arcens, Louise (2011) 'Laughing in the Face of the Past: Satire and Nostalgia in Medieval Heritage Tourism'. *postmedieval* 2 (2) (Special issue: *The Medievalism of Nostalgia*, edited by Helen Dell, Louise D'Arcens and Andrew Lynch): 155–70.
Davis, Fred (1979) *Yearning for Yesterday: A Sociology of Nostalgia*. New York: Macmillan.
Deleuze, Gilles (2004) 'Plato and the Simulacrum'. Appendix 1, *The Logic of Sense*. Translated by Mark Lester with Charles Stivale. Edited by Constantin V. Boundas. London: Continuum.
Deleuze, Gilles (2005) *Francis Bacon: The Logic of Sensation*. Translated by Daniel W. Smith. London: Continuum.

Deleuze, Gilles, and Félix Guattari (1987) *A Thousand Plateaus: Capitalism and Schizophrenia*. Translation and foreword by Brian Massumi. London: Continuum.

Dell, Helen (2011a) 'Nostalgia and Medievalism: Conversations, Contradictions, Impasses'. Editor's introduction. *postmedieval* 2 (2) (Special issue: *The Medievalism of Nostalgia*, edited by Helen Dell, Louise D'Arcens and Andrew Lynch): 115–26.

Dell, Helen (2011b) '"Yearning for the Sweet Beckoning Sound": Musical Longings and the Unsayable in Medievalist Fantasy Fiction'. *postmedieval* 2 (2) (Special issue: *The Medievalism of Nostalgia*, edited by Helen Dell, Louise D'Arcens and Andrew Lynch): 171–85.

Dell, Helen (2016a) 'Musical Medievalism and the Harmony of the Spheres'. In *The Cambridge Companion to Medievalism*, edited by Louise D'Arcens, 60–74. Cambridge: Cambridge University Press.

Dell, Helen (2016b) 'The Medieval Voice'. In *Since Lacan: Papers of the Freudian School of Melbourne 25*, edited by Linda Clifton, 247–58. London: Karnac.

Dell, Helen (2018) 'What to Do with Nostalgia in Medieval and Medievalism Studies?'. *Emotions: History, Culture, Society* 2 (2): 274–91.

Dell, Helen (2019a) 'Music and the Emotions of Medievalism': The Quest for Identity'. *postmedieval* 10 (4) (Special issue: *Music, Emotions, Medievalism*, edited by Helen Dell, Andrew Lynch and Elizabeth Randell Upton: 411–22.

Dell, Helen (2019b) '"A Single, True, Certain Authenticity": The Authenticity Wars in English Twentieth-century Folk and Medieval Music Revivals'. *postmedieval* 10 (4) (Special issue: *Music, Emotions, Medievalism*, edited by Helen Dell, Andrew Lynch and Elizabeth Randell Upton: 439–51.

Dell, Helen, Louise D'Arcens and Andrew Lynch, eds (2011) *The Medievalism of Nostalgia*. (Special issue) *postmedieval* 2 (2).

Dell, Helen, Andrew Lynch and Elizabeth Randell Upton (2019) *Music, Emotions, Medievalism* (Special issue) *postmedieval* 10 (4).

Derrida, Jacques (1988) *Limited Inc*, edited by Gerald Graff, translated by Samuel Weber. Evanston, IL: Northwestern University Press.

Derrida, Jacques (2005) *Writing and Difference*. Translated, introduction and notes by Alan Bass. London: Taylor & Francis. Ebook.

Digou, Mike (2003) 'Hitchcock's Macguffin in the Works of David Mamet'. *Literature Film Quarterly* 31 (4): 270–5.

Dinshaw, Carolyn (1999) *Getting Medieval: Sexualities and Communities, Pre- and Postmodern*. Durham, NC: Duke University Press.

Dinshaw, Carolyn (2011) 'Nostalgia on my Mind'. Book Review Essay. *postmedieval* 2 (2) (Special issue: *The Medievalism of Nostalgia*, edited by Helen Dell, Louise D'Arcens and Andrew Lynch): 225–38.

Dinshaw, Carolyn (2012) *How Soon is Now? Medieval Texts, Amateur Readers, and the Queerness of Time*. Durham, NC: Duke University Press.
Disney, Walt, prod. (1940) *Fantasia*. Burbank: Walt Disney Animation Studios.
Dolar, Mladen (1996) 'The Object Voice'. In *Gaze and Voice as Love Objects*, edited by Renata Salecl and Slavoj Žižek, 7–31. Durham, NC: Duke University Press.
Dolar, Mladen (2006) *A Voice and Nothing More*. Cambridge, MA: MIT Press.
Downing, David C. (2005) *Into the Wardrobe: C. S. Lewis and the Narnia Chronicles*. San Francisco: Jossey Bass.
Drout, Michael D. C. (1996) 'The Influence of J. R. R. Tolkien's Masculinist Medievalism'. *Medieval Feminist Forum: A Journal of Gender and Sexuality* 22 (1): 26–7.
Duffin, Ross, ed. (2000) 'Preface'. In *A Performer's Guide to Medieval Music*, edited by Ross Duffin, ix–1. Bloomington, IN: Indiana University Press.
Dugan, Holly, and Lara Farina (2012) 'Intimate Senses/Sensing Intimacy' (Editors' introduction to special issue *The Intimate Senses*). *postmedieval* 3 (4): 373–9.
Dunsany, Edward John Moreton Drax Plunkett, Lord (1999) *The King of Elfland's Daughter*. New York: Random House.
Dyer, Joseph (1976) 'The Universal Voice'. *Early Music* 4 (4): 489–91.
Eberstadt, Fernanda (2010) 'Who Can Resist a Man who Sings Like a Woman'. *New York Times* (19 November). www.nytimes.com/2010/11/21/magazine/21soprano-t.html. Accessed 15 January 2021.
Eco, Umberto (1986) *Faith in Fakes*. Translated by William Weaver. London: Secker and Warburg.
'Eerie' (1999) Amazon customer review of Mediæval Bæbes, *Worldes Blysse*. www.amazon.com/gp/product/customer-reviews/B00000JMXJ/ref=cm_cr_dp_2_1/103-2919817-8132605?%5Fencoding=UTF8&s=music. Accessed 5 January 2021.
Edel, Uli, dir. (2001) *Mists of Avalon*. Atlanta, GA: TNT.
Edelman, Gilad (2021) 'You Should Listen to CDs'. *Wired*, 23 December. www.wired.com/story/you-should-listen-to-cds/. Accessed 10 June 2022.
Eden, Bradford Lee (2003) '"The Music of the Spheres": Relations between Tolkien's *The Silmarillion* and Medieval Cosmological and Religious Theory'. In *Tolkien the Medievalist*, edited by Jane Chance, 183–93. New York: Routledge.
Eden, Bradford Lee, ed. (2010a) *Middle-earth Minstrel: Essays on Music in Tolkien*. Jefferson, NC: McFarland.
Eden, Bradford Lee (2010b) 'Strains of Elvish Song and Voices: Victorian Medievalism, Music, and Tolkien. In *Middle-earth Minstrel: Essays on*

*Music in Tolkien*, edited by Bradford Lee Eden, loc. 1147. Jefferson, NC: McFarland.

Eidenmuller, Michael (2001) 'American Rhetoric: Rhetorical Figures in Sound'. www.americanrhetoric.com/figures/oxymoron.htm. Accessed 12 January 2021.

Eliade, Mircea (1996) *Patterns in Comparative Religion*. Translated by Rosemary Sheed, Introduction to the Bison books edition by John Clifford Holt. Lincoln, NE: University of Nebraska Press.

Eliot, T. S. (2009) *Four Quartets*. London: Faber. Ebook.

Elliot, Andrew B. R. (2011) *Remaking the Middle Ages: The Methods of Cinema and History in Portraying the Medieval World*. Jefferson, NC: McFarland. Kindle.

Elliot, Andrew B. R. (2017a) *Medievalism, Politics and Mass Media: Appropriating the Middle Ages in the Twenty-First Century*. Woodbridge: D. S. Brewer.

Elliot, Andrew B. R. (2017b) 'A Vile Love Affair: Right Wing Nationalism and the Middle Ages'. Part Two of series 'Race, Racism, and the Middle Ages'. *The Public Medievalist* (14 February). www.publicmedievalist.com/vile-love-affair/. Accessed 4 December 2021.

'Enchanted' (2006) Amazon customer review of Mediæval Bæbes, *Worldes Blysse*. www.amazon.com/gp/product/customer-reviews/B00000JMXJ/ref=cm_cr_dp_2_1/103-2919817-8132605?%5Fencoding=UTF8&s=music. Accessed 5 January 2021.

*Encyclopædia Britannica* (2021) Online. www.britannica.com/EBchecked/topic/333693/leading-note. Accessed 5 February 2021.

Ensemble Gilles Binchois (2001) *Le Vrai Rémède d'amour*. Cantus, ASIN: B00005N890, compact disc.

Eriksen, Niels Nymann (2000) *Kierkegaard's Category of Repetition: A Reconstruction*. Berlin: Walter de Gruyter.

Fallows, David (1998) 'Contradistinctions and Contra–Indications'. *Early Music* 26 (2): 381–2.

Farrell, Eliza (2009) 'Race, Language, and Morality: Does Tolkien's Middle-earth Promote a Racial Myth?' University of Pittsburg. Submitted to the Graduate Faculty of Arts and Sciences in partial fulfillment of the requirements for the degree of Bachelor of Philosophy.

Fast, Susan (2000) 'Days of Future Passed: Rock, Pop, and the Yearning for the Middle Ages'. In *Mittelalter-Sehnsucht?: Texte des interdisziplinaren Symposions zur musikalischen Mittelalterrezeption an der Universitat Heidelberg, April 1998*, edited by Annette Kreutziger-Herr and Dorothea Redepenning, 35–55. Kiel: Vauk.

Ferrara, Lidia Ruth (2020) '"Something More Real than Reality": Picasso's Material Pursuit of the *Sur-Réal* (1926–1933)'. Unpublished masters dissertation, University of California-Los Angeles.

Filmtracks.com (n.d.) 'Mists of Avalon'. www.filmtracks.com/comments/titles/mists_avalon/index.cgi?read=162&expand=1#162. Accessed 15 January 2021.

Fimi, Dimitra (2010) *Tolkien, Race and Cultural History: From Fairies to Hobbbits*. London: Palgrave Macmillan.

Finke, Laurie, and Martin B. Shichtman (2007) 'Inner-city Chivalry in Gil Junger's *Black Knight*: A South City Yankee in King Leo's Court'. In *Race, Class, and Gender in 'Medieval' Cinema*, edited by Lynn T. Ramey and Tison Pugh, 107–21. New York: Palgrave Macmillan.

Finke, Laurie, and Martin B. Shichtman (2014) 'The Romance of Medievalism'. In *Medieval Literature: Criticism and Debates*, edited by Holly A. Crocker and D. Vance Smith, 295–303. London: Routledge.

Finn, Kavita Mudan (2019) '*Game of Thrones* is Based on History – Outdated History'. *The Public Medievalist* (16 May). www.publicmedievalist.com/thrones-outdated-history/. Accessed 10 January 2021.

Finn, Kavita Mudan (2020) 'Queen of Sad Mischance: Medievalism, "Realism", and the Case of Cersei Lannister'. In *Queenship and the Women of Westeros: Female Agency and Advice in Game of Thrones and A Song of Ice and Fire*, edited by Zita Eva Rohr and Lisa Benz, 29–52. London: Palgrave Macmillan.

'First Book' (n.d.) Amazon customer review of *Lord of the Rings*. http://www.amazon.com/gp/product/customer–reviews/0007136587/sr=1-1/qid=1188262275/ref=cm_cr_dp_all_top/105-41587. Accessed 27 August 2007.

Fitzgerald, Thomas, and Siobhan McHugh, presenters (2007) 'And the Music Caught Fire: The Rebirth of Irish Music: The Awakening'. Into the Music. ABC Radio National, 10 March.

Flieger, Verlyn (1997) *A Question of Time: J. R. R. Tolkien's Road to 'Faërie'*. Kent, OH: Kent State University Press.

Flieger, Verlyn (2002) *Splintered Light: Logos and Language in Tolkien's World*. Revised edition. Kent, OH: Kent State University Press.

Fradenburg, L. O. Aranye (1997) '"So That We May Speak of Them": Enjoying the Middle Ages'. *New Literary History* 28 (2): 205–30.

Fradenburg, L. O. Aranye (2002) *Sacrifice Your Love: Psychoanalysis, Historicism, Chaucer*. Minneapolis, MN: University of Minnesota Press.

Fradenburg, L. O. Aranye (2009) '(Dis)continuity: A History of Dreaming'. In *The Post-historical Middle Ages*, edited by Elizabeth Scala and Sylvia Federico, 87–116. New York: Palgrave Macmillan.

Franke, William, ed. (2007) *On What Cannot be Said: Apophatic Discourses in Philosophy, Religion, Literature, and the Arts*. Volume 2: *Modern and Contemporary Transformations* (with theoretical and critical essays by William Franke). Notre Dame, IN: University of Notre Dame Press.

Freitas, Roger (2003) 'The Eroticism of Emasculation: Confronting the Baroque Body of the Castrato'. *The Journal of Musicology* 20 (2): 196–249.

Freud, Sigmund (1917) 'Mourning and Melancholia'. In *The Standard Edition of the Complete Psychological Works of Sigmund Freud*, vol. 14 (1914–16): *On the History of the Psycho-Analytic Movement, Papers on Metapsychology and Other Works*. Translated under the general editorship of James Strachey with Anna Freud, assisted by Alix Strachey and Alan Tyson, 237–58. London: Hogarth Press.

Freud, Sigmund (1961) 'Negation'. In *The Standard Edition of the Complete Psychological Works of Sigmund Freud*, vol. 19. Translated under the general editorship of James Strachey with Anna Freud, assisted by Alix Strachey and Alan Tyson. London: Hogarth Press.

Freud, Sigmund (1990) 'The Uncanny'. In *Art and Literature*. Translated by James Strachey, edited by Albert Dickson, 339–76. London: Penguin. Originally published 1919.

Freud, Sigmund (1991) 'Repression'. In *On Metapsychology: The Theory of Psychoanalysis*. Translated by James Strachey, compiled and edited by Angela Richards, 145–58. London: Penguin.

Fritzman, J. M. (1994) 'The Future of Nostalgia and the Time of the Sublime'. *Clio* 23 (2): 167–89.

Gabriele, Matthew (2018) 'Why the Middle Ages Wasn't More Violent than the Modern World Despite What "Game of Thrones" Says'. *Forbes* (28 November). www.forbes.com/sites/matthewgabriele/2018/11/28/middle-ages-not-murder/#570f96e96bfc. Accessed 1 February 2021.

Gammond, Peter (n.d.) 'Male Altos and Sopranos'. Website no longer accessible.

Ganim, John M. (2005) *Medievalism and Orientalism: Three Essays on Literature, Architecture and Cultural Identity*. New York: Palgrave Macmillan.

Garner, Alan (2006a) *Elidor*. Orlando, FL: Odyssey Classics, Harcourt.

Garner, Alan (2006b) *The Owl Service*. Orlando, FL: Odyssey Classics, Harcourt.

Garner, Alan (2006c) *The Moon of Gomrath*. Orlando, FL: Odyssey Classics, Harcourt.

Garone, Anthony (2020) 'Mediæval Bæbes "Prayers of the Rosary" Interview with Katharine Blake, Charlie Cawood, Michael York'. YouTube, 2 December. www.youtube.com/watch?v=Y3GDA5vT88g. Accessed 5 February 2021.

Garrido, Sandra, and Jane W. Davidson (2019) *Music, Nostalgia and Memory: Historical and Psychological Perspectives*. Cham: Palgrave Macmillan.

Genette, Gérard (1997) *Paratexts: Thresholds of Interpretation*. Translated by Jane E. Lewin. Foreword Richard Macksey. Cambridge: Cambridge University Press.
Giles, Peter (1982) *The Counter Tenor*. With additional material by David Mallinder. London: Muller.
Giles, Peter (*c*.1994) *The History and Technique of the Counter-tenor: A Study of the Male High Voice Family*. Aldershot: Scholar Press; Brookfield, VT: Ashgate.
Godwin, Joscelyn (1987) *Music, Mysticism and Magic: A Sourcebook*. Selected and annotated by Joscelyn Godwin. London: Arkana, Penguin.
Godwin, Joscelyn, ed. (*c*.1993). *The Harmony of the Spheres: A Sourcebook of the Pythagorean Tradition in Music*. Rochester, VT: Inner Traditions International.
Goethe, Johann Wolfgang von (n.d.) Letter to Charlotte von Lengenfeld, 28 December 1787. In *Briefe an Charlotte Stein*, vol. 1, n.p. Project Gutenberg. www.projekt-gutenberg.org/goethe/brstein1/chap108.html. Accessed 13 July 2022.
Goethe, Johann Wolfgang von (2005) *The Sorrows of Young Werther*. Translation and introduction by Burton Pike. New York: Modern Library.
Goldstein, Donna M., and Kira Hall (2017) 'Postelection Surrealism and Nostalgic Racism in the Hands of Donald Trump'. *Hau: Journal of Ethnographic Theory* 7 (1): n.p. www.journals.uchicago.edu/doi/10.14318/hau7.1.026. Accessed 25 January 2021.
Goldthwaite, John (1996) *The Natural History of Make-Believe: A Guide to the Principal Works of Britain, Europe, and America*. New York: Oxford University Press.
Gorbman, Claudia (1987) *Unheard Melodies: Narrative Film Music*. Bloomington, IN: Indiana University Press.
Gothic Voices (1987a) *The Mirror of Narcissus*. Hyperion, CDA66087, compact disc.
Gothic Voices (1987b) *Songs of the Trouvères*. Hyperion, CDA66773, compact disc.
Gould, Stephen Jay (1977) *Ontogeny and Phylogeny*. Cambridge, MA: Belknap Press of Harvard University Press.
Greig, Donald (1995) 'Sight-Readings: Notes on *a cappella* Performance Practice'. *Early Music* 23 (1): 124–48.
Grossman, Lev (2002) 'Feeding on Fantasy'. *Time Magazine* 160 (23): 90–2.
Gunn, James (1998) 'The Other Side of the Mirror: Tigana'. Bright Weavings [website]. https://brightweavings.com/the-other-side-of-the-mirror-tigana/. Accessed 18 January 2021.
Guthrie, Steve (2012) 'Time Travel, Pulp Fictions, and Changing Attitudes toward the Middle Ages: Why You Can't Get Renaissance on Somebody's

Ass'. In *Medieval Afterlives in Popular Culture*, edited by Gail Ashton and Daniel T. Kline, 99–112. New York: Palgrave Macmillan.

Haines, John (2001) 'The Arabic Style of Performing Medieval Music'. *Early Music* 29 (3): 369–78.

Haines, John (2004a) *Eight Centuries of Troubadours and Trouvères: The Changing Identity of Medieval Music*. Cambridge: Cambridge University Press.

Haines, John (2004b) 'Living Troubadours and other Recent Uses for Medieval Music'. *Popular Music* 23 (2): 133–53.

Haines, John (2010) *Medieval Song in Romance Languages*. Cambridge: Cambridge University Press.

Haines, John (2014a) *Music in Films on the Middle Ages: Authenticity vs. Fantasy*. New York: Routledge.

Haines, John (2014b) 'Antiquarian Nostalgia and the Institutionalization of Early Music'. In *The Oxford Handbook of Music Revival*, edited by Caroline Bithell and Juniper Hill, 73–93. Oxford: Oxford University Press.

Hardwick, Michael, and Mollie Hardwick (1980) *Alfred Deller: A Singularity of Voice*. London: Proteus.

Harper, Ralph (1966) *Nostalgia: An Existential Exploration of Longing and Fulfilment in the Modern Age*. Foreword by Richard A. Macksey. Cleveland, OH: Press of Western Reserve University.

Hartley, Jamison (2011) 'Complete Map of Narnia'. www.deviantart.com/jamisonhartley/art/Complete-Map-of-Narnia-200995876. Accessed 22 May 2022.

Harty, Kevin J. (1999) 'Lights! Camelot! Action!', In *King Arthur on Film: New Essays on Arthurian Cinema*, edited by Kevin J. Harty, 5–37. Jefferson, NC: McFarland.

Haskell, Harry (1988) *The Early Music Revival: A History*. London: Thames and Hudson.

'Haunted' (2004) Amazon customer review of This Mortal Coil, *It'll End in Tears*. www.amazon.com/exec/obidos/tg/detail/-/B000007SPT/ref=pd_sbs_gw_6/103-2919818132605?v=glance&s=music&n=507846#product-details. Accessed 17 January 2021.

Haydock, Nickolas (2008) *Movie Medievalism: The Imaginary Middle Ages*. Jefferson, NC: McFarland.

Heap, Imogen (2005) 'Can't Take It In'. Track 14 on *The Chronicles of Narnia: The Lion, the Witch and the Wardrobe (Original Soundtrack Album)*. Walt Disney Records, DIS613747, compact disc.

Hegarty, Paul (*c.*2004) *Jean Baudrillard: Live Theory*. London: Continuum.

Hein, Rolland (2002) *Christian Mythmakers: C. S. Lewis, Madeleine L'Engle, J. R. R. Tolkien, George MacDonald, G. K. Chesterton and Others*. Foreword by Clyde S. Kilby. 2nd edition. Chicago: Cornerstone Press.

Heng, Geraldine (2003) *Empire of Magic: Medieval Romance and the Politics of Cultural Fantasy*. New York: Columbia University Press.
Henriques, Gregg and Daniel Görtz (2020) 'What is Metamodernism?' www.psychologytoday.com/au/blog/theory-knowledge/202004/what-is-metamodernism.
Hespèrion XX (1978) *Llibre vermell de Monserrat*. Erato, LC 7873, compact disc.
Hoeckner, Berthold (c.2002) *Programming the Absolute: Nineteenth-century German Music and the Hermeneutics of the Moment*. Princeton, NJ: Princeton University Press.
Holbrook, David (1991) *The Skeleton in the Wardrobe: C. S. Lewis's Fantasies: A Phenomenological Study*. Lewisburg, PA: Bucknell University Press.
Holdridge, Lee (2001) *Mists of Avalon (Original Television Soundtrack)*. Varèse Sarabande, 302 066 266 2, compact disc.
Holland, Tom (2013) 'Game of Thrones is More Brutally Realistic than Most Historical Novels'. *The Guardian* (25 March). www.guardian.co.uk/tv-and-radio/2013/mar/24/game-of-thrones-realistic-history. Accessed 2 January 2021.
Holmes, John R. (2005) 'Tolkien, *Dustsceawung*, and the Gnomic Tense: Is Timelessness Medieval or Victorian?' In *Tolkien's Modern Middles Ages*, edited by Jane Chance and Alfred K. Siewers, 43–58. New York: Palgrave Macmillan.
Holmes, John R. (2010) '"Inside a Song": Tolkien's Phonaesthetics'. In *Middle-earth Minstrel: Essays on Music in Tolkien*, edited by Bradford Lee Eden, 26–46. Jefferson, NC: McFarland.
Holsinger, Bruce (2001) *Music, Body, and Desire in Medieval Culture: Hildegard of Bingen to Chaucer*. Stanford: Stanford University Press.
Holsinger, Bruce (2005) *The Premodern Condition: Medievalism and the Making of Theory*. Chicago: University of Chicago Press.
Holsinger, Bruce (2007) *Neo-medievalism, Neoconservatism, and the War on Terror*. Chicago: Prickly Paradigm Press.
Huizinga, Johan (1999) *The Waning of the Middle Ages*. Translated and adapted under author's direction by Edward Arnold. Mineola, NY: Dover. Originally published 1924.
Hutcheon, Linda (2000) 'Irony, Nostalgia and the Postmodern'. In *Methods for the Study of Literature as Cultural Meaning*, edited by Raymond Vervliet and Annemarie Estor, 189–207. Leiden: Brill.
Hutcheon, Linda, and Mario J. Valdés (1998–2000) 'Irony, Nostalgia, and the Postmodern: A Dialogue'. *Poligrafías* 3: 18–41.
Hutton, Ronald (2011) 'The Pagan Tolkien'. In *The Ring and the Cross: Christianity and 'The Lord of the Rings'*, edited by Paul Kerry, 57–70. Madison: Fairleigh Dickinson University Press.

Inglis, Fred (1981) *The Promise of Happiness: Value and Meaning in Children's Fiction*. Cambridge: Cambridge University Press.

'Isala' (2004) Amazon customer reviewer for Gothic Voices, *Feather on the Breath of God*. www.amazon.com/Feather-Breath-God-Hildegard-Bingen/product-reviews/B0000CDVR2/ref=cm_cr_arp_d_paging_btm_next_6?pageNumber=6. Accessed 25 January 2021.

Isidore of Seville (2006) *The Etymologies of Isidore of Seville*. Translated by Stephen A. Barney, W. J. Lewis, J. A. Beach and Oliver Berghof, with Muriel Hall. Cambridge: Cambridge University Press.

Itzkoff, Dave (2014) 'George R. R. Martin on "Game of Thrones" and Sexual Violence'. *New York Times* (2 May). https://cn.nytimes.com/film-tv/20140505/t05game/en-us. Accessed January 2021.

Jackson, Peter, dir. (2001–3) *The Lord of the Rings*. Los Angeles: New Line Cinema.

Jackson, Rosemary (1981) *Fantasy: The Literature of Subversion*. London: Routledge.

James, Edward (2012) 'Tolkien, Lewis and the Explosion of Genre Fantasy'. In *The Cambridge Companion to Fantasy Literature*, edited by Edward James and Farah Mendlesohn, 62–78. Cambridge: Cambridge University Press.

James, Henry (2004) 'The Real Thing'. In *The Portable Henry James*, edited by John Auchard, 79–105. New York: Penguin.

James, Jamie (1995) *Music of the Spheres: Music, Science and the Natural Order of the Universe*. New York: Copernicus.

Jameson, Fredric (2002) *A Singular Modernity: Essay on the Ontology of the Present*. New York: Verso.

Jankélévitch, Vladimir (2007) 'Music and Silence'. In William Franck, *On What Cannot be Said: Apophatic Discourses in Philosophy, Religion, Literature, and the Arts*, vol. 2, 283–307. Notre Dame, IN: University of Notre Dame Press.

'jatworks' (2013) 'Nostalgia'. Urban Dictionary. www.urbandictionary.com/define.php?term=Nostalgia. Accessed 5 January 2021.

Jensen, Keith W. (2010) 'Dissonance in the Divine Theme: The Issue of Free Will in Tolkien's *Silmarillion*'. In *Middle-earth Minstrel: Essays on Music in Tolkien*, edited by Bradford Lee Eden, 102–13. Jefferson, NC: McFarland.

John of Garland (Magister de Garlandia) (1991) 'Introductio musice'. Electronic version prepared by Bradley Jon Tucker, Thomas J. Mathiesen and Peter M. Lefferts for the *Thesaurus musicarum latinarum*. From *Scriptorum de musica medii aevi nova series a Gerbertina altera*, 4 vols. Edited by Edmond de Coussemaker. Paris: Durand, 1864–76; reprint Hildesheim: Olms, 1963, 1:1, 57–75. www.chmtl.indiana.edu/tml/13th/GARINT_TEXT.html. Accessed 5 February 2021.

'johnnywalker2001' (n.d.) IMDb boards for *Excalibur*. www.imdb.com/title/tt0082348/board/thread/146277572?d=146277572&p=1#146277572. Accessed 15 August 2020.

Jones, Ashley (2020) 'Mediaeval Baebes Trio – Prayers of the Rosary Launch Show'. YouTube, 7 December. www.youtube.com/watch?v=frNzJ6Mnw50. Accessed 9 July 2022.

Jones, Diana Wynne (1981) *Homeward Bounders*. London: Collins.

Jones, Diana Wynne (1994) *A Sudden Wild Magic*. New York: Avon Books.

Jones, Diana Wynne (1996) *The Tough Guide to Fantasyland*. London: Vista.

Jones, Diana Wynne (2000a) *Fire and Hemlock*. London: Collins.

Jones, Diana Wynne (2000b) *The Lives of Christopher Chant*. London: HarperCollins.

Jones, Diana Wynne (2003) *The Merlin Conspiracy*. London: Collins.

Jones, Diana Wynne (2006) *The Pinhoe Egg*. London: HarperCollins.

Jones, Diana Wynne (2012) 'Inventing the Middle Ages'. In *Reflections of the Magic of Writing*, edited by Diana Wynne Jones, 210–25. Oxford: David Fickling.

Jones, Trevor (2000) *Excalibur (Original Motion Picture Soundtrack) (Millennium Edition)*. Remastered and manufactured AutoGraphic Masterworks. Flying Dutchman, FD-41207, compact disc.

Jones, Trevor (2016) 'Excalibur OST 03 Merlin's Spell'. YouTube, 8 February. www.youtube.com/watch?v=lowvjUZmjRM. Accessed 19 June 2022.

Joy, Eileen, and Craig Dionne (2010) 'Before the Trains of Thought have been Laid Down so Firmly: The Premodern Post/human'. Editor's introduction to special issue, 'When Did We Become Post/human?' *postmedieval* 1 (1/2): 1–9.

Justice, Phyllis (1998) 'Why Celibacy? Odo of Cluny and the Development of a New Sexual Morality'. In *Medieval Purity and Piety: Essays on Medieval Clerical Celibacy and Religious Reform*, edited by Michael Frassetto, 81–118. New York: Garland.

Kalinak, Kathryn (1992) *Settling the Score: Music and the Classical Hollywood Film*. Madison: University of Wisconsin Press.

Kant, Immanuel (c.1978) *Anthropology from a Pragmatic Point of View*. Translated by Victor Lyle Dowdell, revised and edited by Hans H. Rudnick. Introduction by Frederick P. Van De Pitte. Carbondale, IL: Southern Illinois University Press.

Kant, Immanuel (2011) *Observations on the Feeling of the Beautiful and Sublime and Other Writings*. Edited by Patrick Frierson and Paul Guyer. Introduction by Patrick Frierson. Cambridge: Cambridge University Press.

Kassabian, Anahid (2000) *Hearing Film: Tracking Identifications in Contemporary Hollywood Film Music*. New York: Routledge.

Kaufmann, Amy S. (2010) 'Medieval Unmoored'. In *Studies in Medievalism XIX: Defining Neomedievalism(s)*, edited by Karl Fugelso, 1–11. Woodbridge: Boydell & Brewer.

Kaufman, Amy S. (2016) 'Muscular Medievalism'. *The Year's Work in Medievalism* 31: 55–66. https://sites.google.com/site/theyearsworkinmedievalism/all-issues/31-2016?authuser=0. Accessed 21 February 2021.

Kaufman, Amy S., and Paul Sturtevant (2020) *The Devil's Historians: How Modern Extremists Abuse the Medieval Past*. Toronto: University of Toronto Press.

Kay, Guy Gavriel (1996) *The Lions of Al-Rassan*. London: Voyager.

Kay, Guy Gavriel (1999) *Tigana*. New York: Roc.

Kay, Guy Gavriel (2001) *The Darkest Road*. Book 3 of *The Fionavar Tapestry*. New York: Roc.

Kay, Guy Gavriel (2002) *A Song for Arbonne*. New York: Roc.

Kay, Guy Gavriel (2006) *The Summer Tree*. Book 1 of *The Fionavar Tapestry*. London: HarperCollins.

Keats, John (1970) *Poetical Works*. Edited by H. W. Garrod. London: Oxford University Press.

Kenyon, Nicholas (1988) 'Introduction'. In *Authenticity and Early Music: A Symposium*, edited by Nicholas Kenyon, 1–18. Oxford: Oxford University Press.

Kerry, Paul E., ed. (2011) *The Ring and the Cross: Christianity and The Lord of the Rings*. Plymouth: Fairleigh Dickinson University Press.

King, Thomas (2006) 'The Castrato's Castration'. *Studies in English Literature 1500–1900* 46 (3): 563–83.

*King James Bible* (1970) Nashville: Thomas Nelson.

Kitchen, E. F. (2010) *Suburban Knights: A Return to the Middle Ages*. Introduction by Leo Braudy. Brooklyn, NY: PowerHouse Books.

Koelz, Heidi (2013) 'Falsetto'. *Antioch Review* 71 (2): 223–32.

Koenig, John (2021) *The Dictionary of Obscure Sorrows*. New York: Simon & Schuster.

Korrigan, Gabriel (2005) 'Get Medieval'. Urban Dictionary. https://www.urbandictionary.com/define.php?term=get%20medieval. Accessed 20 January 2021.

Kreutziger-Herr, Annette (1998) 'Postmodern Middle Ages: Medieval Music at the Dawn of the Twenty-first Century'. *Florilegium* 15: 187–205.

Kreutziger-Herr, Annette (2005) 'Imagining Medieval Music: A Short History'. In *Studies in Medievalism XIV: Correspondences: Medievalism in Scholarship and the Arts*, edited by Tom Shippey and Martin Arnold, 81–109. Woodbridge: Boydell & Brewer.

Kristeva, Julia (1977) *About Chinese Women*. Translated by Anita Barrows. London: Marion Boyars.

Kristeva, Julia (1981) 'Women's Time'. Translated by Alice Jardine and Harry Blake. *Signs* 7 (1): 13–35.

Kristeva, Julia (1982) *Powers of Horror: An Essay on Abjection*. Translated by Leon S. Roudiez. New York: Columbia University Press.

Kvale, Steinar (1996) 'Themes of Postmodernity'. In *The Fontana Postmodernism Reader*, edited by Walter Truett Anderson, 18–25. London: Fontana.

Labbie, Erin Felicia (2006) *Lacan's Medievalism*. London: University of Minnesota Press.

Lacan, Jacques (1957–58) *The Seminar of Jacques Lacan: Book V: Formations of the Unconscious 1957–1958*. Translated by Cormac Gallagher. Unpublished. www.lacaninireland.com/web/wp-content/uploads/2010/06/Book-05-the-formations-of-the-unconscious.pdf.

Lacan, Jacques (1958–59) *The Seminar of Jacques Lacan, Book VI: Desire and its Interpretation 1958–1959*. Translated by Cormac Gallagher from unedited French typescripts. Unpublished. www.lacaninireland.com/web/wp-content/uploads/2010/06/Book-06-Desire-and-its-interpretation.pdf.

Lacan, Jacques (1962–63) *The Seminar of Jacques Lacan, Book X: Anxiety 1962–1963*. Translated by Cormac Gallagher from unedited French typescripts. Unpublished. www.lacaninireland.com/web/wp-content/uploads/2010/06/Book-10-Anxiety.pdf.

Lacan, Jacques (1966–67) *The Seminar of Jacques, Book XIV: Lacan, the Logic of Phantasy 1966–1967*. Translated by Cormac Gallagher. Unpublished. www.lacaninireland.com/web/wp-content/uploads/2010/06/14-Logic-of-Phantasy-Complete.pdf.

Lacan, Jacques (1967–68) *My Teaching*. Translated by David Macey. London: Verso. www.scribd.com/doc/59808739/Jacques-Lacan-My-Teaching. Accessed 23 January 2021.

Lacan, Jacques (1975) 'The Third' [translation of 'La Troisième'], *Lettres de l'Ecole Freudienne* 16: 177–203.

Lacan, Jacques (1975–76) *The Seminar of Jacques Lacan, Book XXIII: Joyce and the Sinthome 1975–1976*. Translated by Cormac Gallagher from unedited French typescripts. Unpublished. www.lacaninireland.com/web/wp-content/uploads/2010/06/Book-23-Joyce-and-the-Sinthome-Part-1.pdf.

Lacan, Jacques (1977a) *Écrits: A Selection*. Translated by Alan Sheridan. London: Routledge.

Lacan, Jacques (1977b) *The Moment to Conclude*. Translated by Cormac Gallagher. Unpublished. www.lacaninireland.com/web/wp-content/uploads/2014/03/Book-25-The-Moment-to-Conclude.pdf.

Lacan, Jacques (1979) 'The Neurotic's Individual Myth'. *Psychoanalytic Quarterly* 48: 405–25.

Lacan, Jacques (1981) *The Four Fundamental Concepts of Psychoanalysis*. Edited by Jacques-Alain Miller. Translated by Alan Sheridan. New York: Norton.

Lacan, Jacques (1991) *The Ego in Freud's Theory and in the Technique of Psychoanalysis, 1954–1955*. Edited by Jacques-Alain Miller. Translated by Sylvana Tomaselli. Notes by John Forrester. New York: Norton. Book II of *The Seminar of Jacques Lacan*.

Lacan, Jacques (1997) *The Ethics of Psychoanalysis 1959–1960: The Seminar of Jacques Lacan*. Edited by Jacques-Alain Miller. Translated with notes by Dennis Porter. New York: Norton.

Lacan, Jacques (1999) *On Feminine Sexuality: The Limits of Love and Knowledge: Encore, 1972–1973*. Edited by Jacques-Alain Miller. Translation and notes by Bruce Fink. New York: Norton. Book XX of *The Seminar of Jacques Lacan*.

Lacan, Jacques (2006) *Écrits: The First Complete Edition in English*. Translated by Bruce Fink, collected by Héloïse Fink and Russell Grigg. New York: Norton.

Lacan, Jacques (2007) *The Other Side of Psychoanalysis: The Seminar of Jacques Lacan, Book XVII, 1969–1970*. Translated with notes by Russell Grigg. New York: Norton.

Lacan, Jacques (2013) *The Triumph of Religion Preceded by Discourse to Catholics*. Translated by Bruce Fink. London: Polity Press.

Lacan, Jacques (2015) *The Transference 1960–1961: The Seminar of Jacques Lacan, Book VIII*. Edited by Jacques-Alain Miller. Translated by Bruce Fink. Cambridge: Polity Press.

Lacan, Jacques (2020) *The Seminar of Jacques Lacan, Book IV: The Object Relation 1956–1957*. Edited by Jacques-Alain Miller. Translated by A. R. Price. Cambridge: Polity Press.

Lacy, Norris J. (2002) 'Mythopoeia in *Excalibur*'. In *Cinema Arthuriana: Twenty Essays*, edited by Kevin J. Harty (revised edition), 34–43. Jefferson, NC: McFarland.

Larrington, Carolyn (2018) 'Mediating Medieval(ized) Emotion in Game of Thrones'. In *Studies in Medievalism XXVII: Authenticity, Medievalism, Music*, edited by Karl Fugelso, 35–42. Woodbridge: Boydell & Brewer.

Lears, T. J. Jackson (1981) *No Place of Grace: Antimodernism and the Transformation of American Culture, 1880–1920*. New York: Pantheon Books.

Lee, Brian (2016) 'Castrati and Countertenors'. https://vocalability.com/countertenors-vs-castrati/. Accessed 5 January 2021.

Leech-Wilkinson, Daniel (2000) 'Yearning for the Sound of Medieval Music'. In *Mittelalter-Sehnsucht?: Texte des interdisziplinaren Symposions zur musikalischen Mittelalterrezeption an der Universitat Heidelberg, April 1998*, edited by Annette Kreutziger-Herr and Dorothea Redepenning, 295–317. Kiel: Vauk.

Leech-Wilkinson, Daniel (2002) *The Modern Invention of Medieval Music: Scholarship, Ideology, Performance*. Cambridge: Cambridge University Press.

L'Engle, Madeleine (2005a) *Many Waters: A Companion to 'A Wrinkle in Time'*. New York: Yearling.
L'Engle, Madeleine (2005b) *A Swiftly Tilting Planet: A Companion to 'A Wrinkle in Time'*. New York: Yearling.
L'Engle, Madeleine (2005c) *A Wrinkle in Time*. New York: Yearling.
Levitin, Daniel, and Anna K. Tirovolas (2009) 'Current Advances in the Cognitive Neuroscience of Music'. *Annals of the New York Academy of Sciences* 1156: 211–31.
Lewis, C. S. (1946) *The Great Divorce*. New York: Collier.
Lewis, C. S. (1948) 'Priestesses in the Church?' www.episcopalnet.org/TRACTS/priestesses.html. Accessed 19 February 2021.
Lewis, C. S. (1955a) *Surprised by Joy: The Shape of my Early Life*. London: Geoffrey Bles.
Lewis, C. S. (1955b) *That Hideous Strength: A Modern Fairytale for Grownups*. London: Pan.
Lewis, C. S. (1958) *The Allegory of Love: A Study in Medieval Tradition*. Oxford: Clarendon Press.
Lewis, C. S. (1964) *Letters to Malcolm: Chiefly on Prayer*. San Diego: Harvest.
Lewis, C. S. (1966a) *Of Other Worlds: Essays and Stories*. Edited with a preface by Walter Hooper. London: Bles.
Lewis, C. S. (1966b) 'On Stories'. In *Of Other Worlds: Essays and Stories*, edited with a preface by Walter Hooper. London: Bles.
Lewis, C. S. (1966c) 'On Three Ways of Writing for Children'. In *Of Other Worlds: Essays and Stories*, edited with a preface by Walter Hooper. London: Bles.
Lewis, C. S. (1967) *The Discarded Image: An Introduction to Medieval and Renaissance Literature*. Cambridge: Cambridge University Press.
Lewis, C. S. (1970) *God in the Dock: Essays on Theology and Ethics*. Edited by Walter Hooper. Grand Rapids, MI: Eerdmans.
Lewis, C. S. (1977) *Mere Christianity*. Revised edition. London: Fount.
Lewis, C. S. (1980a) *Selected Literary Essays*. Cambridge: Cambridge University Press.
Lewis, C. S. (1980b) *The Weight of Glory and other Addresses*. New York: HarperOne.
Lewis, C. S. (1980c) *Till We Have Faces: A Myth Retold*. Orlando, FL: Harvest Books, Harcourt.
Lewis, C. S. (1986) 'Introduction'. In *Phantastes: A Faerie Romance*, by George MacDonald, v–xii. Grand Rapids, MI: Eerdmans.
Lewis, C. S. (1988) *Letters of C. S. Lewis*. Edited with Memoir by W. H. Lewis. Revised edition by Walter Hooper. New York: Harcourt Brace.

Lewis, C. S. (1992) 'Afterword' to *The Pilgrim's Regress: An Allegorical Apology for Christianity, Reason and Romanticism*. 3rd edition. Grand Rapids, MI: Eerdmans. Ebook.

Lewis, C. S. (1998) *Studies in Medieval and Renaissance Literature*. Collected by Walter Hooper. Cambridge: Cambridge University Press.

Lewis, C. S. (2002) *The Complete C. S. Lewis Signature Classics*. New York: HarperOne.

Lewis, C. S. (2004) 'The Dethronement of Power'. In *Understanding 'The Lord of the Rings': The Best of Tolkien Criticism*, edited by Rose A. Zimbardo and Neil D. Isaacs, 11–15. New York: Houghton Mifflin.

Lewis, C. S. (2005) *The Chronicles of Narnia*. Illustrated by Pauline Baynes. New York: HarperCollins. Originally published 1950–56.

Lewis, C. S. (2007) *Collected Letters*, vol. 3: *Narnia, Cambridge and Joy, 1950–1963*. Edited by Walter Hooper. New York: HarperCollins.

Lewis, C. S. (2009) *The Problem of Pain*. London: HarperCollins. Ebook. Originally published 1940.

Lewis, C. S. (2014) 'Preface' to *George MacDonald: An Anthology*, edited by C. S. Lewis, 17–27. Faded page. Ebook. Originally published 1946.

Lindley, Arthur (1998) 'The Ahistoricism of Medieval Film'. *Screening the Past* 3. www.screeningthepast.com/issue-3-first-release/the-ahistoricism-of-medieval-film/. Accessed 2 February 2021.

Lindley, Arthur (2007) 'Once, Present and Future Kings: *Kingdom of Heaven* and the Multitemporality of Medieval Film'. In *Race, Class and Gender in 'Medieval' Cinema*, edited by Lynn T. Ramey and Tison Pugh, 15–30. New York: Palgrave Macmillan.

Linke, Uli (1999) *Blood and Nation: The European Aesthetics of Race*. Philadelphia: University of Pennsylvania Press.

Livingston, Tamara (1999) 'Music Revivals: Towards a General Theory'. *Ethnomusicology* 43 (1): 66–85.

Lowenthal, David (1985) *The Past is a Foreign Country*. Cambridge: Cambridge University Press.

Lugones, Maria (1994) 'Purity, Impurity, and Separation'. In *Signs: Journal of Women in Culture and Society* 19 (2): 458–79.

'Lulublu' (2001) Amazon customer review of Mediæval Bæbes, *Worldes Blysse*. www.amazon.com/gp/product/customer-reviews/B00000JMXJ/ref=cm_cr_dp_2_1/103-2919817-8132605?%5Fencoding=UTF8&s=music. Accessed 5 January 2021.

Luria, Maxwell S., and Richard L. Hoffman, eds (1974) *Middle English Lyrics*. New York: Norton.

Lynch, Andrew (2005) 'Archaism, Nostalgia, and the Tennysonian War in *Lord of the Rings*'. In *Tolkien's Modern Middle Ages*, edited by Jane Chance and Alfred K Siewers, 77–92. New York: Palgrave Macmillan.

Lynch, Andrew (2011) 'Nostalgia as Critique: Walter Scott's "secret power"'. *postmedieval* 2 (2) (Special issue: *The Medievalism of Nostalgia*, edited by Helen Dell, Louise D'Arcens and Andrew Lynch): 201–15.

McCaffrey, Anne (1978) *Dragonflight*. London: Corgi.

McCamish, Thornton (2008) 'The Reverence of Things Past'. *The Age Extra* (28 December), 15.

McClary, Susan (1991) *Feminine Endings: Music, Gender and Sexuality*. Minneapolis, MN: University of Minnesota Press.

McCoy, Narelle (2014) 'Pagan Communities and the Dissemination of "Celtic" Music'. In *Pop Pagans: Paganism and Popular Music*, edited by Donna Weston and Andy Bennett, 176–88. London: Routledge.

MacDonald, George (2000a) *Lilith: A Romance*. Introduction by C. S. Lewis. Grand Rapids, MI: Eerdmans.

MacDonald, George (2000b) *Phantastes: A Faerie Romance*. Introduction by C. S. Lewis. Grand Rapids, MI: Eerdmans.

MacDonald, George (2001) *At the Back of the North Wind*. New York: Alfred A Knopf. Originally published 1871.

McGee, Timothy (1998) *The Sound of Medieval Song: Ornamentation and Vocal Style According to the Treatises*. Translation from the Latin by Randall A. Rosenfeld. Oxford: Clarendon Press.

McIntyre, Hugh (2018) 'Report: Physical Albums Sell Significantly Better than Digital Ones'. *Forbes* (28 March). www.forbes.com/sites/hughmcintyre/2018/03/28/physical-albums-sell-significantly-better-than-digital-ones-even-today/?sh=42159869b538. Accessed December 2021.

McKennitt, Loreena (2006) *An Ancient Muse*. Quinlan Road, QRCD109, compact disc.

McKennitt, Loreena (2017) 'Loreena McKennitt – The Mystic's Dream'. YouTube, 1 June. www.youtube.com/watch?v=hitsbICdKj4. Accessed 20 February 2021.

Macrobius (*c*.1993) 'Commentary on the Dream of Scipio'. In *The Harmony of the Spheres: A Sourcebook of the Pythagorean Tradition in Music*, edited by Joscelyn Godwin, 64–70. Rochester, VT: Inner Traditions International.

Maly, Michael, Heather Dalmage and Nancy Michaels (2012) 'The End of an Idyllic World: Nostalgia Narratives, Race, and the Construction of White Powerlessness'. *Critical Sociology* 39 (5): 757–79.

Manlove, C. N. (1975) *Modern Fantasy: Five Studies*. Cambridge: Cambridge University Press.

Manlove, C. N. (1992) *Christian Fantasy: From 1200 to the Present*. Notre Dame, IN: University of Notre Dame Press.

Manlove, C. N. (*c*.2003) *From Alice to Harry Potter: Children's Fantasy in England*. Christchurch: Cybereditions.

Mapplethorpe, Robert (2010) 'Self-portrait with Whip'. www.artsy.net/artwork/robert-mapplethorpe-self-portrait-with-whip. Accessed 1 April 2021.

Marcus, Leonard S., ed. (2006) *The Wand in the Word: Conversations with Writers of Fantasy*. Cambridge, MA: Candlewick Press.

Marshall, David W. (2010) 'Getting Reel with Grendel's Mother: The Abject Maternal and Social Critique'. In *Studies in Medievalism XIX: Defining Neomedievalism(s)*, edited by Karl Fugelso, 135–59. Woodbridge: Boydell & Brewer.

Marshall, David W. (2011) 'Neomedievalism, Identification, and the Haze of Medievalisms'. In *Studies in Medievalism XX: Defining Neomedievalism(s) II*, edited by Karl Fugelso, 21–34. Woodbridge: Boydell & Brewer.

Marshall, Melanie L. (2015) 'Voce Bianca: Purity and Whiteness in British Early Music Vocality'. *Women and Music: A Journal of Gender and Culture* 19: 36–44.

Martin Best Mediaeval Ensemble (2015) 'Pax in Nomine Domini'. YouTube, 10 December. www.YouTube.com/watch?v=Klpen360P8k&list=PLUlk6 Ak0JJRbstcS46JnURQxck1Sy0hjq&index=30. Accessed 15 June 2022.

Martin, George R. R. (2003) *A Song of Ice and Fire*. Book 1 of *Game of Thrones* series. London: HarperCollins. Originally published 1996.

Matthews, David (2015) *Medievalism: A Critical History*. Cambridge: D. S. Brewer.

Mediæval Bæbes (1999a) 'All Turns to Yesterday'. Translated by Gareth Williams. *Worldes Blysse*, CD booklet. Virgin, CDVE 941.

Mediæval Bæbes (1999b) 'Kinderly'. Translated by Gareth Williams. *Worldes Blysse*, CD booklet. Virgin, CDVE 941.

Mediæval Bæbes (2008) 'Mediaeval Baebes – Erthe upon Erthe'. YouTube, 16 April. www.youtube.com/watch?v=9eUWs1tDUqY&list=PL64FD4E C747D2EB51&index=6. Accessed 11 January 2021.

Mediæval Bæbes (2009) 'Mediæval Bæbes – Kinderly at the MD Ren Fest on 8-30-2009' [live recording at Maryland Renaissance Festival in Crownsville, MD]. YouTube, 4 September. www.youtube.com/watch?v=WiFrcCSs_B0. Accessed 15 January 2021.

Mediæval Bæbes (2011) 'All Turns to Yesterday'. YouTube, 24 January. www.youtube.com/watch?v=mm7EgiL900o. Accessed 5 February 2021.

Mediæval Bæbes (2021) Website. www.mediaevalbaebes.com. Accessed 5 January 2021.

'Medievil' (n.d.) Information on video game. https://gallowmere.fandom.com/wiki/MediEvil. Accessed 15 January 2021.

'Meditative' (2020) Consumer comment on 'Mediæval Bæbes "Prayers of the Rosary" Interview with Katharine Blake, Charlie Cawood, Michael

York'. YouTube. www.youtube.com/watch?v=Y3GDA5vT88g. Accessed 5 February 2021.

Mendlesohn, Farah (2005) *Diana Wynne Jones: Children's Literature and the Fantastic Tradition*. London: Routledge.

Mendlesohn, Farah (2008) *Rhetorics of Fantasy*. Middletown, CT: Wesleyan University Press.

Menocal, María Rosa (1987) *The Arabic Role In Medieval Literary History: A Forgotten Heritage*. Philadelphia: University of Pennsylvania Press.

*Merriam-Webster Dictionary* (2022) Online. www.merriam-webster.com/dictionary.

Meyer, Stephen C. (2020) 'From the Music of the Ainur to the Music of the Voice-over: Music and Medievalism in *The Lord of the Rings*'. In *The Oxford Handbook of Music and Medievalism*, edited by Stephen C. Meyer and Kirsten Yri, 611–35. Oxford: Oxford University Press.

Meyer, Stephen C., and Kirsten Yri, eds (2020) *The Oxford Handbook of Music and Medievalism*. Oxford: Oxford University Press.

'Michael' (2003) Amazon customer review of Mediæval Bæbes, *Worldes Blysse*. www.amazon.com/gp/product/customer-reviews/B00000JMXJ/ref=cm_cr_dp_2_1/103-2919817-8132605?%5Fencoding=UTF8&s=music. Accessed 5 January 2021.

Miller, Jacques-Alain (2001) 'Jacques Lacan and the Voice'. Translated by Vincent Dachy. *Psychoanalytic Notebooks of the London Circle* 6: 93–104.

Miller, Jacques-Alain (2004) 'Religion, Psychoanalysis'. Translated by Barbara P. Fulks. *Lacanian Ink* 23: n.p. www.lacan.com/frameXXIII2.htm. Accessed 18 February 2020.

Mills, Robert (2018) *Derek Jarman's Medieval Modern*. Woodbridge: D. S. Brewer.

Mimica-Gezzan, Sergio, dir. (2010) *The Pillars of the Earth*. Munich: Tandem Productions.

*Mirabilis* Release Notes (2005) Tolkien Lietuva. www.tolkien.lt. www.forumas.tolkien.lt/viewtopic.php?f=28&t=25&start=200. Accessed 18 January 2021.

Mississippi John Hurt (2010) 'Mississippi John Hurt – The Ballad of Stagolee'. YouTube, 10 July. www.youtube.com/watch?v=4scedJs6hC8. Accessed 21 February 2021.

Morgan, Robert P. (1988) 'Tradition, Anxiety and the Current Musical Scene'. In *Authenticity and Early Music: A Symposium*, edited by Nicholas Kenyon, 57–82. Oxford: Oxford University Press.

Morris, William (1898) *The Sundering Flood*. London: Longmans, Green.

Morrow, Michael (1978) 'Musical Performance and Authenticity'. *Early Music* 6 (2): 233–46.

'Need to relax' (2013) Amazon customer review of Gothic Voices, *Feather on the Breath of God*. www.amazon.com.au/VON-BINGEN-FEATHER-BREATH-GOD/dp/B000002ZGD/ref=cm_cr_arp_d_pl_foot_top?ie=UTF8. Accessed 22 August 2020.

Negus, V. E., Owen Jander and Peter Giles (2001) 'Falsetto (It.; Fr.)'. In *Grove Music Online*. Oxford University Press. https://doi.org/10.1093/gmo/9781561592630.article.09270. Published in print 2001. Accessed 4 January 2021.

Newman, David B., Arthur A. Stone and Norbert Schwarz (2020) 'Nostalgia and Well-being in Daily Life: An Ecological Validity Perspective'. *Journal of Personality and Social Psychology* 118 (2): 325–47.

Nicholas of Cusa (1981) *On Learned Ignorance: A Translation and an appraisal of 'De Docta Ignorantia'*. Translated with an appraisal by Jasper Hopkins. Minneapolis, MN: A. J. Benning Press.

Nicholi, Armand M. (2003) *The Question of God: C. S. Lewis and Sigmund Freud Debate God, Love, Sex, and the Meaning of Life*. New York: Free Press.

O'Malley, Glenn (1957) 'Literary Synesthesia'. *Journal of Aesthetics and Art Criticism*, 15 (4): 391–411.

Orff, Karl (1937) *Carmina Burana*. Boosey & Hawkes.

'Otherworld' (2008) Amazon customer review of Gothic Voices, *Feather on the Breath of God*. www.amazon.com/Feather-Breath-God-Hildegard-Bingen/product-reviews/B0000CDVR2/ref=cm_cr_arp_d_paging_btm_next_6?pageNumber=6. Accessed 25 January 2021.

Otto, Rudolf (1990) *The Idea of the Holy: An Inquiry into the Non-rational Factor in the Idea of the Divine and its Relation to the Rational*. Translated by John W. Harvey. 2nd edition. Oxford: Oxford University Press. Originally published 1923.

Ovid (1955) *Metamorphoses*. Translated by Mary M. Innes. Harmondsworth: Penguin.

*Oxford English Dictionary* (2020) www.oed.com/. Accessed 20 February 2021.

Page, Christopher (1981) 'False Voices'. *Early Music* 9 (1): 71–2. With an addition by Andrew Parrott, p. 72, and a reply by Roger Bowers, pp. 73–5.

Page, Christopher (1986) *Voices & Instruments of the Middle Ages: Instrumental Practice and Songs in France 1100–1300*. Berkeley: University of California Press.

Page, Christopher (1988) 'The Performance of Ars Antiqua Motets'. *Early Music* 16 (2): 147–64.

Page, Christopher (1992) 'The English *a cappella* Heresy'. In *Companion to Medieval and Renaissance Music*, edited by Tess Knighton and David Fallows, 23–9. London: Dent.

Page, Christopher (1993) 'The English *a cappella* Renaissance'. *Early Music* 21: 452–71.
Paolini, Christopher (2008) *Brisingr; or The Seven Promises of Eragon Shadeslayer and Saphira Bjartskular*. Book 3 of *Inheritance* series. London: Doubleday.
Parrott, Andrew (2015) *Composers' Intentions?: Lost Traditions of Musical Performance*. Woodbridge: Boydell & Brewer.
Patterson, Orlando (1982) *Slavery and Social Death: A Comparative Study*. Cambridge, MA: Harvard University Press. Ebook. https://hdl.handle.net/2027/heb.03237.
Paus, Ansgar (1989) 'The Secret Nostalgia of Mircea Eliade for Paradise: Observations on the Method of the History of Religions'. *Religion* 19: 137–49.
Pearsall, Derek (2003) *Arthurian Romances: A Short Introduction*. Malden, MA: Blackwell.
Pearsall, Edward, and Byron Almén (2006) 'The Divining Rod: On Imagination, Interpretation and Analysis'. In *Approaches to Meaning in Music*, edited by Byron Almén and Edward Pearsall, 1–10. Bloomington, IN: Indiana University Press.
Pereira, David (2000) 'The Grammar of the Unconscious and the Perverted Logic of Phantasy'. In *Papers of the Freudian School of Melbourne* 21, edited by David Pereira, 5–19. Melbourne: Freudian School of Melbourne.
Pickering, Michael, and Emily Keightley (2006) 'The Modalities of Nostalgia'. *Current Sociology* 54 (6): 919–41.
Plastow, Michael (2000) 'From Family Myth to Individual Fantasm'. In *Fantasm: Papers of the Freudian School of Melbourne* 21, edited by David Pereira, 21–39. Melbourne: Freudian School of Melbourne.
Plato (1965) *Timaeus and Critias*. Translated by H. D. P. Lee. Middlesex, England: Penguin.
Plato (1994–2009) *Republic*. Translated by Benjamin Jowett. Internet Classics Archive by Daniel C. Stevenson©. https://classics.mit.edu/Plato/republic.html.
Plato (1996) *Sophist: The Professor of Wisdom*. Translation, introduction and glossary by Eva Brann, Peter Kalkavage and Eric Salem. Newport, MA & Indianapolis, IN: Focus/R. Pullins Company.
Plato (2002) *Five Dialogues: Euthyphro, Apology, Crito, Meno, Phaedo*. 2nd edition. Translated by G. M. A. Grube, Rev. John M. Cooper. Indianapolis/Cambridge, IN: Hackett Publishing.
Plotinus (1987) *Music, Mysticism and Magic: A Sourcebook* (Arkana). Selected and annotated by J. Godwin, 20–5. London: Penguin.
Poizat, Michel (1992) *The Angel's Cry: Beyond the Pleasure Principle in Opera*. Translated by Arthur Denner. Ithaca and London: Cornell University Press.

Pratchett, Terry (2002) *Moving Pictures*. New York: HarperTorch.
Pratchett, Terry (2004) *A Hat Full of Sky*. London: Corgi Books.
Pratchett, Terry (2007) 'The fantasy world of Terry Pratchett'. *ABC Radio National*. Sunday 18 February 2007, 7:06 p.m.
Prendergast, Thomas, and Stephanie Trigg (2008) 'What is Happening to the Middle Ages?'. In *New Medieval Literatures* 9: 215–29.
Prendergast, Thomas, and Stephanie Trigg (2019) *Affective Medievalism: Love, Abjection and Discontent*. Manchester: Manchester University Press.
Pugh, Tison, and Angela Jane Weisl (2013) *Medievalisms: Making the Past in the Present*. New York: Routledge.
Pullman, Philip (1998) 'The Dark Side of Narnia', *The Guardian* (1 October), Philip-Pullman-The-Dark-Side-of-Narnia-The-Guardian.docx.
Pullman, Philip (2000) *His Dark Materials, Book Three: The Amber Spyglass*. UK: Scholastic/David Fickling Books.
Purkis, Charlotte (2010) 'Listening for the Sublime: Aural-Visual Improvisations in Nineteenth-Century Musical Art'. *Tate Papers 14* Autumn. www.tate.org.uk/research/publications/tate–papers/14/listening–for–the–sublime–aural–visual–improvisations-in-nineteenth-century-musical-art. Accessed 18 January 2021.
Pyle, Hilary (1991) '"My Unshatterable Friend of Clay": Fantasy in the Paintings of Jack B. Yeats'. In *More Real than Reality: The Fantastic in Irish Literature and the Arts*, edited by Donald E. Morse and Csilla Bertha, 97–110. New York: Greenwood Press.
Quora (n.d.) 'Why Do Some People Still Buy CDs When There's Spotify and iTunes?' www.quora.com/Why-do-some-people-still-buy-CDs-when-theres-Spotify-and-iTunes. Accessed 12 July 2022.
'Rainbow Sphinx' (2006) Amazon customer review of Mediæval Bæbes, *Mirabilis*. www.amazon.com/Mirabilis-Mediaeval-Baebes/product-reviews/B0009VBU5Y/ref=cm_cr_pr_btm_link_2?ie=UTF8&filterBy=addFiveStar&pageNumber=2&showViewpoints=0&sortBy=byRankDescending. Accessed 25 January 2021.
Ralls-MacLeod, Karen (2000) *Music and the Celtic Otherworld*. New York: St Martin's Press.
Ramey, Lynn T., and Tyson Pugh, eds (2007) *Race, Class and Gender in 'Medieval' Cinema*. New York: Palgrave Macmillan.
Randell, Elizabeth J. (1996) 'Hybrid: Countertenors Then and Now'. *Opera News* 59: 25–8.
Randles, Sarah (2008) 'Rebuilding the Middle Ages: Medievalism in Australian Architecture'. In *Medievalism and the Gothic in Australian Culture*, edited by Stephanie Trigg, 147–70. Turnhout: Brepols.
Ravens, Simon (2014) *The Supernatural Voice: A History of High Male Singing*. Woodbridge: Boydell Press.

Rayfield, Ben (n.d.) *Gothic Voices*. https://gothicvoices.co.uk/biography/. Accessed 18 May 2023.

Reid, Robin Anne. 'Light (noun, 1) or Light (adjective, 14b)? Female Bodies and Femininities in the Lord of the Rings'. In *The Body in Tolkein's Legendarium – Essays on Middle-earth Corporeality*, edited by Christopher Vaccaro, 98–118. Jefferson, NC: McFarland.

Richards, Darielle (2010) 'Tolkien: A Fortunate Rhythm'. In *Middle-earth Minstrel: Essays on Music in Tolkien*, edited by Bradford Lee Eden, 61–74. Jefferson, NC: McFarland.

'rmm413c' (n.d.) Commenter on Andreas Scholl's performance of 'Habañera' from Bizet, *Carmen*. YouTube. www.youtube.com/watch?v=tzi_M-Vl_38&feature=related. Accessed 11 August 2013; site no longer accessible.

Roach, Joseph R. (1989) 'Power's Body: The Inscription of Morality as Style'. In *Interpreting the Theatrical Past*, edited by Thomas Postlethwaite and Bruce A. McConachie, 99–118. Iowa City: University of Iowa Press.

Robinson, B. A. (2015) 'New Age Spirituality: Part 1 of 2'. www.religioustolerance.org/newage.htm. Accessed 6 June 2022.

Robinson, Carol L., and Pamela Clements (2009) 'Living with Neomedievalism'. In *Studies in Medievalism: Defining Medievalism(s) II, XVIII*, edited by Karl Fugelso, 55–75. Woodbridge: Boydell & Brewer.

Roesner, Edward (1983) 'Spielmann und Kleriker um 1200: Sequentia. Ensemble für Musik des Mittelalters'. *Early Music* 11 (2): 265–7.

Rohmer, Eric (1978) *Perceval le Gallois*. Paris: Les Films du Losange.

Rosaldo, Renato (1989) 'Imperialist Nostalgia'. *Representations* 26 (Spring): 107–22. Accessed 5 September 2021.

Rosenberg, Samuel N., Margaret Switten and Gérard le Vot, eds (1998) *Songs of the Troubadours and Trouvères: An Anthology of Poems and Melodies*. New York: Garland.

Rosolato, Guy (1974) 'La Voix: entre corps et langage'. *Revue Française de Psychanalyse* 37 (1): 75–94.

Rossi, Lee D. (1984) *Politics of Fantasy: C. S. Lewis and J. R. R. Tolkien*. Ann Arbor, MI: UMI Research Press.

Roszak, Theodore (1995) *The Making of a Counter Culture: Reflections on the Technocratic Society and its Youthful Opposition*. Berkeley: University of California Press. Originally published 1969.

Roth, Norman (1995) *Conversos, Inquisition, and the Expulsion of the Jews from Spain*. Madison: University of Wisconsin Press. Ebook.

Rousseau, Jean-Jacques (1779) *A Complete Dictionary of Music*. Translated by William Waring. 2nd edition. London: John Murray.

Rubino, Carl A. (1985) 'The Invisible Worm: Ancients and Moderns in "The Name of the Rose"'. *SubStance* 14 (2): 54–63.

Ruiz, Raul (2009) 'Three Thrusts at Excalibur'. Translated by Adrian Martin. *Screening the Past* 26: n.p. www.screeningthepast.com/issue-26-special-issue-early-europe/three-thrusts-at%C2%A0excalibur/. Originally published in *Positif* 247 (October 1981): 43.

Said, Edward W. (1979) *Orientalism*. New York: Vintage.

St Germain, Mark (2010) *Freud's Last Session*. Directed by Tyler Marchant. Video Selections. YouTube, 20 July. www.youtube.com/watch?v=__ab5haACWc. Accessed 5 February 2021.

Sammons, Martha C. (1988) *'A Better Country': The Worlds of Religious Fantasy and Science Fiction*. New York: Greenwood.

Saussure, Ferdinand de (1974) *Course in General Linguistics*. Edited by Charles Bally, Albert Sechehaye and Albert Reidlinger. Translated by Wade Baskin. Revised edition. Glasgow: Fontana-Collins.

Scholl, Andreas (2013) 'Andreas Scholl – L'Amour est un oiseau rebelle – Habanera – (Carmen/Bizet)'. YouTube, 29 December. www.youtube.com/watch?v=PP-aqYZ11t0. Accessed 15 January 2021.

Scholz, Piotr O. (2001) *Eunuchs and Castrati: A Cultural History*. Translated by John A. Broadwin and Shelley L Frisch. Princeton, NJ: Marcus Weiner.

Scott, Walter (1819) *Ivanhoe*. (Annotated) Literary Classics Collection, Book 15. Introduction Gillen D'Arcy Wood. G Books.

Sedikides, Constantine, Tim Wildschut, Jamie Arndt and Clay Routledge (2008) 'Nostalgia: Past, Present, and Future'. *Current Directions in Psychological Science* 17: 304–7.

Seiden, Henry M. (2009) 'On the Longing for Home'. *Psychoanalytic Psychology*, 26 (2): 191–205.

Sells, Michael Anthony (1994) *Mystical Languages of Unsaying*. Chicago: University of Chicago Press.

Service, Tom (2010) 'Andreas Scholl and Philippe Jaroussky: Pushing the Envelope for Countertenors'. *The Guardian* (7 December), n.p. www.theguardian.com/music/2010/dec/06/andreas-scholl-phillipe-jaroussky-countertenors. Accessed 15 June 2022.

Shakespeare, William (1960) *The Tragedy of Antony and Cleopatra*. Edited by Maynard Mack. Baltimore: Penguin Books.

Shakespeare, William (1964) *The Tempest*. Edited by Robert Langbaum. New York: New American Library.

Shippey, Tom (2003) *The Road to Middle-earth: How J. R. R. Tolkien Created a New Mythology*. Revised edition. Boston: Houghton Mifflin.

Shippey, Tom (2011) *J. R. R. Tolkien: Author of the Century*. London: HarperCollins.

Shore, Howard (2014) 'The Lord of the Rings – Soundtrack – Lothlorien'. YouTube, 21 November. www.youtube.com/watch?v=1D76LqvYLVA. Accessed 11 July 2022.

Shuker, Roy (2005) *Popular Music: The Key Concepts*. 2nd edition. London: Routledge.

Silverman, Kaja (1988) *The Acoustic Mirror: The Female Voice in Psychoanalysis and Cinema*. Bloomington, IN: Indiana University Press.

Smith, James. L. (2019) 'Interrogating Green Space in Medieval Monasticism: Position, Powers and Politics'. *Open Library of Humanities* 5 (1): 41. http://doi.org/10.16995/olh.283.

Starr, Charlie W. (2007) 'Meaning, Meanings, and Epistemology in C. S. Lewis'. *Mythlore* 25 (3): 161–82.

Steiner, George (1977) *Nostalgia for the Absolute*. Toronto: Anansi Press.

Stewart, Susan (1993) *On Longing: Narratives of the Miniature, the Gigantic, the Souvenir, the Collection*. Durham, NC: Duke University Press.

Stock, Brian (1990) *Listening for the Text: On the Uses of the Past*. Baltimore, MD: Johns Hopkins University Press.

Stone, Ryan (2017) 'The Daily Transcript: Interview with Former White Nationalist Derek Black'. *New York Times* (22 August). www.nytimes.com/2017/08/22/podcasts/the-daily-transcript-derek-black.html.

Strohm, Paul (2000) *Theory and the Premodern Text*. Minneapolis, MN: University of Minnesota Press.

Studio der Frühen Musik (1970) *Chansons der Troubadours: Lieder und Spielmusik aus dem 12. Jahrhunderts*. Telefunken, SAWT 9567-B, LP.

Studio der Frühen Musik (2013) 'Baron, de mon dan covit'. YouTube, 7 August. www.YouTube.com/watch?v=VhbjvTWReYM. Accessed 15 June 2022.

Sturtevant, Paul B. (2017) 'Race, Racism, and the Middle Ages: Tearing down the "Whites Only" Medieval World'. *Public Medievalist* (7 February). www.publicmedievalist.com/race-racism-middle-ages-tearing-whites-medieval-world/. Accessed 15 January 2021.

'Sublime' (2017) Amazon customer review of Gothic Voices, *Feather on the Breath of God*. www.amazon.com.au/VON-BINGEN-FEATHER-BREATH-GOD/dp/B000002ZGD/ref=cm_cr_arp_d_pl_foot_top?ie=UTF8. Accessed 22 August 2020.

'Sweetie' (2002) Amazon customer review of Anonymous 4, *1000: A Mass for the End of Time*. www.amazon.com/1000-Mass-End-Time-4/product-reviews/B00004UFGW?pageNumber=2&reviewerType=all_reviews. Accessed 5 February 2021.

Switchfoot (2008) 'This Is Home'. Track 15 on *Chronicles of Narnia: Prince Caspian (Original Soundtrack)*. Walt Disney Records, D000074202, compact disc.

'SylverOne' (2006) Amazon customer review of Mediæval Bæbes, *Mirabilis*. www.amazon.com/Mirabilis-Mediaeval-Baebes/product-reviews/B0009VBU5Y/ref=cm_cr_pr_btm_link_2?ie=UTF8&filterBy=addFiveSt

ar&pageNumber=2&showViewpoints=0&sortBy=byRankDescending. Accessed 5 February 2021.

Tannock, Stewart (1995) 'Nostalgia Critique'. *Cultural Studies* 9 (3): 453–64.

Tarantino, Quentin, dir. (1994) *Pulp Fiction*. Los Angeles: Miramax.

Taruskin, Richard (1984) 'The Authenticity Movement Can Become a Positivistic Purgatory, Literalistic and Dehumanizing'. *Early Music* 12 (1): 3–12.

Taruskin, Richard (1988) 'The Pastness of the Present and the Presence of the Past'. In *Authenticity and Early Music: A Symposium*, edited by Nicholas Kenyon, 137–207. Oxford: Oxford University Press.

'Tokaji' (n.d.) Amazon customer review of Mediæval Bæbes, *Mirabilis*. http://www.amazon.com/Mirabilis-Mediaeval-Baebes/product-reviews/B0009VBU5Y/ref=cm_cr_pr_btm_link_2?ie=UTF8&filterBy=addFiveStar&pageNumber=2&showViewpoints=0&sortBy=byRankDescending. Accessed 22 August 2013. Comment no longer accessible.

Tolkien, J. R. R. (1936) 'Beowulf: The Monsters and the Critics'. https://jenniferjsnow.files.wordpress.com/2011/01/11790039-jrr-tolkien-beowulf-the-monsters-and-the-critics.pdf.

Tolkien, J. R. R. (1966) 'On Fairy-Stories'. In *The Tolkien Reader*, 33–99. New York: Ballantyne.

Tolkien, J. R. R. (1987) *The Lost Road and Other Writings*. Edited by Christopher Tolkien. London: Unwin Hyman.

Tolkien, J. R. R. (1991) *The Silmarillon*. Edited by Christopher Tolkien. London: Grafton Books.

Tolkien, J. R. R. (1993) *The Lord of the Rings*. London: HarperCollins. Originally published 1954–55.

Tolkien, J. R. R. (1995) *The Letters of J. R. R. Tolkien*. A selection, edited by Humphrey Carpenter, assisted by Christopher Tolkien. Boston: Houghton Mifflin.

Tomlinson, Gary (1988) 'The Historian, the Performer, and Authentic Meaning in Music'. In *Authenticity and Early Music: A Symposium*, edited by Nicholas Kenyon, 115–36. Oxford: Oxford University Press.

Trilling, Renée (2011) 'Medievalism and its Discontents'. *postmedieval* 2 (2) (Special issue: *The Medievalism of Nostalgia*, edited by Helen Dell, Louise D'Arcens and Andrew Lynch): 216–24.

'tuulari' (2011) Consumer comment on 'Avatar Soundtrack 14 – I See You (theme from Avatar)'. YouTube. www.youtube.com/watch?v=5fEvay1mljE. Accessed 5 February 2021.

TV Tropes (n.d.) 'One-Woman Wail'. https://tvtropes.org/pmwiki/pmwiki.php/Main/OneWomanWail. Accessed 11 July 2022.

Tzigany, Becca (n.d.) 'Return of Morgaine'. http://venusandherlover.com/pilllowbook/returnofmorgaine. Accessed 30 July 2013. Site no longer accessible.

Tzigany, Becca (2013) 'Venus and her Lover: Transforming Myth, Sexuality and Ourselves'. YouTube. www.youtube.com/shorts/QTkyCoTppFI. Accessed 30 July 2013.

'u/dacara1615' (2018) 'Do You Still Buy CD's? If So, Why Do You Still Enjoy Buying Them?'. Reddit, 6 August. www.reddit.com/r/LetsTalkMusic/comments/94zf3y/do_you_still_buy_cds_if_so_why_do_you_still_enjoy/. Accessed 12 July 2022.

Upton, Elizabeth Randell (2012) 'Concepts of Authenticity in Early Music and Popular Music Communities'. *Ethnomusicology Review* 17 (2). http://ethnomusicologyreview.ucla.edu/journal/volume/17/piece/591. Accessed 15 January 2020.

Urban Dictionary (n.d.) www.urbandictionary.com.

Utz, Richard (2011) 'Coming to Terms with Medievalism: Towards a Conceptual History'. *European Journal of English Studies* 15 (2): 101–13.

Utz, Richard (2017) *Medievalism: A Manifesto*. Kalamazoo: Arc Humanities Press.

Vinson, Liz (2021) '"Waking up to Racism": New Documentary Tells Truth about Confederacy, Tracks Root of "Lost Cause" Myth'. Southern Poverty Law Center, 5 August. www.splcenter.org/news/2021/08/05/waking-racism-new-documentary-tells-truth-about-confederacy-tracks-root-lost-cause-myth. Accessed 11 July 2022.

Wagner, Tamara (c.2004) *Longing: Narratives of Nostalgia in the British Novel, 1740–1890*. Lewisburg, PA: Bucknell University Press.

Walker, Alison Tara (2009) 'Towards a Theory of Medieval Film Music'. In *Medieval Film*, edited by Anke Bernau and Bettina Bildhauer, 137–57. New York: Palgrave Macmillan.

Walker, Jessica (2015) '"Just Songs in the End": Historical Discourses in Shakespeare and Martin'. In *Mastering the Game of Thrones: Essays on George R. R. Martin's 'A Song of Ice and Fire'*, edited by Jes Battis and Susan Johnston, 71–91. Jefferson, NC: McFarland.

Wallenstein, Sven-Olov (n.d.) *Tropes of Nostalgia: Winckelmann, Hegel, Heidegger, and the Quest for Origins*. ThinkLink. http://iloapp.philosophy.se/blog/thinklink?ShowFile&doc=1212586706.pdf. Accessed 20 June 2011; no longer accessible.

Ward, Adolphus William (1879) *Chaucer*. London: Macmillan.

Weever, Jacqueline de (2002) 'Morgan and the Problem of Incest'. In *Cinema Arthuriana: Twenty Essays*, edited by Kevin J. Harty (revised edition), 54–63. Jefferson, NC: McFarland.

Weisl, Angela Jane (2003) *The Persistence of Medievalism: Narrative Adventures in Contemporary Culture.* New York: Palgrave Macmillan.
Weiss, Allen S. (2002) *Breathless: Sound Recording, Disembodiment, and the Transformation of Lyrical Nostalgia.* Middletown, CT: Wesleyan University Press.
Werf, Hendrik van der (1972) 'Review *Chansons der Troubadours*'. *Musical Quarterly* 58 (2): 338–41.
Whistler, Theresa (1976) *The River Boy.* London: Oxford University Press.
White, T. H. (1996) *The Once and Future King.* New York: Ace Books. Originally published 1958.
Whitehead, Gregory (1992) 'Out of the Dark: Notes on the Nobodies of Radio Art'. In *Wireless Imagination: Sound, Radio and the Avant-garde*, edited by Douglas Kahn and Gregory Whitehead, 253–63. Cambridge, MA: MIT Press.
Willin, Melvyn (2012) *Music, Witchcraft and the Paranormal: A Series of Essays on Parapsychology and Psychical Research with Special Reference to Paganism and Witchcraft from the Perspective of MUSIC.* FW Media. Kindle.
Wilson, Janelle L. (2005) *Nostalgia: Sanctuary of Meaning.* Lewisburg, PA: Bucknell University Press.
Wittgenstein, Ludwig (2010). *Tractatus Logico-Philosophicus.* Project Gutenburg. www.gutenberg.org/ebooks/5740. Accessed 20 January 2021. Originally published 1922.
Wolfe, Gary K. (2002) 'Evaporating Genre: Strategies of Dissolution in the Postmodern Fantastic'. In *Edging into the Future: Science Fiction and Contemporary Cultural Transformation*, edited by Veronica Hollinger and Joan Gordon, 11–29. Philadelphia, PA: University of Pennsylvania Press.
'Woman of faith' (2020) Consumer comment on 'Mediæval Bæbes "Prayers of the Rosary" Interview with Katharine Blake, Charlie Cawood, Michael York'. YouTube. www.youtube.com/watch?v=Y3GDA5vT88g. Accessed 5 February 2021.
Wordsworth, William (1977) *The Poems.* Edited by John O. Hayden. Vol. 1. New Haven, CT: Yale University Press.
Young, Helen (2015a) 'Introduction: Dreams of the Middle Ages'. In *Fantasy and Science Fiction Medievalisms: From Isaac Asimov to 'A Game of Thrones'*, edited by Helen Young, loc. 25–160. New York: Cambria. Ebook.
Young, Helen (2015b) 'Introduction: Multiple Middle Ages'. In *The Middle Ages in Popular Culture: Medievalism and Genre*, edited by Helen Young, 1–10. Amherst, NY: Cambria.
Young, Helen (2016) *Race and Popular Fantasy Literature: Habits of Whiteness.* New York: Routledge.

Young, Helen (2021) 'Why the Far-right and White Supremacists Have Embraced the Middle Ages and their Symbols'. *The Conversation* (14 January). https://theconversation.com/why-the-far-right-and-white-supremacists-have-embraced-the-middle-ages-and-their-symbols-152968. Accessed 11 July 2022.

Yri, Kirsten (2008a) 'Medievalism and Exoticism in the Music of Dead Can Dance'. *Current Musicology* 85: 53–73.

Yri, Kirsten (2008b) 'Remaking the Past: Feminist Spirituality in Anonymous 4 and Sequentia's Vox Feminae'. *Women and Music: A Journal of Gender and Culture* 12: 1–21.

Yri, Kirsten (2010) 'Thomas Binkley and the Studio der Frühen Musik: Challenging "the Myth of Westernness"'. *Early Music* 38 (2): 273–80.

Yri, Kirsten (2019) 'Black Sabbath *Purgatus*: Medievalizing Heavy Metal'. *postmedieval* 10 (4) (Special issue *Music, Emotions, Medievalism*, edited by Helen Dell, Andrew Lynch and Elizabeth Randell Upton): 466–81.

Zentner, Oscar (2000) 'Borges and the Fantasm of Reality'. In *Fantasm: Papers of the Freudian School of Melbourne* 21, edited by David Pereira, 67–84. Melbourne: Freudian School of Melbourne.

Zimbardo, Rose A., and Neil D. Isaacs, eds (2004) *Understanding 'The Lord of the Rings': The Best of Tolkien Criticism*. Boston: Houghton Mifflin.

Zink, Michel (1998) *The Enchantment of the Middle Ages*. Translated by Jane Marie Todd. Baltimore: Johns Hopkins University Press.

Žižek, Slavoj (1998) 'The Seven Veils of Fantasy'. In *Key Concepts of Lacanian Psychoanalysis*, edited by Dany Nobus, 190–218. London: Rebus Press.

# Index

*13th Warrior, The* (film) 193

Abel, Sam 160
Aberth, John 177
absolute music 103
acousmatism, acousmatic sound and voice 88, 90–1, 98, 112, 138n7, 151–2
Adams, Doug 189–90
Addison, Joseph 95, 97
Adorno, Theodor 13–14, 102, 103, 174, 197n15, 198n19
Aelred of Rievaulx 144
Aeone 188, 190, 192
Ahmed, Saladin 18
Alexander, Lloyd 56, 82–3
Almén, Byron 102
ambiguity 13–14, 141–2, 150, 200, 201, 203
Anderson, Walter Truett 53–4
anemoia 2, 32n2
Anonymous 4 116
Anonymous XI 146
Anselmi, Giorgio 93
Aristotle 36n32, 204n1
Aronstein, Susan 198n23
Arthurian tradition 197n9, 198n23
  *see also Excalibur* (film); *Mists of Avalon* (TV miniseries)
Austin, Linda 5
authenticity 44, 71n6, 75n41, 118–19, 147, 149–50, 169–70n9, 201
*Avatar* (film) 67, 174, 196n5

Bacon, Francis 39, 203
Balkun, Mary McAleer 71n6
Barnhouse, Rebecca 39
Barrett, Frederick S. 32n1
Barrett-Peacock, Ruth 23
Barthes, Roland 94, 105n14, 110, 152, 161, 164
Bataille, George 69, 81
Baudrillard, Jean 62, 63, 65–6, 76n55
Benjamin, Walter 26–7, 66, 82
Bennett, Alana 22
Bernard of Clairvaux 144
Bernau, Anke 22
between-ness, indicating 86–93
Bevan, Edwyn 98
Bildhauer, Bettina 22
Binkley, Thomas 148, 155
Blake, Katharine 114–15, 116–17, 118, 120, 122, 131
Blake, William 95
body, the 8, 106n32, 130, 154, 201–3
Boethius 93, 94, 95
Bonnett, Alistair 14
Boston Camerata 156
Bowers, Roger 143–4, 145
Bowman, James 157–8
Boym, Svetlana 4, 12, 13, 14, 15, 67
Bradley, Marion Zimmer *see Mists of Avalon* (Bradley)
Burke, Edmund 139n27
Burney, Charles 164
Butler, Charles 38

Butler, Judith 136
Byatt, A. S. 56

Caldwell, John 144–5
calling voice, the 187–96
Camille, Michael 54
Carpenter, Humphrey 41
Carroll, Shiloh 44
Casanova 166
Cassin, Barbara 105n16
castrati 31, 157–68
castration 160, 165–7, 171n30, 173–4
Celtic Woman 187
Cerquiglini, Bernard 10
Chance, Michael 157
Chandler, Alice 74n32
Chastelain de Couci 123, 127
Chaucer, Geoffrey 144–5
childhood 49–51, 52, 73n23, 73n25
Chion, Michel 131, 132, 133, 201
Christianity 7, 57–8, 88–9, 133
*Chronicles of Narnia* (films) 38, 191–2
*Chronicles of Narnia* (Lewis) 2–3, 17, 65
  *The Horse and his Boy* 19, 20
  *The Last Battle* 19, 21, 40, 56, 56–7, 89, 107n38
  *The Lion, the Witch and the Wardrobe* 58, 82, 89, 133
  *The Magician's Nephew* 98–9
  *Prince Caspian* 90
  *The Silver Chair* 133
  *The Voyage of the Dawn Treader* 58, 70, 89, 91, 113
citation value 186
Clements, Pamela 11
Clute, John 40
*coincidentia oppositorum* 100–4
concept albums 2
conspiracy theory 176–7

Cooper, Susan (Cooper) 56, 86, 89, 97, 105n12
  see also *Dark is Rising, The*
Copland, Aaron 108n44
countertenor, the 8, 31, 141–68
  ambiguity of 141–2
  and castrati 157–68
  English choral tradition 148–54, 162–3, 170n16
  evidence and interpretation 143–54, 169n7
  and oriental music 154–5
  sexual ambiguity 155–6, 157–68, 166–8, 201
  and the space between 141–2
courtly love 125–6
creation music 97–8
cultural forms 29

Dame, Joke 161
Daniels, David 158–9
Daniels, E. B. 5
*Dark is Rising, The* (Cooper) 30, 78, 80–1, 83, 90–1
*das Ding* 131–4, 134–5, 140n36, 193, 194
Davidson, Jane W. 1–2, 3, 5
Dean, Jonathon 197n14
Deleuze, Gilles 62, 203
Deller, Alfred 157, 167, 168, 172n31
desire 23–7, 37n44, 47, 69–71, 122–3, 178, 201
Dinshaw, Carolyn 7, 10, 104n5
*Doctor Who* (TV series) 62, 63, 64
Dolar, Mladen 86, 130
Downing, David C. 42
Doyle, Arthur Conan 43
Drout, Michael D. C. 20
Duffin, Ross 149
Dunsany, Lord 82
Dyer, Joseph 145–6

Eberstadt, Fernanda 160
Eckhart, Meister 101

# Index

Eco, Umberto 75n40
ecstasy 101–2, 104, 122
Eden, Bradford Lee 95, 107n39
Eisler, Hanns 174, 198n19
Eliade, Mircea 66, 68, 96
Eliot, T. S. 31, 200
Elliot, Andrew 14, 120
emotion 162–3
enchantment 3, 87, 91
English choral tradition 148–54, 162–3, 170n16
Enlightenment, the 73n27
*Excalibur* (film) 31–2, 173, 174–5, 176, 196n7, 197n8
   backstairs music 182–3
   calling voice 187–8
   Edenic time 178, 178–9, 181
   masculine fantasy 192
   music 182–3, 185–6, 187–8, 194, 195, 196, 197n10, 198n20
   paranoiac tendencies 177–8
   primeval being 180–1

faith 63–4
Fallows, David 145
*Fantasia* (film) 99
fantasy 2
   default setting 38–9
   disenchanted 64
   and narrative 175–6
   role of 47–8
   transcendentalist 39–40
Farinelli 159, 160, 164
*Farinelli* (film) 172n37
Farrell, Eliza 17–18
Father Parmenides' law 86
feminine archaic, the 190
Ferrara, Lidia Ruth 39
film music 174, 182–96, 198n19
Findley, Marie 135
Finke, Laurie 9–10, 10
Finn, Kavita Mudan 45–6
Fox, Phil 115
Fradenburg, L. O. Aranye 85–6, 101

Freitas, Roger 165
Freud, Sigmund 5, 6, 34n15, 46–7, 55, 129, 168, 201
Fritzman, J. M. 42

Gabriele, Matthew 44–5
*Game of Thrones* (TV series) 43–6
Ganim, John 5–6, 7, 141–2, 150
garden of Eden fantasy 174
Garner, Alan 79, 90, 92, 124
Garrido, Sandra 1–2, 3, 5
Gavriel Kay, Guy Gavriel 7
gender 20–1
Gerrard, Lisa 114
Giles, Peter 143, 145, 154, 158, 159, 160, 162
Gizmodo.com 43–4
God 88–9, 98, 99–100, 101, 202
Godwin, Joscelyn 3
Goldthwaite, John 20
Gorbman, Claudia 174, 186
Gothic Voices 116–17, 124, 145, 146–7, 152–3, 153–4, 156
Green, Roger Lancelyn 41
Greig, Donald 151, 152, 153, 162
Grossman, Lev 24–5
Guthrie, Steve 75n39

Haeckel, Haeckel 50
Hagen, Ross 23
Haines, John 5, 43, 144, 155, 184
Harper, Ralph 40
Harty, Kevin J. 197n9
Haydock, Nickolas 39, 196n7
Hein, Rolland 133
Hespèrion XX 2
Hildegard of Bingen 116
Hilliard Ensemble 117
Hitler, Adolf 13–14
Hofer, Johannes 4
Hoffmann, E. T. A. 102
Holdridge, Lee 186, 188
Holsinger, Bruce 51, 106n32, 154, 204n2
Huizinga, Johan 50

human dimension 183–4
Hutcheon, Linda 12, 53, 76n52

Inglis, Fred 71n3
Isidore of Seville 204n1

Jackson, Rosemary 39–40, 64, 66, 73n20
James, Edward 3
James, Henry 186
James, Jamie 95–6
Jameson, Fredric 52
Jaroussky, Phillippe 158, 159, 160, 167, 171n28
John of Garland 143
John the Scot Eriugena 100
Jones, Diana Wynne 33n7, 59–60, 97, 104n3, 105n12
  *Chrestomanci* series 84, 85
  *The Homeward Bounders* 60–1, 63, 66, 88, 92–3, 177
Jones, Trevor 182
*jouissance* 31, 85–6, 101, 103, 134–5
joy 49, 72n9

Kalinak, Kathryn 91
Kant, Immanuel 4
Kay, Guy Gavriel 56, 92
Keats, John 95
Keightley, Emily 4
Keyser, Dorothy 161
Kierkegaard, Soren 29
King, Catherine 152
King, Thomas 164
Koelz, Heidi 160
Kowalski-Wallace, Beth 165
Kristeva, Julia 84–5, 134, 173–4, 193, 194, 203–4
Kvale, Steinar 64

Labbie, Erin 23
Lacan, Jacques 5, 7, 8, 25, 27, 46, 51, 54, 67, 69, 85, 96, 101, 103, 110–11, 123, 129, 130, 165–6, 172n35, 195

and *das Ding* 131–4, 140n36, 193
and desire 23–4, 25, 47
*Formations of the Unconscious* 85–6
and language 25–6, 137, 192
on myth 175, 178
on nostalgia 66–7
and the Real 46–9, 78, 84, 134–5, 175
and reality 29, 47–8
Lacy, Norris J. 186
Lang, Paul Henry 162
language 25–6, 54, 86, 130, 137, 173–4, 192
Lears, T. J. Jackson 50, 52–3, 54–5, 74n35
Ledroit, Henri 156
Leech-Wilkinson, Daniel 6, 114
L'Engle, Madeleine 92
Levitt, Richard 155–6
Lewis, C. S. 7, 43, 72n11, 77n61, 88–9, 107n37, 133, 175, 201–2
  creation music 96
  and desire 23–7, 122–3
  and faith 63
  *The Great Divorce* 56
  impact 38–9
  medieval model 99–100
  *Mere Christianity* 63
  and music 95, 98–100
  'On Stories' 40–1, 82
  *The Pilgrim's Regress* 70
  *The Problem of Pain* 3
  and the Real 46–7, 48–9
  and reality 29
  and religion 20, 42
  Space trilogy 106n20
  *That Hideous Strength* 89
  *Till We Have Faces* 68
  understanding of meaning 57–8
  and violence 45
  *see also Chronicles of Narnia*
Liège, Jacques de 93

listener response analysis
  methodology 205–8
listening 29
Livingston, Tamara 147,
  169–70n9
*Lord of the Rings, The* (film) 38,
  80, 189–90, 197n14
*Lord of the Rings, The* (Tolkien)
  1, 11, 48, 61, 65, 69–70,
  73n21, 83, 115, 116, 151–2,
  179, 202
  colour coding 35n26
  elven music 88
  Galadriel 132–3
  and gender 20–1
  Lothlórien (Lórien) 58–9, 64,
    68–9, 79–80, 125–6
  oxymoron 124
  publication 2–3
  racism 16–9, 35n26, 36n30
  and renunciation 125–6
  temporal distortion 104n2
  and tendency to repetition
    124–5
loss 24, 27, 178
lost object, the 69–71
Lowenthal, David 66
Lynch, Andrew 66

McCaffrey, Anne 105n9
MacDonald, George 86, 88–9, 93,
  133, 136, 175
McGee, Timothy 146
McKennitt, Loreena 188–9
Maly, Michael 36n29
Mapplethorpe, Robert 161
Marshall, David 11–12, 193
Marshall, Melanie M. 153
Martin, George R. R. 8, 43–6
masculinity 156, 157–9, 167, 194,
  198n23
maternal body, the 31, 32
maternal voice, the 131–2, 194–5
Matthews, David 8, 11, 140n34
Mediæval Bæbes, the 114–15,
  117, 117–22, 128–9, 135,
  136, 155

medievalism 9–15, 21–3, 74n32,
  74n33, 85
Medievalism Studies 10
medievalist film 173
medieval music 6, 109–14, 185–6
  promotional material 114–23
  responses to 114–23
medieval, the 7, 29–30, 33n10
  associations and implications
    49–54
  invocation 195–6
  space between 82–6
medieval unconscious 54–6
Menocal, María Rosa 20
*Merlin* (TV series) 179–80
methodology 27–29
Miller, Jacques-Alain 129
Mills, Robert 33n10
Minter, Drew 159
*Mists of Avalon* (Bradley) 56
*Mists of Avalon* (TV miniseries)
  31–2, 173, 174–5, 176, 181
  calling voice 188–9, 192–6
  castle dance cue 183
  Edenic time 178, 179–81
  music 182, 183–5, 186–7,
    188–96
  paranoiac tendencies 177
  primeval being 180–1
  the sign foretold 183–4
modernity 51, 52
Morrison, Richard 156
Morrow, Michael 150
*Moving Pictures* (Pratchett) 61–2
music
  allure of 86
  imaginary in 105n14
  meaning in 101–4, 108n44
  and medievalism 21–3
  and nostalgia 1–2, 22
  power of 3, 33n7, 110
  *see also* film music; medieval
    music
musical décor 182–83
musical enjoyment 134–7
musical-literary symbolism
  107n39

musical object, the 86–93
music of the spheres 93–100, 154
musicology 21–2
Mustafa, Domenico 162
myth 59, 175, 177–8, 180, 195–6, 197n8
mythopoeic moments 184–5

narrative 175–6
Nazi ideology 13–14, 17, 176
negativity 55
Negus, V. E. 143
neomedievalism 11–2
neo-medieval music 34n20
neuropsychology 137n3
Nicholas of Cusa 100
Nicholi, Armand M., Jr 46–7
non-European influences, erasures of 20
nostalgia
  and the academy 9–15
  ambiguities 13
  and desire 69–71
  distinctions 12
  and irony 12–13
  for the medieval 4–9
  and music 1–2, 22
  narrativisation 175–6
  and purity 142–3
  for reality 65–9
  temporality 191–2
  Tolkien 51
  understanding 4–5, 26–7, 34–5n21, 51–2
nostalgic longing 3
nostalgic medievalism 4
numinous experiences
numinous, the 3, 42–3, 50

Orff, Carl 185, 187, 198n18
Orientalism 73n23, 170n17, 170n18
oriental music 154–5
otherworld, access to 79
Otto, Rudolf 42, 202
Ovid 84
oxymoron 86–7, 124, 201

Page, Christopher 145, 146–7, 147–9, 151, 152–4, 162–3, 170n16
Paradise, longing for 174
paranoia 176–8
Parrott, Andrew 145, 146, 147, 149–50, 155
patriarchy 194
Paul, Jean 92
Paus, Ansgar 66
Pearsall, Derek 180
Pearsall, Edward 102
Philpot, Margaret 152
Pickering, Michael 4
Plato 68, 69, 91, 110, 135
Plotinus 98
Poizat, Michel 135–6
postmodernism 53
post-reality 59–65
Pratchett, Terry 61–2, 106n28
Prendergast, Thomas 9, 10, 15–16
*Problem of Pain, The* (Lewis) 3
psychoanalysis 5, 23–7, 46, 46–7, 54, 68
Pugh, Tison 22, 34n17
Pullman, Philip 21, 196n2
*Pulp Fiction* (film) 7, 34n16
purity 16, 35n26, 35–6n28, 142–3, 150, 201–3
Purkis, Charlotte 42

racism 15–20, 35n25, 35n26, 35–6n28, 36n29, 36n30
Ragin, Derek Lee 159
Ralls-MacLeod, Karen 79, 82
Randell, Elizabeth 159
reality 29, 39–41, 47–8, 65–9, 76n47
Real, the 29, 39–40, 43, 46–9, 78, 84, 101, 134–5, 137, 175
recorded music 30–1, 37n45, 109–14, 128–9
  promotional material 114
  reception 111
  and renunciation 126–7
  and repetition 123–5
  responses to 114–23

reviews 114
structures 111–12
reflective nostalgia 12, 13
religion 23–27, 41–2, 46–7, 72n8, 72n11, 73n20
Renaissance, the 29–30, 51, 73n27, 117, 142, 148, 170n16, 197n12, 200
renunciation 125–7
repetition 123–5, 127
repression 168
restorative nostalgia 12, 13
return, fantasies of 173–4
Rice, Anne 161–2
Robinson, Carol L. 11
Roesner, Edward 146
romanticism 42–3
Rosaldo, Renato 169n4
Rosolato, Guy 201
Rossi, Lee D. 37n41
Roszak, Theodore 24
Rubino, Carl 52
Ruiz, Raúl 196n4

sacred, the 41–2
Said, Edward 19–20, 169n4
Sartre, Jean-Paul 64
Saussure, Ferdinand 86, 130
Schiller, Friedrich 49–50
*Scholica enchiriadis* 94, 95, 203
Scholl, Andreas 167–8, 171n28, 172n37
Scholz, Piotr O. 160
Sedikides, Constantine 34–5n21
Seiden, Henry M. 68
Sells, Michael 100–1
sexism 20–1
sexual violence 43–5
Shichtman, Martin B. 9–10, 10
Shippey, Tom 104n2
Shore, Howard 190, 197n14
Shuker, Roy 2
silence 92–3
silent music 86
  *coincidentia oppositorum* 100–4
  music of the spheres 93–100

*Silmarillion* (Tolkien) 97–8
Silverman, Kaja 131, 192
soul, the 8, 203
sources 27–29, 37n45
space between, the 30, 31, 32, 48, 49, 50, 51, 81, 82–6, 86–93, 100, 103, 131, 141–2, 173, 200, 201
spirituality 94–5
Starr, Charlie W. 57
Steiner, George 68
Stewart, Susan 37n44, 70–1, 75n41
Stock, Brian 73n27
Strick, Philip 177
Strohm, Paul 54
Studio der Frühen Musik 154–5, 155–6
sublime, the 42, 103, 139n27
super-real, the 56–9

Tannock, Stuart 175–6
Taruskin Richard 149–50
temporality 30, 31, 81–2, 104n2, 191–2
temptation 63–4
time travel 81–2
Tippett, Michael 157, 168
Tolkien, J. R. R. 3, 7, 8, 11, 43, 72n9, 72n11, 77n61, 107n41, 108n43, 133, 201–2
  creation music 97–8
  and desire 23–7
  and faith 63
  impact 38–9
  and music 94–5
  musical-literary symbolism 107n39
  nostalgia 51
  'On Fairy-Stories' 40, 41, 86–7
  and the Real 46–7, 48–9
  and reality 29
  regret 11
  and religion 41

Romantic ancestry 69–70
and violence 45
*see also* Lord of the Rings, The
(Tolkien); *Silmarillion*
(Tolkien)
Tolkien/Lewis tradition 38–39, 41,
46–7, 50–1, 56, 58–9, 64–5,
78, 86
Tomlinson, Gary 150
Tosi, Pietro Francesco 162
transcendence 100
Trigg, Stephanie 9, 10, 15–16
Trump, Donald 35n25
Tzigany, Becca 181

Ugolino of Orvieto 93
unconscious, the 54–6, 201
Upton, Elizabeth Randell 29

Vidal, Peire 155–6
violence 7, 34n16, 43–6,
75n39
voiceless song 190
voice, the 129–31, 137, 138n7,
202–3

acousmatic 98, 138n7, 151–2
calling 187–196
feminine 131–4, 184, 187–96

Wagner, Richard 42, 185, 186–7,
197n15, 198n20
Wallenstein, Sven-Olov 51
Warmbrunn, Christina 16–19
Weisl, Angela Jane 22, 34n17
Weiss, Allen S. 138n7
Werf, Hendrik van der 146
West, Christian 154
Whitehead, Gregory 112
Wittgenstein, Ludwig 100
Wordsworth, William 49, 58
World of Warcraft 192

Yeats, Jack B. 39
Young, Helen 16, 18

Zink, Michel 49, 130
Žižek, Slavoj 27, 175–6, 188
Zwinger, Theodor 4

EU authorised representative for GPSR:
Easy Access System Europe, Mustamäe tee 50,
10621 Tallinn, Estonia
gpsr.requests@easproject.com

www.ingramcontent.com/pod-product-compliance
Lightning Source LLC
Chambersburg PA
CBHW051609230426
43668CB00013B/2036